The Postdevelopmental State

SERIES EDITOR: YOUNGJU RYU

Perspectives on Contemporary Korea is devoted to scholarship that advances the understanding of critical issues in contemporary Korean society, culture, politics, and economy. The series is sponsored by The Nam Center for Korean Studies at the University of Michigan.

Smartland Korea: Mobile Communication, Culture, and Society
    Dal Yong Jin

Transgression in Korea: Beyond Resistance and Control
    Juhn Y. Ahn, editor

Cultures of Yusin: South Korea in the 1970s
    Youngju Ryu, editor

Entrepreneurial Seoulite: Culture and Subjectivity in Hongdae, Seoul
    Mihye Cho

Revisiting Minjung: New Perspectives on the Cultural History of 1980s South Korea
    Sunyoung Park, editor

Rediscovering Korean Cinema
    Sangjoon Lee, editor

Korean Families Yesterday and Today
    Hyunjoon Park and Hyeyoung Woo, editors

Mediating the South Korean Other: Representations and Discourses of Difference in the Post/Neocolonial Nation-State
    David C. Oh, editor

Mediating Gender in Post-Authoritarian South Korea
    Michelle Cho and Jesook Song, editors

The South Korean Film Industry
    Sangjoon Lee, Dal Yong Jin, and Junhyoung Cho, editors

The Postdevelopmental State: Dilemmas of Economic Democratization in Contemporary South Korea
    Jamie Doucette

The Postdevelopmental State

Dilemmas of Economic Democratization
in Contemporary South Korea

Jamie Doucette

UNIVERSITY OF MICHIGAN PRESS

Ann Arbor

Copyright © 2024 by Jamie Doucette
Some rights reserved

This work is licensed under a Creative Commons Attribution-NonCommercial 4.0 International License. *Note to users:* A Creative Commons license is only valid when it is applied by the person or entity that holds rights to the licensed work. Works may contain components (e.g., photographs, illustrations, or quotations) to which the rightsholder in the work cannot apply the license. It is ultimately your responsibility to independently evaluate the copyright status of any work or component part of a work you use, in light of your intended use. To view a copy of this license, visit http://creativecommons.org/licenses/by-nc/4.0/

For questions or permissions, please contact um.press.perms@umich.edu

Published in the United States of America by the
University of Michigan Press
Manufactured in the United States of America
Printed on acid-free paper
First published September 2024

A CIP catalog record for this book is available from the British Library.

Library of Congress Cataloging-in-Publication Data

Names: Doucette, Jamie, author. | Michigan Publishing (University of Michigan), publisher.
Title: The postdevelopmental state : dilemmas of economic democratization in contemporary South Korea / Jamie Doucette.
Other titles: Perspectives on contemporary Korea.
Description: Ann Arbor [Michigan] : University of Michigan Press, 2024. | Series: Perspectives on contemporary Korea | Includes bibliographical references (pages 189–210) and index.
Identifiers: LCCN 2024021579 (print) | LCCN 2024021580 (ebook) | ISBN 9780472077083 (hardcover) | ISBN 9780472057085 (paperback) | ISBN 9780472904686 (ebook other)
Subjects: LCSH: Management—Employee participation—Korea (South) | Labor—Korea (South) | Employees—Korea (South) | Korea (South)—Economic conditions—21st century. | Korea (South)—Economic policy—2002–
Classification: LCC HD5660.K6 D68 2024 (print) | LCC HD5660.K6 (ebook) | DDC 330.95195—dc23/eng/20240612
LC record available at https://lccn.loc.gov/2024021579
LC ebook record available at https://lccn.loc.gov/2024021580

DOI: https://doi.org/10.3998/mpub.12875326

This work was supported by the Core University Program for Korean Studies through the Ministry of Education of the Republic of Korea and Korean Studies Promotion Service of the Academy of Korean Studies (AKS-2024-P-013).

The University of Michigan Press's open access publishing program is made possible thanks to additional funding from the University of Michigan Office of the Provost and the generous support of contributing libraries.

Cover photograph by Noh Suntag, used by permission.

Contents

List of Illustrations	vii
List of Abbreviations	ix
Acknowledgments	xi
Introduction: After the Revolution	1
1 The Democratic Deficit of Developmental State Theory	23
2 The Political Economy of the Postdevelopmental State	53
3 Debating Economic Democracy	78
4 Social Democracy without Labor?	111
5 The Integral State of the Conservative Bloc	141
Conclusion: The Future of a Problematic?	165
Methodological Appendix	183
References	189
Index	211

Digital materials related to this title can be found on the Fulcrum platform via the following citable URL: https://doi.org/10.3998/mpub.12875326

Illustrations

Figures

1	The end of the high debt model? Debt ratios of manufacturing firms (1970–2021)	58
2	Growth rates of Korean GDP	60
3	The continuation of circular ownership: the structure of the Samsung group	63
4	The explosion of household debt and decline of household savings (1992–2022)	65
5	Increasing income inequality: Shares of pre-tax national income (1992–2021)	67
6	The increase of irregular workers following the IMF crisis	68
7	The high incidence of nonregular work (total and by gender, 2004–2022)	69
8	Uneven social protection among workers: Social insurance coverage (2022 vs. 2007)	71
9	Deepening export dependency? GDP spending structure (1953–2022)	74
10	Uneven consumption dynamics	75
11	Cross-shareholding structure of the chaebol (simplified)	88
12	Damage claims: constraining workers' rights	123

Tables

1	Outstanding damage claims and provisional seizure of worker assets in KCTU-affiliated workplaces (March 2015)	125
A1	Research informants	187

Abbreviations

CCEJ	Citizen's Coalition for Economic Justice
CFA	Committee on Freedom of Association
CGCG	Center for Good Corporate Governance
CSO	civil society organization
EDCF	Economic Development and Cooperation Fund
ESDC	Economic and Social Development Commission
ESLC	Economic, Social, and Labor Council
ETU-MB	Equality Trade Union—Migrants' Branch
FKI	Federation of Korean Industries
FKTU	Federation of Korean Trade Unions
GDP	gross domestic product
ILO	International Labour Organization
IMF	International Monetary Fund
KCTU	Korean Confederation of Trade Unions
KDI	Korea Development Institute
KDLP	Korean Democratic Labor Party
KLI	Korea Labor Institute
KLSI	Korea Labour and Society Institute
KOICA	Korea International Cooperation Agency
KOILAF	Korea International Labor Foundation
KRWU	Korean Railway Workers' Union
KTC	Korean Tripartite Commission
KTU	Korean Teachers and Education Workers' Union
KTUC	Korean Trade Union Congress
KTX	Korea's high speed rail system
KWWA	Korean Women Workers Association
MITI	Ministry of International Trade and Industry
MMP	mixed-member proportionate representation system
MOFE	Ministry of Finance and Economy

x | Abbreviations

MSM	Minority Shareholder Movement
MTU	Migrant Trade Union
NAPD	National Association of Professors for Democracy
NBFI	nonbank financial institutions
NGO	nongovernmental organization
NHRC	National Human Rights Commission
NIS	National Intelligence Service
NL	National Liberation
ODA	official development assistance
OECD	Organisation for Economic Co-operation and Development
PD	People's Democracy
PSPD	People's Solidarity for Participatory Democracy
PSSP	People's Solidarity for Social Progress
SER	Solidarity for Economic Reform
SERI	Samsung Economic Research Institute
SLAPP	Strategic Lawsuit Against Public Participation
SMG	Seoul Metropolitan Government
STEPI	Science and Technology Policy Institute
TRC	Truth and Reconciliation Commission
TULRAA	Trade Union and Labor Relations Adjustment Act
UPP	United Progressive Party
WSC	welfare state camp

Acknowledgments

The origins of this book can be found in a sharing of the sympathies and frustrations of my peers and colleagues who have traveled through a variety of social and political movements, through the "movement-sphere," as the Korean term *undongkwon* captures rather poetically. The book itself would not have been possible to write without the support of the wider network of friends, coworkers, and family it is embedded within. While the work of writing is often solitary, I often tell my students that no person is an island: knowledge is social. Ideas have practical purposes and are produced through interaction, not so much with theory and abstract facts, but with people and the passions that motivate them to seek change in the world. In my case, the social backdrop of this work precedes the days of my graduate studies and extends back to my own experience in the student, alter-globalization, and global justice movements of the mid-1990s to early 2000s, and subsequent interaction with members of the movement-sphere in South Korea. For I arrived in Korea in the summer of 2001 rather exhausted following a long series of mobilizations that led up to historic events for the alter-globalization or "anti-(corporate) globalization" movement as it was then known (not to be confused with today's bizarre anti "globalist" discourse): the sequence of protests that began in Seattle in 1999 through to cognate events in 2001 in Quebec City, Gothenburg, and then Genoa. I then witnessed from afar its rapid decline and demoralization following 9/11. At the same time, I became curious about the very different conjuncture and sense of optimism experienced by my peers in Korean social movements and the opportunities for change and transformation they sensed. On topics such as unions, political parties, and the potential for progressive change at the national scale—and in the sheer continuity of activism around global trade and inequality—their experiences contrasted deeply with my own and that of my North American peers, and I wanted to know why. Little did I know that what seemed

xii | Acknowledgments

like a small gesture of solidarity and a desire for understanding would become a longer labor of scholarship and inquiry.

For that first introduction, I remain deeply indebted to my old friends Moona Lee, Yoo Byeong-seo, Cho Yak-gol, Nancy Hayne, and Kabir Uddin, along with various former members and supporters of the Equality Trade Union—Migrant's Branch (later to become the Migrant Trade Union) including Devon Ayers, Mahbub Alam, Masum Moniruzzaman, Jeong Yeoungsup, and many others. As I began to think about the broader projects of Korean reformers and progressive activists after entering graduate school, I benefited from a range of supportive people and resources in various institutions of higher education. At the University of British Columbia, Jim Glassman first guided and encouraged me to engage with the broader debates about the developmental state and shared my interest in the long march of Korean social movements on both the street and through the institutions. I also benefited from the support of members on my doctoral committee and examiners, including Geraldine Pratt, Dan Hiebert, Baik Tae-ung, Don Baker, Leonora Angeles, Jamie Peck, Aihwa Ong, and John Agnew. The friendship of other graduate students and visitors from my UBC days (now long past) cannot go unrecognized, including Mona Atia, Kathryn Furlong, Junjia Ye, Heather Frost, Pablo Mendez, Bjorn Surborg, Simon Parker, Sara Koopman, Andrew Shmuely, Kristina Lee Podesva, Alan McConchie, Wes Attewell, and Christian Abrahamsson, among others. I may not have considered a PhD at all had it not been for the examples of scholarly commitment and curiosity during my undergraduate days provided by Julie Cruikshank and the late Blanca Muratorio at the UBC Anthropology Department and the support and encouragement of Gillian Hart, Jean Lave, and the late Allan Pred at UC Berkeley. It was Allan above all who encouraged me to become a geographer and allowed me to complete my undergraduate thesis with him despite being a visiting anthropology student on international exchange: "you are here to get an education, not a degree" was his quip. Allan's iconoclasm continues to inspire my understanding of academic life.

In the mid-2000s, an invitation to spend a year at the Democracy and Social Movements Institute at Sungkonghoe University from the progressive sociologist and reformer Cho Hee-yeon proved to be a valuable resource. I am grateful for the interaction with the nexus between political and civil society in South Korea this experience offered, and for the friendships with Lee Sun-ok, Song Yong-han, Rebecca Kim, Robert Prey, and Hur Seong-woo whom I met there. During that year, participation in the "Reading group on critical geographic thoughts" organized by Park Bae-

Acknowledgments | xiii

gyoon at Seoul National University provided me with close connections to other critical geographers in Korea and East Asia, including Choi Young-jin, Jung Hyun-joo, Dougless Gress, and Kim Sook-jin. These relations developed further through attending the East Asian Regional Conference on Alternative Geographies, the main East Asia critical geography group, since 2006. I have benefited enormously from my colleagues and participants at those events, including Choi Byung-doo, Jinn-yuh Hsu, Ji Joo-hyoung, Hwang Jin-tae, June Wang, Takashi Yamazaki, Laam Hae, James Sidaway, Wing Shing Tang, Park Se-hoon, Yi-ling Chen, Szu-yun Hsu, Joel Wainwright, Dongwan Gimm, Choi Young-rae, and many more.

There are too many people to thank in a long work such as this, and I will inevitably miss many. Nonetheless, there are many friends, colleagues, and collaborators both inside and outside of academia, and in geography, Korean and Asian studies, and the wider social sciences and humanities who I'd like to recognize for their support and inspiration. In no particular order, these include Owen Miller, Lee Seung-Ook, Chang Dae-oup, Oiwan Lam, Ip Iam Chong, Se-woong Koo, Jeong Seong-jin, Choi Young-chan, Shin Hyun-bang, Christina Moon, Seo Bong-man, Susan Kang, Kim So-Yeun, Sara Westin, Sonn Jung-won, Shin Hae-ran, Shin Kwang-yeong, Han Yoonai, Erik Mobrand, Nan Kim, Dan Bousfield, Song Jesook, Alice Kim, Joseph Jeon, Eva Hansson, Meredith Weiss, Matt Van Volkenberg, Tom Rainey Smith, Jesse Proudfoot, Greg Sharzer, Farwa Sial, Alex Loftus, Kean Fan Lim, Karen Lai, Anders Riel Müller (Song Yeonjun), Emma Mawdsley, Amy Levine, Holly Stephens, Bonnie Tilland, Jihoon Park, Lim Sojin, Youngmi Kim, John Lee, Patrick Neveling, David Fasenfest, Kevin Hewison, Mark Selden, Jenny Chan, Dennis Arnold, Aaron Moore, Bridget Martin, Byun Jung-pil, Bob Jessop, Ngai-ling Sum, among others. I'd like to add that, in recent years, conversations with Hyeng-joon Park, Hong Gibin, Lee Byeong-cheon, Myung-joon Park, Aelim Yun, Choi Jeong-koo, Mikyoung Ryu, Youngjin Choi, Gareth Dale, and the late Chung Tae-in have been an enormous benefit for my understanding of economic democracy and the politics of labor reform, more than I can fully express here. Nonetheless, all interpretations are my own. At the University of Manchester, where I have worked since late 2012, I have also been fortunate to have a wonderful group of colleagues to bounce ideas off, including Aurora Fredriksen, Cristina Temenos, Martin Hess, Caitlin Henry, Joe Blakey, Will Fletcher, Abi Stone, Ali Browne, Sarah Hall, Stefan Bouzarovski, Saska Petrova, Kevin Ward, Ross Jones, Mark Usher, Clancy Wilmott, Felipe Irarrázaval, Ian Bruff, Pritish Behuria, Jonny Darling, Helen Wilson, Kelly Kay, Noel Castree, Mercè Cortina Oriol, Martin Evans, Phil Hughes, Sarah Lindley,

Gareth Clay, Emma Shuttleworth, Mario Hernandez Trejo, Filippo Menga, Erik Swyngedouw, Adrienne Roberts, Jinsoo Lee, Tianshu Liu, Jeongseong Lee, Ben Knight, Matt Varco, Bill Kutz, Ola Demkowicz, Aya Homei, and Ed Pulford, among others. Outside of these circles, the company of my small crew of all-season, North and Irish Sea surfers in Manchester, Pedro Labanca and Bertrand Houchot, has been a much-needed salve to the pressures of professional life.

The research for this book benefited enormously from a range of financial supports. These include a generous Leverhulme Trust Research Fellowship (RF-2018-263\7) in 2018–19, the support of the National Research Foundation of Korea (NRF-2017S1A3A2066514), and various small grants from the University of Manchester. This publication was also supported by the 2024 Korean Studies Grant Program of the Academy of Korean Studies (AKS-2024-P-013). Some of the research for this book benefited from the assistance of Woo-cheol Kim, Yu Cheong-hee, and Hanee Choi, while Hyeng-joon Park also helped me to navigate a few of the statistical databases used in chapter 2. While the book represents a cohesive work on its own, it is also indebted to some of my earlier work. Chapter 3 incorporates, in revised and updated form, several sections of a previous article, "Debating Economic Democracy in South Korea: The Costs of Commensurability," *Critical Asian Studies* 47 (3) (2015): 388–413. Two sections of chapter 4 include revised text from an article originally written with my colleague Susan Kang, "Legal Geographies of Labour and Postdemocracy: Reinforcing Non-Standard Work in South Korea," *Transactions of the Institute of British Geographers* 43 (2) (2018): 200–214. Likewise, parts of chapter 5 include revised and updated text from an article originally written with Se-Woong Koo, "Pursuing Post-Democratisation: The Resilience of Politics by Public Security in Contemporary South Korea," *Journal of Contemporary Asia* 46 (2) (2016): 198–221. Thanks to both my coauthors for permission to rework these texts for this book. Most of the earlier, original text in these passages was written by myself; as such, all errors and interpretations are my own. Finally, chapter 5 also includes fragments from a reworked paragraph from "The Occult of Personality: Korea's Candlelight Protests and the Impeachment of Park Geun-hye," *Journal of Asian Studies* 76 (4) (2017): 851–60. Some of the arguments in this book were first presented in talks at the London School of Economics, York University, Lund University, Gyeongsang National University, SOAS University of London, Sungkonghoe University, Ecole des Hautes Etudes en Sciences Sociales, and the Academy of Korean Studies Europe (Rome conference). I would like to thank audiences there for their engagement.

Acknowledgments | xv

At the University of Michigan Press, I'd like to thank series editor Youngju Ryu for recognizing a kindred project to her own critical scholarship, and to Katie LaPlant for her definitive editorial guidance and advice in helping bring this project through to completion, along with the excellent feedback of three anonymous readers. I also want to thank the artist Noh Suntag for the use of one of his photos as a poignant cover image for this book. I have long been a fan of his work and the way it speaks to the politics of memory, emotional force of democratic events, and ironies of the present moment in ways that are hard to describe in words. Finally, I would be remiss if I did not mention the love and support of my extended family, especially Mary and Len Doucette and Cecilia and Stanley Chong. Their support through the ups and downs of a scholarly life and its various migrations has been much appreciated, along with that of my two brothers, Andrew and the late Tim Doucette, whose gut sense of justice and fairness is recognized here. Lastly, the love, kindness, and sense of humor of my partner, Tiffany, and children, Alma and Simone, make life truly worth living and provide daily optimism of the will that a better world is there for the making.

Introduction

After the Revolution

In the autumn and winter of late 2016 and early 2017, South Korea was rocked by the largest mass protests witnessed in decades. They began as a series of candlelight vigils against influence peddling by President Park Geun-hye's shamanistic spiritual "advisor," Choi Soon-sil, and quickly flared into an episode of prolonged nonviolent civil disobedience, one that spurred Park's impeachment by the National Assembly and sustained an enormous popular mobilization until that decision was upheld by the Constitutional Court in March 2017.[1] Although international media coverage of the protests focused on the sharing of state secrets with Choi, and delegation of considerable policy-making power to her, several intersecting events and their attendant mobilizations provoked the Candlelight Revolution, as it came to be called (Park A 2022). These included the Park administration's ill-fated reaction to the Sewŏl ferry disaster and the hostile treatment of its victims' families (Kim N 2018; Park HO 2022; Suh and Kim 2017); the blacklisting of thousands of critics and liberal-left public figures within politics, arts, and culture (Yuk 2019); earlier revelations about interference by the National Intelligence Service and other state agencies during the 2012 presidential election (Seo 2018; Choi SW 2022); and bribery and collusion with Korea's large, family-led conglomerate

---

1. This book uses McCune-Reischauer romanization except in cases where a person, author, or common word (e.g., chaebol) is known using revised romanization or otherwise. Likewise, Korean names are written with the surname followed by first name with a dash between syllables (e.g., Park Geun-hye) except for in cases where an author is known for the inverse or by a different spelling or name order (e.g., Ha-joon Chang). Finally, in-text referencing for some authors includes initials after the surname (e.g., Lee BC 2006). The purpose here is to avoid confusion around the identity of authors who share a common surname and may have works that share the same publication dates.

2 | The Postdevelopmental State

groups, the chaebol (Doucette 2017), among other related issues (Han JJH 2022). This conjunction of events shaped a wave of mobilization that led to Park's impeachment, and, in quick succession, the election of a liberal administration led by veteran pro-democracy politician and human rights lawyer Moon Jae-in who embraced an ambitious program of reforms to safeguard democracy and prevent similar collusion in the future.

Specifically, the Moon administration quickly pledged to institutionalize the spirit of the Candlelight Revolution by addressing the "deep-rooted evils" (*jŏkp'ye chŏngsan*) that have long haunted Korea's politics and economy. Principal among them was the sense of inequality and injustice in Korean society that animated the protests and was illustrated by the slogan "*Hell Chosŏn.*" This phrase was used by the demonstrators and more widely by the nation's youth to describe feelings of social paralysis and immobility. A reference to Korea's feudal past, it connotes a divided society where those born into rich families of the economic, political, and cultural elite—"gold spoons"—marginalize and exploit the rest, the "dirt spoons" (Kim H 2017). But while the actions of Park's administration and her advisors triggered the use of this phrase, they were not the sole cause of it. For the inequalities it was directed toward involve the wider structural changes that have taken place in the Korean economy since the Asian financial crisis of the late 1990s—an event that left significant economic restructuring, slowing rates of economic growth, and increasing levels of income and wealth inequality in its wake. As Korea's economy became more, rather than less, dependent on its large, export-focused chaebol since the crisis, abuses of power by their ruling families have become the source of much popular ire and resentment. In parallel, the expansion of nonstandard employment relations—temporary contracts, gig economy jobs, disguised subcontracting, dispatched and day labor—has triggered anxiety about fairness within employment relations. Speculative investment in real estate and the financial market has widened the wealth gap between rich and poor and has been fueled by a historic increase in household debt that has created concerns of larger impending crises. Meanwhile, countervailing protections in the form of spending on welfare and social protection have remained low by Organisation of Economic Co-operation and Development (OECD) standards (Yang 2017). Frustratingly, a conservative public security apparatus, itself a product of the Cold War, continues to harass pro-democratic actors in a manner that obscures egalitarian demands for social justice as threats to public order (Jayasuriya 2018).

Because of their comprehensive nature, addressing the "evils" that spurred the Candlelight Revolution required more than simply retributive

Introduction | 3

justice in the form of prosecuting individuals from the Park administration for their crimes. Instead, the Moon administration regarded this task to be part of a broader *transformative* project that would reorient the foundations of Korean politics and the economy toward "economic democracy and peace" (Moon 2017a). This broad platform included creating a "people-centered economy" and reforming the security apparatus of the state to create a society in which "opportunities are equal, processes are fair, and outcomes are just" (Moon 2017b). To do so, Moon pledged to tackle the power of the conglomerates through corporate governance reform and regulation; pursue a "society that respects labor" by raising the minimum wage, encouraging social dialogue with labor, and promoting the regularization of workers on nonstandard and temporary contracts; correct for abuses of power by the public security apparatus by reorganizing the prosecution, police, and the intelligence service; and work to minimize the effects of Cold War antagonism on the peninsula by promoting peaceful engagement and dialogue with North Korea.

While this vision of "Candlelight Democracy," as it was also called, provided a novel break with the policies of the conservative Park administration, it did not appear out of thin air. Rather, it can be understood as the culmination of long-standing ideas about the nature and limits of Korea's democratization, the legacy of its authoritarian, anticommunist "developmental state" model of economic growth, and that model's neoliberal restructuring. In other words, the Candlelight Revolution did not give birth to a new type of politics or ideology per se but provided an opportunity for liberal and progressive reformers to finally *institutionalize* their existing ideas about the problems of Korean politics and economy, and how they might be overcome. For Korean reformers, the slogan of "economic democracy" signaled this project. Yet as is explored in this book, despite enhanced parliamentary power, the pro-democratic bloc largely failed to effectively implement this project in a manner that might secure them the broad and long-lasting public support and legitimacy they assumed would follow. While many spoke of a Rooseveltian, New Deal coalition that might ensure the bloc a 20-year reign, by spring 2022 the Conservative Party were able to claim victory in the presidential elections by capitalizing on growing disillusionment with the Democratic Party.[2]

---

2. Korean political parties share a tendency to frequently change their names, sometimes several times per administration. This usually occurs following splits and schisms that eventually lead to new alliances and reformation or simply as a means to refresh a

The Postdevelopmental State

This book takes this moment of failure as its point of departure in order to accomplish two interconnected empirical and conceptual tasks: (1) to describe and unpack the dilemmas involved in and challenges encountered by the project of economic democratization, and (2) to reframe the way that the political economy of development and democratization in Korea, and by extension East Asia, is studied so as to better align it with the normative concerns, democratic desires, and practical goals of progressive actors who seek a more egalitarian economic system. The title of this book names both the problem and an approach: that is, I use it to describe the *dilemmas* of contemporary efforts to democratize the economy, and to signal an *approach* that predicates itself on a more relational and processual understanding of political and civil society than previous work on the developmental state. As an *empirical* phenomenon, the postdevelopmental state connotes a sense of both continuity and change within the structural relations that shape the Korean economy: the high-growth, high-debt "model" pursued under authoritarian regimes has indeed been transformed, but the power of many actors associated with it remains strong, such as the chaebol, public security apparatus, and conservative bloc. The economy features elements of both developmentalism—powerful conglomerates, active subordination of labor, and export-orientation—and neoliberalism—corporate governance reform, financial transformation, and the proliferation of nonstandard employment relations. While these structural conditions are explored in this book, the postdevelopmental state has an even greater salience for describing a key *practical* challenge that comes with seeking to address their effects and that I put *relatively* more weight on here as a phenomenon to be examined: the fact that despite efforts to include progressive actors in the state to provide policy ideas and to help secure legitimacy, liberal administrations have lacked a clear vision of an alternative to developmentalism and neoliberalism. The post- prefix in this case symbolizes the lack of substantive break with the politics of developmentalism and neoliberalism, one that

---

party's image. For example, in the six years preceding the 2022 presidential election, which it won, the conservative People Power Party had been known as the United Future Party, Liberty Korea Party, and Saenuri Party. For the sake of clarity and to maintain a sense of continuity, in this book I refer to the two major ruling and opposition parties that have governed since the late 1990s as the Conservative Party and the Democratic Party.

Introduction | 5

can be seen by a narrowing vision of what constitutes economic democracy among pro-democratic forces, the ambiguous space accorded to workers within this vision, and a problematic "politics of personality" that has been used to pursue legitimacy in lieu of effective alliance-building. Overall, it is the manner in which these *objective* and *subjective* (or structural and practical) aspects of political economic transformation interact that the terminology employed here seeks to capture.

While the postdevelopmental state is a useful term for descriptive purposes, the way it is described above also signals that a reorientation in the priorities of research on developmental states is necessary for grasping the practical challenges encountered by progressive reformers. Specifically, it implies a shift in the object of inquiry away from the idealized structure of elite bureaucracies and institutions of rapid GDP growth toward the dynamics of actual historical blocs and the contours of socioeconomic inequality. As the dominant framework used to understand Korea's economic growth, the developmental state approach has long neglected the influence of pro-democratic actors in favor of a focus on the structure and organization of elite economic bureaucracies and a largely *quantitative* understanding of development (as GDP growth and industrial expansion). This standpoint is politically problematic, for it separates development from democracy in a troubling manner and quietly aligns itself with the perspectives of the elites it studies. Consequently, it says little about what the *experience* of development meant to many actors negatively affected by it, and, by extension, their efforts to challenge it, neglecting key sources of transformation. This *democratic deficit* as I call it is of particular concern because without grasping the ways political and civil society have shaped political-economic reform during the last three decades, it is difficult to critically understand the challenges involved in creating alternatives to the status quo.[3]

---

3. Unfortunately, this problem extends even beyond the classic literature on developmental states to include recent work that seeks to account for their democratization (e.g., Slater and Wong 2013, 2022). Much of this literature lacks a strong consideration of debates about democratization among public intellectuals in the countries under study and replicates antiquated ideas about strong states and elite cohesion and combines them with claims inherited from modernization theory: that (state-led) development begets a strong middle class with a preference for liberal democracy; that democracy is a matter of elections that provide for elite competition and their periodic rotation (a minimalist definition); or that democratic consolidation proceeds in a linear direction (see Gilman 2007, 2018).

6 | The Postdevelopmental State

This democratic deficit is examined below in the context of the neo-Weberian theorists who developed the idea of the developmental state. These theorists argued that the state was explicitly *not* something that was understood as a balance of forces within political and civil society. Instead, they identified the *state* with its internal structure and organization, and its *developmental* variety with an ideal type of economic bureaucracy, one that was *autonomous* from society and sufficiently *insulated* from outside pressures. In Gramscian terms, the state appeared as a "rational absolute" capable of solving the problem of development through direct intervention in the market (Gramsci 1971, 116; see also Liguori 2015, 3). This representation is typified by the neo-Weberian obsession with bureaucratic rationality—understood as a matter of meritocratic recruitment, a calculative, results-oriented mentality, and long-term career rewards—as the core feature of developmental states. For developmental state theorists, this "rationality" allowed bureaucrats to enjoy the autonomy and cohesion necessary to "govern the market," using tools such as policy loans, access to foreign exchange, licensing authority, and import/export credits to pursue industrial transformation (Johnson 1982; Wade 1990). But this idealization belied the more complex reality under its surface. By identifying "rationality" with state structure and organization, it omitted the standpoints of actors situated beyond the bureaucracy, including those of the various social forces that pressured authoritarian regimes to seek to *legitimize* themselves through development, to pursue specific policies, and even to relinquish power in the face of democratic upheaval.

Progressive Korean intellectuals have made cognate arguments in debates surrounding the historiography of the Park Chung-hee dictatorship (1962–79), for Park is often considered as the architect behind the Korean developmental state. For instance, Paik Nak-chung (2011, 85–86) argues that no scholarly account of the period would be adequate unless it sought to pay attention to the living voices of those victims who were suppressed under his regime and whose voices do not easily translate into the type of "objective data" that scholars of development like to deal with. As Paik continues, "A serene disregard of their suffering as 'collateral damage' in any march to modernization would not only be infuriating to those who had suffered, but would, in all probability, negatively affect the quality of the scholarly work in question" (86). Likewise, progressive economist and democracy activist Lee Byeong-cheon (2006) argues that the triumphalist take on Korea's development in the Park era needs to be reconciled with the perspectives of the movements that fought against what he calls Park's "developmental dictatorship," in order to balance the shadows and

Introduction | 7

light of the period.[4] Finally, Cho Hee-yeon (2000, 2010) proposes the replacement of the concept of the developmental "state" altogether in favor of a developmentalist "regime" to better account for how diverse forces have interacted within state and society, including the dynamics of repression, regimentation, and contestation that shaped the Park era.[5] What these scholars share is a critique of approaches that regard politics and economics, state and society, as discrete phenomenon (Kayatekin 2009), and a desire for concepts that can better account for the standpoints of actors affected by developmentalist politics and ideology—an intervention that resonates with a broader postcolonial critique of political economy in the social sciences (Chen 2010; Song JS and Hae L 2020; Kaiwar 2014; Wang H 2011).

This book takes this contextualizing task to heart. To do so, it employs a Gramscian approach to geographical political economy that foregrounds the fluid nexus between political and civil society and engages critically with the standpoints of progressive political actors by centering the project of economic democratization.[6] Antonio Gramsci's concept of the *integral state* is particularly useful here. Rather than regarding political and civil society as fixed in their identity and external to one another as much previous research on East Asian political economy has done, Gramsci provides an approach that is both *relational* (attuned to their interaction) and *processual* (attentive to their mutual transformation through time and

---

4. For some, however, Lee's approach comes at the risk of an apologia for dictatorship through assuming that such a balance can be struck or even disentangled analytically to begin with (see Kim SH and Park SH 2007).

5. Cho's explicitly Gramscian approach is a direct inspiration for the current study as it is focused on the production and disintegration of hegemony to understand the political dynamics of particular regimes (see Cho HY 2008, 2009).

6. By *geographical* political economy I mean that grasping the dilemmas of the prodemocratic bloc requires an understanding of the institutions that have shaped Korea's economic history and that make it stand out as a place-specific instance or "variety" of capitalist development. Important here is the legacy of Korea's position under the aegis of the United States in the Cold War, and its anticommunist, authoritarian "developmental state" or "developmental dictatorship" as Korean scholars have more critically put it (Lee BC 2006). The institutions of rapid development inherited from this period—such as the export-oriented economy, large chaebol, the public security apparatus, authoritarian labor control regimes, and the division system (the logic of antagonism that maintains the division of the Korean peninsula into two states), among others—and their neoliberal restructuring and realignment are all "geographical" in some sense. They are structured by relations that extend beyond the national territory, are constitutive of various scales and practices of governance, and reveal how capitalist institutions are varied, uneven, and differential across place.

8 | The Postdevelopmental State

space). As such, a focus on the nexus between political and civil society can help reveal the changing composition of the state, the effect of popular struggles on the policies it enacts, and the challenges involved in crafting substantive alternatives to the status quo. Such an approach is particularly suited for grasping the dynamics of Korea's pro-democratic historical bloc and its efforts to transform Korea's political economy compared to conventional perspectives. In the next chapter, I draw out the difference a Gramscian approach makes and discuss its relevance for a geographically sensitive, postcolonial political economy in more detail. But one key prescription worth mentioning in advance is that its conceptual and empirical strategy requires critical engagement with practical, real-world political struggles, and the ideas and imaginaries that shape their activity: it's an activity that itself requires the researcher to *translate* between difficult political conjunctures and broader social theories in a spirit of revision and recontextualization (Ekers et al. 2020; Hart 2023).

Conservative Democratization?

Guided by this strategy, one key idea that is essential for understanding the reasons behind the Candlelight protests, the nature and urgency of Moon's proposed reforms, and his party's subsequent loss in the 2022 presidential elections that needs to be introduced here is the theory of conservative democratization. This is a concept associated with veteran public intellectual, and periodic advisor to liberal politicians, Choi Jangjip. This notion is useful to first review before detailing some of the specific arguments made in this book about why exactly the project of economic democratization failed to secure hegemony for the pro-democratic bloc, for such arguments partially rework Choi's explanation. Commenting on earlier episodes of candlelight protests that prefigured the events of 2016–17, Choi (2012) argued that the system of representative democracy in Korea was not functioning properly. The system provided little room for diverse ideological viewpoints and horizontal checks on power: this made it difficult to address problems created by neoliberalism and the growing inequality associated with it. Factional competition over patronage and an entrenched regionalism prevented political parties from raising substantive alternatives. As a result, the system came to fixate too heavily upon the personality of the president, who, invested with considerable executive power, came to be seen by the public as personally responsible for the cycle of enthusiasm, disappointment, and

Introduction | 9

resistance that followed various regimes (Choi JJ 2012a; cf. Kang JM 2008). The result was a politics divided between the "plaza" of street protests and the president, the latter seen as either directly responsive to or responsible for the former. In Choi's opinion, what was needed as a solution to the problem was stronger democratic institutions that could allow for the representation of working-class interests in politics and facilitate broader ideological competition within the representative system: a solution that had been obscured by the prioritization of anticommunism over liberal democracy during Korea's Cold War experience of development, and by the extremely slow pace of reforms made to "authoritarian bureaucratic apparatuses and their behavioural norms" since the democratic transition (Choi JJ 2009, 6; see also Song HY 2013; Shin KY 2010; Suh et al. 2012).

The general contours of this argument are shared by a variety of prodemocratic forces active within and beyond the Moon administration, many of whom use the term "'87 regime" to describe the structural foundations they see at the root of the problem (Paik 2013; Kim CY 2009). This "regime" denotes the political settlement among elites that led to free elections but left concerns about conservative hegemony, national division, expanding socioeconomic inequality, poor labor rights, and other limits on democratic participation unresolved (Park HO 2015, 62–64). While intellectuals have been divided on which of these concerns to prioritize to overcome the '87 regime, they generally agree that a broad progressive transformation is needed (Kang JI 2017; Ko 2011) and have been supportive of efforts to enhance participation by civil society organizations (CSOs) and labor and democracy movement activists within the state. Likewise, the CSOs that emerged in the wake of the broad-based people's (*minjung*) or democracy movements (Lee N 2011) have advocated for visions of a participatory society (*ch'amyŏ sahoe*) and economic democracy (*kyŏngje minjujuŭi*) as the solution to the power of the domestic conglomerates and the old conservative elite, not to mention enduring concerns surrounding environmental degradation, low levels of social welfare, and the expansion of inequality, among others. Consequently, the liberal administrations that developed out of the democracy movement have sought to draw legitimacy from these aspirations and have recognized them in their reform plans (Park HS 2017). For instance, the electoral manifesto of President Kim Dae-jung (1998–2003) was called the "Mass Participatory Economy," and President Roh Moo-hyun's administration (2003–8) named itself the "Participatory Government." These administrations included the participation of large numbers of public intellectuals, civil society activists, and democracy movement veterans from CSOs, who served as policy advisors, ministers, and members of the national assembly.

And yet, despite fealty to the criticisms of conservative democratization and the '87-regime and the incorporation of CSOs, veteran activists, and progressive intellectuals and their reform slogans into policy, liberal administrations have largely failed to satisfy their promises to substantially transform Korean politics and economy. This "failure" has led to claims that they have not lived up to their democratic credentials—a predicament that the Candlelight administration of Moon Jae-in also came to face. While he initially sought to distance his policies from the neoliberal reforms of previous administrations—with promises to expand wages, regularize precarious workers, reform the chaebol, and address rising housing costs and real estate speculation—by the spring of 2019 Moon's reform efforts had either stalled or begun to backtrack. Moon countenanced complaints from within and without of not living up to the democratic goals and desires of the Candlelight Revolution. Consequently, the government became a target of protest from progressive labor and civil society activists frustrated by his policies toward workers and the chaebol, and by a newly re-emboldened conservative bloc opposed to his proposed reforms of the prosecution service. The latter capitalized on a series of scandals involving high-profile democratic reformers by pointing out the hypocrisy of those involved. The result was that mobilization both in support of and opposition to legal reform devolved into a culture war over the virtues or vices of specific reformers' personalities that obscured the wider political purpose of reforming the prosecution service to begin with. This reversal signaled that the Moon administration would likely follow the pattern of his liberal predecessors whose administrations were also inaugurated with excitement by pro-democratic forces, but whose policies eventually led to fragmentation and disillusionment within the wider democratic bloc that undermined their legitimacy. Despite a strong start, by the later stages of the Moon administration it was clear that neither the symptoms of conservative democratization described by Choi—who continued to criticize Korea's party system and concentration of political authority in the president during the Moon administration (see Choi JJ 2020; 2018)—nor the features of the '87 regime described by others had been overcome.

These enduring criticisms and the cyclical nature of enthusiasm and disappointment they help describe raise the question of why liberal administrations have faced such difficulties in creating a more substantive, pro-democratic alternative to the *status quo*. In other words, what

Introduction | 11

accounts for the failure to institutionalize a more participatory and egalitarian system that might address the long-standing exclusion of labor and allow pro-democratic actors to have a more substantive influence? And by influence here, I am talking in broad terms about not only the formal institutions of representative democracy such as elections and political parties, but of wider areas of economic and social policy that might help stimulate progressive political economic change. In short, I see the dilemma outlined by Choi and others as best answered using the description of the postdevelopmental state identified above, for it involves both the *effects* of economic processes and *interaction* between political forces that extend beyond the party system and thereby subtend the politics of conservative democratization and the '87 regime. In other words, the challenges encountered by Moon Jae-in's Candlelight reforms, as well as the ambitions of preceding liberal administrations, are, broadly speaking, problems of *political* economy. Simply put, the pro-democratic bloc has been unable to reform the economy in such a way as to create an alternative economic model that might secure them the hegemony they desire.[7]

The Dilemmas of Economic Democratization

While this book is inspired by the spirit of Choi's arguments concerning conservative democratization, it also departs from them. Besides his preference for an analytical focus on the formal institutions of representative democracy, I find the way Choi regards a contentious public sphere, or the "politics of the street," as signs of a deficiency within party politics rather limiting. Phenomenon such as protest and contention help to shape and reorient the relations between political and civil society and should thus be seen as part of broader historical struggles for hegemony rather than simply a sign of lack or deficiency. In these regards, the political problem of conservative democratization—and by extension the residual effects of the Cold War developmental state and its neoliberal restructuring—is not simply confined to a lack of ideological diversity and the subversion of liberal democracy, as Choi would find it. Rather, beyond the very real

---

7. This book's usage of the term "pro-democratic bloc" to delineate the wider grouping of progressive, liberal, regional (and even some moderate conservatives) forces within political and civil society follows Shin Kwang-yeong's (2021) cognate usage of it to delineate between pro-democratic and conservative blocs. The pro-democratic bloc includes politicians, intellectuals, trade unions, the Democratic Party and minor progressive parties, civil society organizations, and other actors.

material consequences of socioeconomic inequality, it involves broader relations within the wider pro-democratic historical bloc, including the content of its reform policies, the economic imaginaries that shape them, and specific forms of formal and informal coordination between political and civil society.

In the empirical chapters that follow, I examine the structural contours of the postdevelopmental state and relations between political and civil society that have informed efforts to address it in more detail. In doing so, I argue that there are three specific practical reasons why the project of economic democratization failed to overcome the problem of the postdevelopmental state when considered from the viewpoint of the integral state. The first involves the very *imaginaries* of reform that progressive actors working within the nexus between political and civil society have embraced. The book highlights how the two main visions of economic democracy within the pro-democratic bloc—visions that, in part, have their origins in Korea's radical social formation debates of the late 1980s—have become increasingly narrow in scope. As such, they have come to neglect long-standing concerns about the subordination of labor and other historical injustices associated with Korea's history of rapid industrialization and neoliberal restructuring. This problem has been clearly visible in strategies to tackle the power of the chaebol, which is the main task that the slogan has come to reference. But it has also animated cognate projects that are explicitly concerned with improving the participation of labor, including the Moon administration's plan to create a "society that respects labor." A narrowing, capital-centric vision of economic democracy and a problematic politics of participation and coordination with labor and popular interests in the implementation of policies meant to correct for corporate power and improve labor standards, I argue, reveal the limitations in how alternatives to developmentalism and neoliberalism have been imagined and practiced within the integral state.

The second reason involves the broader politics of *legitimation* in which these visions of economic democracy are embedded, a problem that involves how the pro-democratic bloc has been organized. Specially, I argue that progressive forces such as intellectuals, CSO officials, trade unions, and notable activists from the democracy movement have been mobilized to provide legitimacy to liberal administrations often in lieu of a substantive transformative vision of democratic reform. As Yoonkyung Lee (2022) remarks, the Democratic Party has looked to these forces to provide "new blood" to revitalize the organization and ensure it remains

Introduction | 13

relevant. But the ways that these figures have been incorporated remain problematic for the wider egalitarian demands that have shaped this bloc. For the party itself has often remained susceptible to Korea's strong regionalism rather than united by ideology and, despite the incorporation of progressives into the party, the latter do not share a common political vision. As such, Lee argues, the logic of personal calculation dominates over progressive coordination, and the boss-like system of party heavyweights continues despite the party's venerable democracy movement history (Lee Y 2022, 129–39). This book similarly finds that the appointment of progressive intellectuals, politicians, and CSO activists to important posts has been used to secure broad consent for the Democratic Party. However, despite these appointments, the policy initiatives pursued by progressive figures—which include many post-Keynesian economists, former student activists, and veteran trade unionists—have not been able to satisfy demands for an egalitarian solution to chaebol power, irregular work, and the public security apparatus. In some cases, the problem has involved the very imaginary of reform being embraced by reformers themselves, as the debate on chaebol reform reveals. In others, the problem has more to do with broader coordination within the integral state, including the failure of progressives to create a "control tower" (a cohesive strategy for progressive policy advocacy and internal coordination) that can help to implement substantive reform (Park SY and Cho SE 2021a). Such a failure is seen particularly in the manner that the liberal administrations have sought to both include and limit the voice of labor in its reform plans.

In addition, the inclusion of famous progressive activists to legitimize policy has devolved, at times, into a problematic politics of personality, especially when contradictions are found between the espoused beliefs and personal practices of specific historically significant individuals. The reaction to the Cho Kuk controversy surrounding prosecution reform discussed in the final chapter is a particularly poignant case as have been several prominent #MeToo cases among key reformers. The uncritical defense of some of these figures obscures the actual challenges of producing substantive policy and, unfortunately, has helped the conservative bloc to regain some of its political capital. Consequently, the pursuit of legitimation through inclusion of activists and CSOs by the Democratic Party has created anxieties about co-optation by social movements and reformers. As Amy Levine in her study of South Korea "civil movement organizations" points out, CSO activists have constantly and reflexively interro-

14 | The Postdevelopmental State

gated the "site" or "field" (*hyŏnjang*) of their practice with considerable gravity. As "the privileged site of praxis shifted from farm or factory during the *minjung* [people's] movements to offices, even those inside the government, during the *simin* [citizens] movements," Levine (2016, 42) recounts, the question of how to advance broadly transformative goals within the constraints offered by democratization and liberal administrations has been a constant concern.[8] Likewise, scholars interested in what has happened to the broad goals of the democracy movement after formal democratization (Kim A 2011; Lee N 2011, 2019; Song J 2009; Song and Hae 2019) have noted that similar tensions and contradictions have come with participation in multiple policy areas—from the environment to welfare—that make progressives uneasy about the terms of their incorporation into the ethical-political projects of liberal regimes. Consequently, the *nexus* between political and civil society within the pro-democratic bloc itself has become a *site* of protest and contestation.

The third reason involves the *resilience* of conservative forces associated with the old regime. This factor extends beyond the internal structure and content of the pro-democratic bloc but nevertheless demonstrates the importance of a Gramscian focus on historical blocs and the contours of the integral state. For conservatives have also cultivated their own strategic alliances between political and civil society through inclusion of actors such as the New Right to create obstacles for progressive reform. This coordination has allowed conservatives to promote a cultural politics that casts doubt on the legacy of pro-democracy, labor, and civil society movements using anticommunist rhetoric; revise the official historiography of Korea's development and democratization to accord greater prestige to past dictatorships (Miller 2010; Tikhonov 2019; Yang M 2021); and use the public security apparatus to maintain existing economic, social, and political monopolies (Cho HY 2012b). These obstacles act as an external constraint on pro-democratic forces—including, at times, some moderative conservatives—making it necessary for liberal and progressive forces to act together as a historical bloc. Hence, an understanding of the manner that progressives have also targeted conservative influence over the residual institutions of the authoritarian state is salient for grasping the challenges associated with the project of economic democracy, not to mention broader ambitions such as peaceful engagement with North Korea. For, unfortunately, the lack of an effective strategy in this area helped shape

---

8. See Kim W (2011) for an account of how radical academic communities have debated their participation in the Democratic Party.

Introduction | 15

conservative renewal and success in the 2022 elections, further deferring the promise of economic democratization and perhaps scuttling its status as a future project for the pro-democratic bloc.

Researching the Postdevelopmental State

The arguments above are explored in this book through a series of interconnected chapters that examine the dilemmas encountered by the project of economic democratization and its interconnected struggles through a long view that stretches back over roughly the last 25 years since the Asian financial crisis (or "IMF crisis" as it is often known in Korea). To do so, the book uses a range of materials and data gathering strategies. The structural contours of the postdevelopmental state described in chapter 2 have been constructed from analysis of statistics from the Bank of Korea, Korean Statistical Information Service, World Inequality Database, World Bank, Ministry of Employment and Labor, and the Fair Trade Commission, among other sources. They help to paint a picture of socioeconomic inequality, as well the changing dynamics of savings and debt, government spending, exports, and capital formation that is useful for situating the strategies of progressive, pro-democratic reformers. Meanwhile, the challenges encountered by the project of economic democratization, and which inform the substantive chapters that follow the structural description of the postdevelopmental state, have been reconstructed, in part, from key informant interviews and informal conversations and encounters with civil society activists, intellectuals, reform politicians, policymakers, officials, advisors, and bureaucrats involved in various areas of political economic reform undertaken over the last decade and a half. These interviews and conversations have been useful for identifying other sources of data, including legislation, policy reports, statistics, secondary literature, and published exchanges in the progressive press that I use to build a narrative and to verify and substantiate some of the insights provided in interviews.

This approach to case formation is inspired by the extended case method approach pioneered by the sociologist Michael Burawoy and his students (Burawoy et al. 2000; Burawoy 2009). This is a reflexive method oriented toward understanding a case site not as a localized example that can be deduced from a generic, homogenous process, but as a site through which broader processes—such as globalization, development, and democratization—are actualized in a heterogenous, place-specific manner. In other words, the case is used to critique, revise, and reposition theory in a manner that resembles the Gramscian principles described above and in chapter 1. In practice, Burawoy and his students have often used participant observation as their preferred technique for this method, for their goal is to engage with the everyday lifeworlds of their participants, although they also supplement it with additional strategies when dealing with complex historical events. Nonetheless, the principles of the method apply to a variety of data gathering strategies. The key point is to be reflexive about the techniques that are being used to understand the case site and the ideas and theories that are being critiqued and revised by doing so. For instance, scholars within critical human geography and other social sciences have found Burawoy's approach to be a useful guide for case construction using multiple methods, including key informant interviews, policy analysis, and archival research (Peck and Theodore 2012). Such a strategy is necessary when dealing with historical events and expansive geographical processes or with elite actors whom it might be difficult to engage with in participant observation.

While my approach to case formation does not formally involve ethnography in the traditional sense, it has benefited a great deal from observation or "deep hanging-out"—a shorthand borrowed from Renato Rosaldo by James Clifford (1996) to describe participant observation—among progressive intellectuals and CSO and labor activists over the last 20 years. This process of "hanging out" or "fellow-traveling" (to adopt another phrase I like to use to describe it) has included observation of many protests, campaigns, government forums, and CSO events over the years (see methodological appendix for further description). I have participated in some of these in a very modest fashion, including some of the events that led up to the Candlelight Revolution and that discussed the priorities of Candlelight Democracy afterwards. This experience predates the research for this book and built upon my time as a young activist in the alter-globalization movements of the late 1990s. That participation helped to form broader networks among older cohorts of pro-democracy, labor and civil society activists, and intellectuals, and led to an invitation to carry out my doctoral fieldwork as a visiting researcher at the Democracy and Social Movements Institute at Sungkonghoe University, a small but venerable institution with deep roots in the democracy movement. Many of the informants I interviewed at the time played or came to play key roles in liberal administrations (particularly that of Presidents Roh Moohyun and Moon Jae-in), and I have followed their careers and those of their colleagues over time to better understand the dynamics of both sides

Introduction | 17

of the integral state, in addition to recruiting new informants involved in a variety of policy areas (see table A1 in the appendix for a sample of informants). In most of the chapters, however, I cite only documents and published materials instead of interviews because in many cases the published record is more precise, and because it allows me to identify key actors involved in the debate without revealing the identities of my informants even though, of course, many of the public intellectuals I have spoken with expressed that they would be happy to be identified.

The sensitivity to progressive standpoints advocated for in this book is very much one that comes out of witnessing the challenges and frustrations experienced by my close peers in various movements and CSOs, particularly those who have been active in smaller organizations that have not benefited from the large budgets of the more prominent universities and organizations. I have often found that these peers, many of whom have spent more than a decade as CSO staffers, have been keenly aware of the strategic dilemmas of the integral state. Often working on insecure contracts under the directorship of more charismatic figures from the 586 generation (the generation of activists born in the 1960s, who fought for democracy in the 1980s, and are now in their late 50s and early 60s), these friends have been highly attuned to the ironies and contradictions of contemporary Korean politics. I find that their emotional experience of the hopes for and frustrations of development and democracy provides a much better starting point for analysis of contemporary Korean political economy than abstract claims about the rationality of the state and economic planning. This is not to claim, however, that this book is written *directly* from the standpoints of my peers within these movements but rather through interaction with them and other critical voices. The book does not seek to essentialize, or even valorize, the views of specific political organizations even though it is *aligned* with their goals and objectives for a more democratic and egalitarian society. Instead, the standpoint from which this book is written has been produced by an "interested interaction" (Pels 2004) with such movements. This interaction is one that has its own specific context or "site" formed between a desire to understand this experience of democratic struggles and a broader wariness of the politics implied by an uncritical celebration of the developmental state as a "successful" alternative to neoliberalism. For I have long found that this claim, one often repeated in the social sciences, belies the real-life challenges faced by actual political struggles. Hence, my desire in this book is to reorient knowledge about so-called developmental states with an analytical framework sensitive to the concrete experiences, dilemmas,

18 | The Postdevelopmental State

concerns, and understandings of movements seeking to create a more democratic and egalitarian economic model on their own terms.

Outline of the Present Work

Chapter 1 begins by revisiting some of the classic studies on the developmental state to both examine its practical critique of neoliberal approaches to development and what this book calls its democratic deficit: that is, its neglect of pro-democratic struggles and a variety of social standpoints that would have been useful for assessing the experience of development and identifying sources of change and transformation. Consequently, the result is that the celebratory image of the state provided by its theorists is one that awkwardly aligns with many of the views of conservative economists and politicians who celebrate the legacy of the "developmental dictator" Park Chung-hee. Moreover, the chapter argues, the neglect of both an understanding of the integral nature of political and civil society and the politics of legitimation (or, rather, hegemony) contributed to the decline of the developmental state research program when its idealized vision of state autonomy could not be found. As such a focus was explicitly rejected by several of its key theorists, the chapter explores Gramsci's understanding of the integral state in greater detail so that the difference between these approaches and the latter's utility for understanding the present conjuncture is made clear. The remainder of the chapter then extends beyond the usual empirical critique of developmental state research to examine the very different approaches to knowledge, ideas, and politics represented by each perspective. Drawing on recent scholarship and the postcolonial critique of Max Weber, the chapter makes a contrast between the epistemology that underlies the ideal-type method preferred by the neo-Weberian state theorists who crafted the theory of the developmental state and the "politico-gnoseology" that shapes this book's Gramscian approach. Rather than delineating the conditions for "successful" development from a standpoint external to social and political struggles, the latter, it argues, provides a reflexive approach that can help address the democratic deficit by loosening the hold of such parsimonious paradigms and aligning analysis with the projects of progressive actors and their shared concerns about equality and emancipation.[9]

---

9. Readers who are more interested in the empirical narrative of continuity and change this book provides can feel free to skip over this chapter. But reading it will provide a much deeper sense of the book's political and philosophical rationale.

Departing from the conceptual register of chapter 1, chapter 2 explores the political *economy* of the postdevelopmental state in order to outline the broad structural transformation that has conditioned the pro-democratic bloc's project of economic democracy and to set the stage for the more granular reading of the politics of reform in the chapters that follow. To do so, the chapter examines some of the major changes made to the Korean economy following the 1997–98 Asian financial crisis, changes that belie a simplistic either/or description as purely a neoliberal or developmentalist model. While the Korean economy has undergone a financial transformation, it has not necessarily "financialized" in the extensive manner that the term often implies. The export economy persists and so does the power of the super-chaebol that both benefited from the crisis and have increasingly consolidated their hold over their conglomerates. Several drivers of inequality are discussed. These include a historic rise in household debt that has helped fuel wealth inequality and speculative urban development. Most importantly, this chapter discusses the expansion of nonstandard or "irregular" work following the crisis, for as this book argues, the position of labor within the project of economic democracy, and by extension the integral state, is key for understanding the challenges of pursuing substantive reform in the contemporary period. This challenge is one that does not simply involve the question of employment status, and the forms of social difference that shape it, but also the contours of social welfare and social insurance coverage and the context of their expansion. The initial exploration of these topics in this chapter will help the reader to better grasp the heated nature of debates about the nature of the Korean economy among reformers, and the possible solutions to inequality that have animated their imaginaries of economic democracy.

Chapter 3 turns its attention to these intense debates in order to examine the different ways in which the project of economic democracy has been construed. It does so by beginning with the presidential elections of 2012 where the slogan of "economic democratization" animated the campaigns of both major parties. To better understand the specific visions of economic democracy advanced during this campaign, and rekindled following the Candlelight events of 2016–17, the chapter traces how the term has been used since the late 1980s and some of the political practices and events it has informed. The discussion shows how the meaning of economic democratization has increasingly narrowed its horizon since the days of the democracy movement and broad-based citizens movements of the 1990s. It also reveals a rather fluid movement of ideas and political actors between state and civil society that is instructive for broader arguments advanced in this book about the importance of the integral state.

The chapter shows how the idea of economic democracy has become increasingly fixated on technical questions of corporate governance, neglecting many of the demands for equality and social justice historically associated with it. As a result, I argue, debates concerning economic democracy have fallen into a relatively simplistic pro- and anti-chaebol register that neglects broader *inter*-class relations that shape finance and the chaebol, especially the role of labor. Consequently, the inability to think about chaebol reform from the standpoint of labor as a key actor and participant within reform strategy weakens such imaginaries and belies the actual historical experiences (e.g., the various forms of social democracy) that many reformers draw their inspiration from. The chapter discusses how this problem came to animate not only the 2012 elections but also chaebol reform under the Moon administration. Despite being led by some of the key progressive intellectuals from the 2012 debate and broader civil society organizations, these reforms did little to address the question of labor's role in reshaping the power of the chaebol or to advance a vision of economic democracy that might address many of the demands of social justice raised by Candlelight movements.

If chapter 3 raises questions about the narrowing vision of chaebol reform and the dilemma of what role workers should play in economic democracy, chapter 4 extends this concern to policies that directly concern work and employment. It does so by looking backwards from the Moon administration's attempt to create a "society that respects labor" to understand why, despite efforts to promote social partnership and social dialogue, the pro-democratic bloc has had difficulty in addressing the problem of irregular work. The chapter argues that while liberal administrations have tended to promote labor reforms and mechanisms of deliberation that appear social democratic in *form*—and, indeed, they are often inspired by policies associated with Scandinavian and Northern European institutions—they rarely do so in *content*. That is, labor is rarely treated as a substantive, agonistic partner in these processes; consequently, the actual reforms that result leave much to be desired. To better understand this dilemma, the chapter charts how social dialogue between labor, business, and the state has been organized since the Asian financial crisis and has shaped policies toward irregular or nonstandard workers. It also discusses the use of new punitive policies such as civil suits for damages that have been used to constrain activism by irregular workers. The manner that labor market reform and social dialogue have shaped one another in a process that involves coercion and consent, I argue, has left unions distrustful of the intent and purposes of social dialogue and their status as a

Introduction | 21

substantive "partner" to begin with. To better situate the Moon administration's attempt to remedy this problem, the chapter then explores how local experiments in social dialogue, such as Seoul's Urban Labor Policy, provided an alternative framework of labor inclusion that, in many ways, inspired Moon's vision of a "society that respects labor." Yet despite similar policies and progressive leadership, Moon's new dialogue body, the Economic, Social and Labor Council broke down in disagreement. The result was that Moon's labor reforms became a glass half empty. While it shifted the terrain of labor struggle by raising the minimum wage and promoting regularization through indefinite term contracts, its instrumental approach to social dialogue, and lack of substantive participation by the democratic labor movement, meant that it was unable to provide a satisfactory alternative to the status quo.

The final empirical chapter examines how the project of economic democracy also involves the broader question of the public security apparatus inherited from the developmentalist dictatorships of the past. To do so, it details how the projects of liberal and progressive reformers, and, by extension, their pursuit of labor and chaebol reform, have been frustrated by the use of a "politics by public security." This is a form of politics that grew to prominence during the recent conservative administrations of Lee Myung-bak and Park Geun-hye, and that partly provoked the Candlelight Revolution. The discussion reveals how the Korean conservative bloc's own "integral state," that is, its own nexus between state and civil society, has, in many ways, shaped the necessity for "bloc politics" to begin with: that is, the need for liberal and progressive forces to form their own cohesive historical bloc to pursue pro-democratic reforms. The chapter then looks at how the Moon administration sought to reform the public security apparatus, and how, here too, problems emerged regarding its vision of reform and the contradictions involved in the politics of legitimation it pursued through the inclusion of progressive actors. The chapter argues that, ultimately, Moon's attempt at prosecution reform devolved into a problematic "politics of personality" that revolved around the figure of Moon's advisor, and progressive legal scholar, Cho Kuk. In this case, the inclusion of Cho as a charismatic, pro-democratic personality initially helped to legitimize Moon's policies, but the controversy surrounding his personal life and mobilizations for and against his role that resulted ultimately distracted from the more substantive question of what sort of legal reforms might be necessary to realize economic democracy. The chapter ends by arguing that the Cho affair provided a means for the conservative bloc to appropriate the discourse of fairness and has helped to prolong the cycle of conservative democratization noted by Choi and other observers above.

The conclusion revisits the main arguments of the book and then surveys recent progressive discussions about the failures of the project of economic democratization and Moon's vision of Candlelight Democracy before making its own prescriptive remarks. It then steps back to reflect on the implications of the research for the broader interdisciplinary field of research in Korean studies and geographical political economy. It argues that the dilemmas outlined in this book do not exhaust the meaning of the postdevelopmental state as a problematic for research, for it is one that is useful for describing the conjunctural problem of overcoming the intersecting legacies of neoliberalism and developmentalism in the context of democratization. For in multiple areas, cognate dilemmas, frustrations, and challenges can be seen, especially in urban, environmental, and gender politics in Korea among other topics. The chapter then discusses how its critique and reframing of developmental theory provides a timely intervention given the recent rise of the developmental state as a *prescriptive* policy model in international development cooperation, for it strengthens the utility of both the conceptual critique of the democratic deficit and the relational and processual focus on the integral state provided in this book. For despite all its promises of a "democratic developmentalism," the policy vision of the developmental state often remains even more celebratory of Korea's developmentalist dictatorship and less critical than its academic precursor. Unfortunately, it also risks replicating the democratic deficit criticized here by focusing too narrowly on the "successes" of state planning to the neglect of the actual dynamics of the social forces that embed development. The book concludes with the hope that the approach provided here can help to stimulate a more critical and reflexive turn in studies on rapid development and East Asian political economy, one that aligns them more closely with the projects, concepts, experiences, and standpoints of progressive forces, and that, by extension, helps work toward a more democratic and egalitarian future.

1

The Democratic Deficit
of Developmental State Theory

The title of this book signifies two interconnected empirical and conceptual tasks: (1) to describe the dilemmas encountered by the project of economic democratization, and (2) to reframe the way that the political economy of development and democratization in Korea, and by extension East Asia, is studied to better situate and align its standpoint in relation to progressive actors involved in democratic struggles. The introduction has already provided a preliminary description of these dilemmas and they will be unpacked further in the empirical chapters that follow. Meanwhile, this chapter is focused largely on the second task. For while the theory of the developmental state has helped to identify many of the place-specific institutions (elite economic ministries, the chaebol, export-led growth orientation) with which such progressive strategies have had to contend, it tells us remarkably little about the agency of progressive actors themselves. Moreover, it lost much of its explanatory value following the Asian financial crisis of the late 1990s, despite the often ritual invocation of it since then as a shorthand for almost any kind of state intervention in East Asian economies. Moreover, the neglect of the complex social composition of various states and the manner in which pro-democratic forces sought to change them blinded its theorists to the experience of non-elite actors and, by extension, the role of contentious politics in shaping developmental politics. Consequently, and perhaps despite the intentions of its proponents, the praise of authoritarian efforts to promote rapid economic growth by developmental state theorists came to share an awkward affinity with and an apologia for the self-congratulatory pro-growth politics of autocratic leaders who separated economic development from democratization.

24 | The Postdevelopmental State

This chapter explores the origin of this "democratic deficit," as I call it, in greater detail. Its source can be found within the very concept of *state autonomy* embraced by the neo-Weberian theorists who constructed the idea of the developmental state as well as within their adaption of Weber's ideal type method. For the concept itself was used to externalize state from society and identify the former primarily with the structure and organization of elite ministries. Consequently, this understanding of the state blinded its theorists to key relations of exploitation and the relational interaction of political and civil society even in its revised form of "embedded autonomy," as discussed below. In what follows, I contrast the neo-Weberian understanding of the state to the rival understandings it rejected, including both structural accounts within the Marxian tradition and, most importantly, Gramsci's understanding of the "integral state." Drawing on recent critical scholarship on Weber and Gramsci, I argue that the difference between neo-Weberian approaches to state autonomy and Gramsci's notion of the integral state is much more than simply that between two rival ideal *types*. Rather, it is one between two very distinct philosophical *approaches* to concept formation. The first is based on a method—the ideal type—that comes at the cost of obscuring the practical link between concepts and reality. The other is based upon a "politico-gnoseology," or a political theory of knowledge, that sees ideas as practical "conceptions of the world" that are struggled over and that, consequently, help to shape part of broader reality in which they seek to make an intervention.

In the spirit of immanent critique, this chapter begins by situating developmental state theory in its *practical* context to grasp the theory's potential for political transformation and its limits. As discussed below, developmental state theorists sought to make an important intervention into the neoliberal and neoclassical orthodoxy of the 1980s and 1990s by recognizing the substantial role played by the state in shaping economic development. Against the chaos of market society, they found coherence in the politics of state-led development, an insight that had potentially progressive implications for defending economies against structural adjustment and recognizing the geographical diversity of economic institutions. The chapter then examines the concept of state autonomy and its revision by neo-Weberian state theorists to understand how important concerns surrounding legitimacy and hegemony, and consequently democracy, were bracketed off from the analysis of rapid growth. It then explores the roads not taken in terms of Gramsci's concept of the integral state. This discussion is complemented in the final sections of the chapter by a deeper look at the epistemology that informs the ideal

The Democratic Deficit of Developmental State Theory | 25

type method used by neo-Weberian theorists and its contrasts with the more practice-oriented approach associated with Gramsci. Drawing on recent critical and postcolonial scholarship on both Gramsci and Weber, I argue that Gramsci's ideas can help to loosen the hold of powerful frameworks that have dominated the study of East Asian development to better align itself with the standpoints of pro-democratic reformers and, consequently, can help to grasp problems they seek to overcome. Such a reorientation can aid in the postcolonial reframing of geographical political economy by closely engaging with specific political projects within Korea and East Asia, and beyond, that are aimed at securing a more egalitarian economic model and expanding the parameters of popular democratic participation.

Awkward Affinities

The origins of the democratic deficit are to be found in what, ironically, was an important practical contribution to the politics of development, and one with potential progressive implications, made by theorists of the developmental state. For the theory emerged, in part, from a critique of neoliberal theories of East Asian economic growth, and by extension the Washington Consensus, that provided a powerful intervention into the neoliberal climate of the 1980s and 1990s. Much like the German historical school of economics in the late nineteenth century, developmental state theorists mounted an important defense of uneven institutional development against the "flat world" approaches of free market economists and their idealistic vision of self-regulating markets (Friedman 2005). They grasped that there was no single way to organize economic institutions and that uneven or "late" development in time and space could be an asset as much as a hindrance to economic growth. In contrast to mainstream neoliberal prescriptions that attributed East Asia's rapid development to the liberalization of trade policies and flexible exchange rate policies (see, for instance, Krueger 1987, 42–44; Bhagwati and Krueger 1973; Nam 1995; cf. Chang DO 2009, 9–13), they argued that state intervention had succeeded in producing rapid economic growth in the region. Writing at a time of intense pressure for a rollback of state intervention and regulation, these theorists detailed how states had used their control over financial resources to allocate scarce capital to infant industries in return for meeting performance targets such as the expansion of export markets and the increase of domestic production, rather than the profit-

26 | The Postdevelopmental State

ability of individual firms per se (Woo 1991). Against neoliberal wisdom, they showed that the state had gone much further than just simulating markets, it had actually "gotten prices wrong" (Amsden 1989) by using strict control or "repression" of the financial market to channel financial resources to exporting firms and harness the potential that came with access to external markets, foreign currency, and technology (cf. Amsden 1989, 139–55; Woo 1991, 159–76).

The powerful defense of state intervention against efforts to roll it back—or to "kick away the ladder" (Chang HJ 2002) of state-led industrial policy—from developing countries earned the idea of the developmental state a prominent place in discussions of alternatives to neoliberalism. At the same time, however, the very notion of the state embraced by these theorists and their largely pro-growth orientation limited its applicability to more egalitarian, democratic ends. For at the heart of the state's control of the market, developmental state theorists fixated to the point of idealization on the power of a highly professionalized economic bureaucracy— one based on selective meritocratic recruitment, long-term career rewards, and a sense of corporate coherence through shared values and social ties (Evans 1995, 12; Wade 1990, 339)—that served for them as an example of, even a paragon for, *rationality*. As such, the origins and evolution of various nodal bureaucracies occupied a great deal of attention in this research. Johnson's (1982) study of Japan's Ministry of International Trade and Industry, for instance, reads much like a yearbook of elite bureaucrats while Woo's classic study of Korea's rapid development (1991) traces the roots of Korean industrial policy back to tight cohorts of postwar bureaucrats who emulated colonial-era policies. This corporate coherence, they argued, allowed the bureaucracy to exercise the foresight and clarity to pursue economic planning without falling prey to the interests of individuals or particular social groups (what Cumings 1999 would later call a "spider without a web"). The effectiveness of state policy was seen as a function of the degree of the bureaucracy's insulation (or "autonomy") from the surrounding social structure: a developmental state was one that had an autonomous bureaucracy that could pursue industrial policy.

The standpoint of developmental state research, in other words, embraced an anti-neoliberal politics (albeit one many hoped had democratic ends) that tailored itself to the behavior of elite bureaucracies for whom the economy was conceived as an object that they exercised control over, and that could be measured in terms of industrial expansion and rapid economic growth. And here is where the contours of the democratic deficit begin to be seen. For in the "strong" version of this thesis, states that

The Democratic Deficit of Developmental State Theory | 27

were not only autonomous but that *actively* limited autonomous public organization were seen as being more cohesive and, by extension, better able to pursue coherent and consistent industrial policies (Haggard 1990, 45). As Wade (1990, 375) put it, the coherence of state policies is difficult to maintain when important parts of the state are beholden to sectoral, ethnic, or regional interests. Wade went so far as to *prescribe* insulation in the face of pressures for democratization, arguing that states should "develop corporatist institutions as or before the system is democratized," and wondered aloud whether or not groups excluded under authoritarian regimes such as labor unions and civil society actors should be included in such arrangements. "Labour exclusion," he argues, "gives a government more room to maneuver when austerity comes, and that latitude can be used to restore fast growth more quickly" (Wade 2004, 376n18; as cited in Selwyn 2014, 44). Awkwardly enough, and despite the social democratic complexion of many (but not all) developmental state theorists, this sort of prescription shares an affinity with that of authoritarian regimes and their apologists. For instance, the Korean economist and chairman of the Park Chung-hee Memorial Foundation, Jwa Sung-hee, similarly praises such insulation and exclusion. He argues that Park put "economics above politics" or, rather, "economized Korean politics for the sake of national economic development" (Jwa 2017, 94), and even goes so far as to assert that both Park's coup d'etat (1961) and dictatorial Yushin Constitution (1972) "can be reinterpreted as a vivid example of his efforts to keep the political sector from becoming a stumbling block in the achievement of the nation's long-term economic goals as well as national security" (Jwa 2017, 93).[1]

The awkward affinity between Wade and Jwa here reveals a fine line between description and prescription, analysis and apologia, that raised questions about the democratic credentials of developmental state theory and created some anxiety among its theorists. For instance, Chalmers Johnson admitted to the worry that he was becoming the Ministry of International Trade and Industry's "captive propagandist" after his book on its role in Japan's postwar development was translated into Japanese by

---

1. For an excellent account of the depoliticizing force of the Yushin Constitution, and its roots in Schmittian ideas concerning dictatorship and political authority, see Yi 2022. For a critique of its organicism, anticommunism, statism, militarist and fascist aspects, and the separation of development from democracy as an absolute value, see Ryu Y 2018. Ryu (2016) in particular provides an excellent account of how literary writers came to contest this separation, one that has unfortunately been mimicked by developmental state theorists, and shows how engagement with such literary works can provide a powerful critique of the separation of economic developmentalism from democracy.

the ministry to instruct new officials and to promote the political careers of former senior bureaucrats who were running for seats in the Diet (Johnson 1999, 43–47). Discomfort with how easily the descriptions of its theorists resonated with the prescriptions of conservative actors likely spurred further revisions to the theory, such as Peter Evans's concept of "embedded autonomy." With this concept, Evans relaxed the view of state autonomy-as-insulation by noting how the state's "embeddedness"—its connections to particular social groups—was equally important in the pursuit of developmental goals.[2] The internal organization of developmental states are *not* insulated from society, he argued.

> They are embedded in a concrete set of social ties that binds the state to society and provides institutionalized channels for the continual negotiation and renegotiation of goals and policies. Either side of the combination by itself would not work. A state that was only autonomous would lack both sources of intelligence and the ability to rely on decentralized private implementation. Dense connecting networks without a robust internal structure would leave the state incapable of resolving "collective action" problems, of transcending the individual interests of its private counterparts. Only when embeddedness and autonomy are joined together can a state be called developmental. (Evans 1995, 12)

For some observers, this theory of embedded autonomy opened the research program toward a more democratic vision as development seemed to rest on a coalition of actors that were essential for communication and coordination in Evans's view (cf. Mkandiwire 2001).[3] But in substituting insulation for embeddedness, Evans (1995, 58–59) in no way rejected the underlying neo-Weberian understanding of autonomy. While embedded autonomy hinted at the importance of other social actors (to put the spider back in its web, so to speak), it remained trapped in a narrow view of state autonomy that identified it primarily with the bureaucratic corps and externalized it from society. As such, it lacked a critical understanding of the dynamic social composition of the state, and of those forces that would seek to change it.

---

2. See Krippner et al. (2004) for an excellent forum, one that includes Evans, on the uses and abuses of Karl Polanyi's concept of embeddedness.

3. Evans's work in part inspired a whole new set of literatures on the "political settlements" that lead to state capacity in strategic sectors and shape development, see Kelsell et al. 2022.

Against Legitimacy

The problem with this deficit becomes more visible when seen through Evans's dismissal of rival approaches, such as that of Castells (1992) who sought to define developmental states as ones that base their legitimacy, and national identity, on their ability to promote and sustain economic development. Evans (1995, 257n29) argued that the problem with this definition is that it conflates a *desire* to build legitimacy through economic development with the *ability* to do so, which, for Evans, rested on the question of bureaucratic coherence embedded within strategic partnerships with social groups. But why was Evans so quick to dismiss this view? On the one hand it seemed to accord with his argument that rapid economic development might constitute a shared project of transformation. It offered the potential to look at how a variety of political forces beyond the elite bureaucracies interacted with one another and could perhaps better account for emergent processes of change in the form of conflict and discontent. But on the other hand, by prioritizing an understanding of economic development that situates it *politically*—that is, as a nationalist project of identity construction aimed at securing legitimacy, both domestically and internationally—Castells's reading of development might have undermined Evans's understanding of autonomy and embeddedness, for the latter centered strongly on national economic bureaucracies and their strategic societal partners rather than on the broader relations of forces that shaped the nationalist project. Hence, Evans dismissed Castells's understanding of the developmental state as a *developmentalist* state—an approach that prioritizes ideology and the pursuit of legitimacy through development—alongside other cognate approaches.

Specifically, Evans (1995, 59) rejected two other rival approaches to his understanding of embedded autonomy that might have further complicated his narrow view of state autonomy: the "structural Marxist" view of the "relative autonomy" of the state and the Gramscian understanding of hegemony as an "organic interpenetration of state and society." Evans saw the Marxian insistence on the class character of the state as lacking *specificity* and criticized its perspective on the state as being "constrained by the generic requirements of capital accumulation." Likewise, he saw embeddedness as more *specific* than hegemony. In contrast to these two perspectives, Evans preferred a view of autonomy based on the structure and coherence of the bureaucracy itself, albeit one understood as embedded in "a concrete set of social ties that bind the state to society and provide institutionalized channels for the continual negotiation and renegotiation of goals and policies" (59). Embeddedness, for Evans, implied an "effective amalgam," "a concrete set of connections that link the state intimately and aggressively to particular social groups with whom the state shares a joint project of transformation" (59). In his rejection of these rival understandings of the state, Evans closely replicates the language of other comparative politics and political sociology scholars from his cohort (see Munck and Snyder 2007) who embraced a neo-Kantian distinction between *ideographic* (the unique and specific) and *nomothetic* (following general laws and tendencies) explanations. Their focus was on producing an analysis of what was unique about specific state structures and their underlying connections to societal actors in a manner that facilitates comparison rather than general laws and tendencies. But if all it was concerned with was a simple, empirical description of state institutions and policies at a particular moment in time, this comparative focus on state structures and policies might not be a problem. But since the theory of the developmental state focused on a more generalizing and prescriptive set of claims about the role of the state and processes of late capitalist development itself, its elision of a focus on the genetic *and* generic, the general and specific, was problematic and remains so. For it blinded the theory to broader processes of change that undergirded development and the experiences of multiple actors beyond the bureaucracy it negatively affected and who, consequently, sought to overcome authoritarian developmentalism. It also perpetuated a myth that development was merely the result of a meritocratic, development-oriented bureaucracy rather than a more dense and contradictory ensemble of political and economic actors, anticommunist imaginaries, and complex social relations across scale.

In his rejection of a focus on legitimacy, Evans was not alone among state theorists. Rather, he closely follows the language of Theda Skocpol, whose pioneering work on state autonomy catalyzed the neo-Weberian campaign of "bringing the state back in" to the social sciences in the late 1970s (Evans et al. 1985). Skocpol (1979, 31–32) rejected "approaches that treat the legitimacy of political authorities as an important explanatory concept." An indicative approach of what Skocpol was rejecting here is that of her mentor, Seymour Martin Lipset, who understood legitimacy as the capacity of a political system to engender and maintain the belief that existing political institutions are the most appropriate or proper ones for society (Lipset 1959, 86). Lipset put equal weight both on effectiveness—which he understood as an instrumental dimension of government that included an efficient bureaucracy and decision-making system (86)—and legitimacy, understood as more affective and evaluative in terms of how

The Democratic Deficit of Developmental State Theory | 31

groups understand a political system according to their values. As she was trying to distinguish her *comparative* approach from postwar systems theory and other "society-centered" approaches, Skocpol prioritized effectiveness and the organization of the bureaucracy over the dimension of legitimacy and the wider values and actors that configure political systems so that the specificity of the state could be attended to. Likewise, neo-Weberian scholars have tended to distance themselves from the work of other state theorists such as Jürgen Habermas and his student Claus Offe (key influences on Manuel Castells) who sought to account for both the *general* and *specific* contours of the capitalist state. These thinkers also regarded the state in Weberian terms, as a system of rational administration, but argued that the state performed an important but contradictory role in both stabilizing capital accumulation and securing legitimation from society. This meant that the state had to seek to satisfy both *popular* aspirations and the interests of capital, a process that resulted in conflict and contradiction between its legitimation and accumulation functions. In short, analysis of the state required an explicit focus on the intersection between the state, capital, and popular struggle (Clarke 1991, 6–8). Again, such an approach was deemed to be too "society-centered," that is, too generic compared to the more limited, comparative focus on state structure that Skocpol was trying to promote at the time.

It should come as no surprise then that Skocpol preferred to focus on the structures of state organizations and their capacities themselves and, at best, their elite partners instead of processes of legitimation between state and society. If she was concerned with legitimacy at all, it was only in terms of how it might derive from the structure of the state itself rather than through broad societal processes. "If state organizations cope with whatever tasks they already claim smoothly and efficiently," Skocpol (1979, 31–32) argues, "legitimacy will probably be accorded to the state's form and rulers by most groups in society." In her view, what matters most is not the manner in which the state is viewed by the majority, but by "politically powerful and mobilized groups, invariably including the regime's own cadres." Loss of legitimacy by elite groups tends to occur when the state fails to cope with existing tasks or with new tasks suddenly thrust upon it. However, Skocpol asserts, even after great loss of legitimacy has occurred, a state can remain quite stable if its "coercive organizations remain coherent and effective."

> Consequently, the *structure of those organizations*, their place within the state apparatus as a whole, and their linkages to class

32 | The Postdevelopmental State

forces and to politically mobilized groups in society are all important issues for the analyst of states in revolutionary situations, actual or potential. Such an analytic focus seems certain to prove more fruitful than any focus primarily or exclusively upon political legitimation. (Skocpol 1979, 32, emphasis added)

It is clear here that Evans's theory of embedded autonomy and its rejection of legitimation in favor of a focus on the state and its elite societal partners had already been prefigured by Skocpol avant la lettre. It is this rejection, I believe, that firmly marks out the theory of state autonomy, and by extension the theory of developmental state, as a *neo*-Weberian theory.

Traditionally, neo-Weberians have embraced the *neo-* prefix based on their distinct views of the autonomous role of the state. Following Evans (1995, 30), what makes the developmental state a *neo*-Weberian theory is that while Weber saw the state as an adjunct to private capital, they saw it as transformative agent that played a much more active and interventionist role. Economic bureaucracies exercised Johnson's "plan rationality" or, as, as Thurbon (2016) puts it, a virtuous "developmental mindset" to spur development. But these theorists are also strongly *neo*-Weberian inasmuch as they dropped the Weberian concern with legitimacy and legitimation. So much is visible not only from the discussion above, but also in their abridged use of Weber's definition of the state as a "compulsory association claiming control over territories and the people within them" (Skocpol 1985, 7, also cited in Evans 1995, 5). This paraphrased adaptation elides Weber's original emphasis by substituting "association" for "human community" (*menschliche gemeinschaft*) and by omitting Weber's reference to legitimacy from the original: "Today, however, we have to say that a state is a human community that (successfully) claims the monopoly of the legitimate use of physical force within a given territory" (Weber 1946, 78). As Kalberg (1980) points out, Weber understood legitimacy not solely as an effect of organizations but as a product of individuals ascribing legitimacy to them. In short, the legitimacy of an organization is something to be examined in terms of the "elective affinities" that exist between it and other forms of social action, other value spheres and orientations. If neo-Weberian theorists of the developmental state were interested in remaining true to their Weberian origins, they might have given stronger consideration to how nonstate actors, such as pro-democracy movements and their value spheres, come to shape the state's legitimacy, or to contest particular state activities they deem illegitimate, or both. But instead, by neglecting to look for elective affinities between state and nonstate actors,

The Democratic Deficit of Developmental State Theory | 33

their theories came to share an awkward correspondence with politicians seeking to derive their authority from the organization of the state itself.[4]

Decline of a Research Program

One consequence of this relatively limited focus on state structure and organization by developmental state theorists was the gradual decline of their research program. Their understanding of state autonomy proved to be an Achilles heel, for when its "rationality" could not be found it was difficult to defend the theory.[5] This was particularly the case in the face of the 1997–98 financial crisis, among other events. This event led developmental state theorists into a series of inconsistent and retrospective revisions: tell-tale signs of a research program in decline (Lakatos 1970; Jayasuriya 2005; Buroway 2009). If autonomy could not be found in the economic bureaucracies, it was suddenly to be seen in other areas of state capacity, such as biotech (Wong 2005), knowledge-based industries (Chu 2002), and crisis management and construction (Kalinowski 2015). Some admitted that neoliberal reform had fundamentally altered the economy, but still saw a role for the elite bureaucracies in defending against the worst of neoliberal policy (Shin JS and Chang HJ 2003). Others saw the family-controlled conglomerates as an important vestige of the developmental state, one whose close, interlinked form of cross-shareholding held a potential developmental function that encouraged patient capital and fended off a regime of shareholder value that might stymie innovation (Jeong SI 2004). Despite their diversity, what these different views have in

---

4. For a cognate critique of the priorities of neo-Weberian social science, see Brown 2023, 91–93.

5. It should also be clear that this definition of "rationality" lacks any clear psychological basis beyond the orientation of staff toward a particular set of "developmental" values. What is not considered here, however, are the various psychological processes, including anxiety, resentment, and other feelings and emotions, and social pressures that shape them, that affect planning bureaucracies and individual officials in a differential and conflicted manner, what Sioh (2010) calls the "not-said" that surrounds planning and development. In contrast, a more critical view of embodied rationality might have paid attention to unconscious drives and processes as a "necessary correlate to consciously held knowledge and a mediator between individual subjectivity and socio-historical processes" (Bloch 2019, 521). It is beyond the scope of the present work to explore the psychoanalytical aspects of bureaucracy in more detail, but see Doucette (2020a) for a fuller examination of elite bureaucrats' anxious and conflicted feelings about representations of the Korean "model."

common is an ad hoc and post hoc revision of the core empirical claims of developmental state theory about the autonomous nature of Korea's economic planning ministries. If that autonomy could not be found, it had to be located elsewhere, or else the role of the state could not be justified. For the theory was largely based on the tautology that an autonomous state is the precondition for rapid development, and rapid development is the product of an autonomous state rather than a political regime seeking legitimacy. And if the state was not autonomous and developmental, it was likely captured and predatory (Evans 1995). Such tautologies, however, made it difficult to use the rubric of developmental state theory to account for processes of adaptation where autonomy became much less straightforward (Wong 2011; cf. Pirie 2018). In such scenarios the developmental state was mostly seen as something that had declined in the face of the structural constraints brought about by new global market realities. There was no way to effectively adapt the theory to changed realities by altering its core claims about autonomy and embeddedness in a manner that could better account for relations of coordination, contestation, and conflict in the pursuit of hegemony.

Ironically, the basis for such revision is precisely what the two perspectives that Evans and others sought to avoid seemed to provide. For they showed that the state was a product of hegemonic struggles, and, by extension, it was not as independent from the dynamics of capital accumulation as had been let on. As Dae-oup Chang (2009) discusses, the value of a Marxist focus on what Evans calls the "requirements of capital accumulation"—in the form of class relations between the state, labor, and capital—is that it allows us to see that while the Korean state's interventions may have disciplined individual capitalists within a particular transnational context, they were generally oriented toward extending capitalist relations in society at large and took place not only through industrial policy but, importantly, through the active subordination of labor to capital by varied means. To paraphrase Marx (1982, 926), the capital that was so skilfully allocated by the economic bureaucracy "comes dripping from head to foot, from every pore, with blood and dirt." But yet developmental state theorists preferred to reify capital as a *quantitative* entity over which bureaucracies could demonstrate "rational" control (e.g., as money and finance) rather than as a *qualitative* social relation (e.g., the wage labor relation) in which they were embedded. In this regard, Chang argues that developmental state theorists *mystified* the class nature of state intervention by *mistaking* relations between businesses and bureaucrats with state-capital relations. "In consequence, the state appears to be class neutral and exist above class relations as long as the state has leadership over private capital" (Chang 2009, 24). The result was a focus that neglected the role of the state in repressing labor for the *benefit* of capital, as well as the attempts of labor to effectively contest managerial and state power over them. Such a focus might have tempered claims about state autonomy, but it was rejected in favor of an approach that focused on those interventions in finance and industrial policy where the state appeared to be playing a directive role (cf. Hart-Landsberg 1993; Jeong SJ 2007).

The Marxist approach, however, was not the only approach to the "requirements of capital accumulation" rejected by developmental state theorists. Their work also fails to engage with cognate critiques by feminist scholars who examined the role of the state in shaping the gendered nature of the labor process and relegating social reproduction to the private sphere. For instance, Gottfried (2015) argues that the secret to the "enigma" of Japanese capitalism lies in its "reproductive bargain": the subordination of women workers to unpaid reproductive work and precarious, nonstandard employment. Seungsook Moon (2005) developed similar insights into the context of Korean developmentalism by noting how its regime of gendered citizenship mobilized men to be "martial and productive" in the military and the workplace and women to be marginalized in production and mobilized in the domestic sphere (see also Hur 2013). These arguments are complemented by that of other scholars who have looked at how women workers have contested these dynamics from the days of the developmental dictatorship to the expansion of nonstandard forms of work following the Asian financial crisis to the present moment (Chun JJ 2003, 2011; Kim SK 1997; Nam 2021). What this Marxist and feminist work on East Asian development shows us is that understanding the role of the state requires a focus that is sensitive not only to economic bureaucracies but also to the wider interactions within political and civil society that shape and contest the broader politics of development. It is precisely here where Gramsci's concept of hegemony, and his understanding of the state and civil society as being "organically" related and mutually constitutive, is most useful. For his notion of the *integral state* allows us to think about how the state is constituted as an interpenetration of civil and political society and to align scholarship with the goals, practices, and concerns of pro-democratic movements. As the approach taken in this book is based upon it, it deserves greater attention here. Hence, the second half of this chapter explores this notion in greater depth both to contrast it to neo-Weberian state theory and to reveal the very different set of philosophical assumptions about concepts and ideas on which it rests.

An Integral Analysis

As Liguori (2015) notes, Gramsci's discovery of the integral state first occurred in his study on intellectuals. It was here that Gramsci first extended his definition of the state to include both political and civil society. This study surveyed the role that intellectuals played as producers of political and economic ideas at a variety of scales. This study helped Gramsci to clarify his theory of hegemony—of dominance and leadership through a balance of coercion and consent—by accounting for the diverse role that intellectuals played in helping dominant groups to secure it through both the practical role they played in political and civil society—including the political party, trade unions, and educational institutions—and their production of or alignment with particular conceptions of the world, or both, including the concept of the state. Writing from his prison cell to his sister-in-law Tatiana Schucht in 1931, Gramsci notes that his study has come to address

> certain determinations of the concept of the state, which is usually understood as political society (a dictatorship, or a coercive apparatus to make the mass of the people conform to the type of production and of the economy of some given moment) and *not as a balance of political society with civil society* (or, the hegemony of a social group over the entire national society, exercised by means of the so-called private organizations, such as the church, trade unions, schools and so on), and indeed, intellectuals are especially active in civil society. (Gramsci to Tatiana Schucht as cited in Liguori 2015, 8, emphasis added)

As Liguori (2015, 3) writes, Gramsci was particularly concerned with how in the Italian context some intellectuals had "absolutized" the concept of the state in a manner that attributed to it an omniscient form of rationality. Gramsci saw this representation as one bound up with situations of uneven geographical development that produced a weak bourgeois and a stratum of intellectuals seeking to ally or even identify themselves with the state itself.

Gramsci argued that this phenomenon often takes place where the international situation is favorable to change but where there is a lack of strong local forces pushing for development, and, as a corollary, where intellectuals are not strongly tied to any particular economic group. In this context, intellectuals are more likely to be the bearer of new ideas:

The problem can be formulated as follows: since the State is the concrete form of a productive world and since the intellectuals are the social element from which the governing personnel is drawn, the intellectual who is not firmly anchored to a strong economic group will tend to present the State as an absolute; in this way the function of the intellectuals is itself conceived of as absolute and pre-eminent, and their historical existence and dignity are abstractly rationalized. (Gramsci 1971, 117)

Pierre Bourdieu (1998, 38) once described this idealistic understanding of the state as a symptom of the bureaucratic thinker (*penseur fonctionnaire*), a figure obsessed with the "official representation of the official" who portrays "bureaucracy as a 'universal group' endowed with the intuition of, and a will to, universal interest; or as an 'organ of reflection' and a rational instrument in charge of realizing the general interest." Gramsci was particularly concerned that this idealized concept of the state could be used to obscure the relational balance of forces that shape it. While he was thinking here about the view of the state promoted in the fascist, neo-Hegelian idealism of Italian thinkers such as Giovanni Gentile, it is easy to see how his critique can extend to the views of developmental state theorists and the authoritarian apologists whose views they share an awkward affinity with.

Elsewhere in *The Prison Notebooks*, Gramsci notes how laissez-faire liberalism evinced a similar problem by attributing rationality not to the state, but primarily to the market economy, which it equates with civil society as a normative sphere of freedom. Gramsci points out here, however, that "laissez-faire too is a form of State 'regulation,' introduced and maintained by legislative and coercive means."

It is a deliberate policy, conscious of its own ends, and not the spontaneous, automatic expression of economic facts. Consequently, laissez-faire liberalism is a political programme, designed to change—in so far as it is victorious—a State's leading personnel, and to change the economic programme of the State itself—in other words the distribution of the national income. (Gramsci 1971, 160)

By pointing out that laissez-faire, like neoliberalism or developmentalism, is an ideological project, one aimed at securing the hegemony of one social group over another (despite differences in whether or not this hegemony is to be maintained relatively more through the consent of various so-called private organizations or through the coercive apparatus of the state itself), Gramsci extends his understanding of the integral state—conceived of as a balance of forces—to both politics and economics. This second extension is relevant to the economic imaginaries of both developmentalism and neoliberalism for it reveals that the state and market cannot be reduced to an autonomous set of laws and tendencies—that is, to a self-regulating market in the sphere of civil society, or the mindset of a supposedly virtuous economic bureaucracy—confined to either sphere. Instead, the state and the market must be understood as a *relational* balance of social forces.

This dialectical nature of Gramsci's conception of the integral state should not be ignored. While he stressed that the state was composed of a balance of political and civil society, Gramsci (1971, 160) warned that the distinction between the two of them should not be regarded as organic, however, but merely methodological. While Gramsci often appears to position civil society as the site of consent and political society as a site of coercion, it is important not to interpret these identities as ontologically distinct—civil society as the sphere of freedom and the state as a sphere of domination—but as *relational* and *processual*. The functions performed by, the relations between, and the identity of, actors that compose political and civil society are variable, transformable, and even, at times, interchangeable. As Liguori (2015, 4) writes, "The complexity of the role of the ('integral') state lies in the fact that it holds force and consent together in a dialectical nexus, one of 'unity-distinction.'" There is "unity" to this nexus because the conjunction between political and civil society is what often legitimizes the state or provides it with allies and ideas—political and civil society can work in tandem—and "distinction" because the two are separately institutionalized (e.g., as politics and economics) and can exhibit coercion and conflict. Because they are relational and processual, the ties that bind state to civil society into a cohesive historical bloc with a clear hegemonic project are not something to be taken for granted, for they are shaped by multiple historical and geographical processes and subject to change and transformation. This contingency also means that the forms of consent and coercion involved in the integral state are always changing and specific to context (Whitehead 2015). In some, coercion predominates, while in others consent is crucial.

By way of illustration, the policies promoted by a specific actor, such as a corporation, nongovernmental organization, consumer cooperative, or trade union, might be accepted or appropriated by state actors (political parties and bureaucrats) seeking a broader basis of consent,

The Democratic Deficit of Developmental State Theory | 39

thus helping to legitimize a particular regime. Conversely, these groups might even be brought into the state, in an extended sense, to provide services at some times and places (but not others) or to participate in decision-making bodies (such as social dialogue bodies), in this sense complicating these functions as solely belonging to political or civil society. In other instances, some of these actors may be repressed by or excluded from political society in the interests of a specific class project such as rapid development or austerity. In some cases, civil society itself might be the coercive force and the state the site of new ethical relations, such as in cases of right-wing reaction against forces and policies associated with equality, diversity, and democratization. Furthermore, even the identity of particular historical actors might be associated at different times and places with both political and civil society, as in the case when dissident intellectuals are elected by a political party and become part of the state, or when former politicians and bureaucrats join social movements or civil society organizations. The elusiveness of stable boundaries here should not be taken as a problem of conceptual precision but, rather, as the product of social and spatial processes. As Timothy Mitchell (1999, 77) remarks, to understand the state we should not seek to find a "definition that will fix the state-society boundary (as a preliminary to demonstrating how the object on one side of it influences or is autonomous from what lies on the other)." What needs to be examined instead, he argues, are the "processes through which the uncertain yet powerful distinction between state and society is produced." Gramsci's dialectical approach provides a method to do.

There is a third extension to this integral conception of the state that is important for our purposes here, and this regards its spatial dimensions, which extend beyond a fixed conception of scale. In other words, the state should not be idealized as merely a national phenomenon but analyzed in light of the processes that produce coherence along multiple geographic registers. As Jessop (2005, 425) remarks, despite Gramsci's concern with various national political conjunctures, his focus on the national level should not be taken as a symptom of methodological nationalism.

Gramsci was extremely sensitive to issues of scale, scalar hierarchies of economic, political, intellectual and moral power, and their territorial and non-territorial expressions. He was not a "methodological nationalist" who took the national scale for granted but typically analysed any particular scale in terms of its connection with other scales.

40 | The Postdevelopmental State

This is an important insight for the present study, which examines what might be relatively construed as domestic political struggles over the direction of economic reform. While they may be methodologically defined as "domestic," the activity of these actors and the forces that shape them should not be considered as simply *confined* to national borders (cf. Hart 2020b; Goswami 2020). The transnational reach of capital and migration flows, and the complex geographies of solidarity and governance across place and scale, for instance, can affect the capacities of even the most "local" actors. By way of example, the mobility of social movements and other civil society actors in Korea during the Park Chung-hee regime was relatively constrained due to restrictions on travel. This phenomenon did not mean, however, that their agency or the source of the structures they sought to change should be seen as being territorially confined. As McCormack (2011) remarks, the transnational reach of the Park Chung-hee regime—in terms of both its repressive activities, labor migration policies, and political economic networks—helped to germinate a transborder, cross-nation civil society concerned about Korean politics. Crackdowns on Korean students abroad and the abduction of famous dissidents in foreign countries in the 1960s and 1970s led to solidarity movements that helped the fight for democracy and, in some ways, stimulated later developments within global civil society (for instance, as a precursor of the global justice protests of the mid-90s to early 2000s and contemporary movements against military bases). Even under rigid dictatorship, we should not assume that the agency of social forces is necessarily confined to the local or domestic scale.

This final point resonates with the critique of developmental state theory within human geography. Geographers have mostly focused on its "territorially trapped" nature, that is, its tendency to view the national and the international as discrete phenomena (Agnew and Corbridge 1995, 78–102; Agnew 1994). It's a problem that stems from the narrow focus on state structure and organization. To overcome this trap, geographers and other critics have argued for a more relational, transnational, and multiscalar lens (Park, Hill, and Saito 2011; Hart 2018) that is sensitive to multiscalar interaction between actors that shape the state's role in development and democratization (Doucette and Lee 2015; Hwang 2016; Hwang and Park 2014; Park BG and Choi YJ 2014) and that have produced distributed, contested, and complex relations of authority. The work of Jim Glassman is particularly instructive here. Drawing upon Gramsci's relational understanding of politics and economy, Glassman (2018) advocates that the

The Democratic Deficit of Developmental State Theory | 41

(geo)politics and economics of East Asian development be regarded as *integrally* related, as bound together through *transnational* class processes that integrated economic development with militarism and repressive capacity (see also Meulbroek and Akhter 2019). The enrollment of Korean firms into transpacific and inter-Asian processes of class formation through war-marking and overseas procurement, he argues, were crucial to Korea's industrial transformation. In this case, what is normally regarded as a background context for state autonomy (e.g., Woo 1991) here takes on the quality of an explanation independent of specific activities often associated with developmental states (Glassman 2018, 12; cf. Song HY 2019a).[6] In making this argument, however, Glassman does not reject the idea of a "developmental state" so much as he revises or modifies it, loosening its core claims about autonomy. Here he uses the term to describe states that pursue industrial policy through strict control of specific fractions of capital such as finance, often called "financial repression," and the funneling of the surplus denied to them to other class fractions (e.g., industrial capital). The difference is that, for Glassman, these activities take place within a wider set of (transnational) class relations that a narrow focus on state structure and elite organization (state autonomy)

---

6. This attention to the *transnational* scale of the forces behind Korea's industrial transformation also resonates with Henry Yeung's (2016) recent revision and reworking of developmental state theory to better account for the role of global production networks. Yeung argues that while Korean businesses may have benefited from the initial industrial policies of the developmental state, their later success was as much dependent on their own efforts to articulate themselves within global production networks through developing strong relationships with global lead firms. This argument is most persuasive in Yeung's analysis of the electronics industry that shows how firms like Samsung have made concerted efforts to deepen capacity, establish an international brand and market presence, and link up to global players like Apple. While Yeung's account revises developmental state theory to provide a broader picture of industrial evolution in the midst of globalization, it still works closely along the grain of previous developmental state research and retains the strong claims about the role of the national state—that is, those moderated by Glassman—for the initial period of industrial takeoff. And while Yeung tempers some of the hard claims about state autonomy in East Asian development by noting that not only firm-level initiatives but also dissent from labor and democracy movements restricted the abilities of state actors, he also largely provides an elite- and firm-centered focus on industrial upgrading that is concerned with what is more or less a success story of strategic coupling, one that tells us little of normative and political concerns about equality and democracy, and the standpoints of the actors who advocate for them.

elides.[7] In this sense, continuity and change in so-called developmental states can be understood as a function of broader changes in those relations, rather than simply the presence or absence of an autonomous state.[8]

While geographers have revealed the spatial complexity of the state by paying attention to transnational class processes that have shaped East Asian development, they have often had less to say about the strategies of progressive political forces to contest Cold War legacies at the national level. This is not to say that literature in geography, however, has been blind to a spatially sensitive reading of domestic politics in its critique of developmental state theory. Urban geographers and urban studies scholars have focused on other aspects of developmentalist politics. Their focus on the production of urban space has shown how construction and investment in the built environment provided a crucial site of capital accumulation to affirm strategic state-business ties within Korea, and created a tacit class alliance between middle-class apartment owners and ruling political parties that helped the latter to retain hegemony (Sonn and Shin 2019; Doucette and Park 2019). The work of these scholars shows that class alliances are not merely discursive, or confined to the level of formal politics, but also spatially selective (Park BG 2005, following Brenner 2004, 72). Nonetheless, there remains room in this literature to focus more closely on broader democratic imaginaries that extend beyond the urban to include stronger visions of social and economic democracy, especially in contexts such as Korea where there remains very strong, nationally organized, progressive movements and civil society. The Gramscian approach described here provides a powerful way to do so.

---

7. Gray (2013) makes a similar point and argues that Gramsci's framework of passive revolution recognizes social relations and geopolitics as being mutually constitutive in a manner that corrects for methodological nationalism. Passive revolution, in Gray's view, involves a response to geopolitical pressures by the state that secures the power of capital by selectively adopting some demands from subaltern forces. See also Morton (2007).

8. The reason for this framing, argues Glassman, is that discussions of what constitutes a developmental state have routinely been expanded in a haphazard fashion that "begins to gut the concept of any real analytical utility" (Glassman 2018, 7), including states that merely have high growth rates instead of industrial policies. As Glassman notes, "Thailand, which has had comparatively little in the way of overt industrial policy but has had high growth rates, is counted as a developmental state, while the Philippines, which has had more in the way of overt industrial policy but low growth rates, is not." Glassman cites Amsden (1995) and Leftwich (1995) as examples of this tendency, but his critique is relevant for other work that seeks to associate an ideal type Weberian bureaucracy per se with developmental outcomes (e.g., Evans and Rauch 1999; Henderson et al. 2007).

Epistemology vs. Politico-Gnoseology

From the discussion above, it should be clear that the difference between the neo-Weberian idea of the developmental state and Gramsci's integral perspective is not one between two rival "types" of state in the sense of discrete, comparable phenomenon. For while the former seeks to fix the identity of the state in a parsimonious, either/or fashion, the latter avoids fixing a static identity for the state and emphasizes instead that a relational and processual examination is necessary to grasp the forces that compose and shape state policy. Underlying this distinction are thus two very different philosophical *approaches* to concept formation. As discussed below, the neo-Weberian approach idealizes social institutions in a manner that makes it difficult to grasp their relational construction, for it rests on an epistemology that separates concepts from reality and contributes to the democratic deficit by disguising the standpoint of the observer. In contrast, the Gramscian approach sees concepts as inextricably and practically tied to the world they describe. It demands that the intellectual activity of both the observer and the observed be taken seriously. Consequently, it is an approach that can help aid in the progressive, postcolonial reconstruction of the political economy of democratization and development through greater interaction with the standpoints of democratic reformers and other progressive actors seeking alternatives to both developmentalism and neoliberalism.

Although they do not expand on it at length, the neo-Weberian theorists of the developmental state are explicit about the origins of their method. As Evans (1995, 64) explains, following Weber, actually existing developmental states are empirical *approximations* of an ideal type. He then reminds his reader that ideal types have no solid basis in reality but are merely mental constructs. For Weber regarded the ideal type as explicitly not the "average" of the phenomena it describes. Rather, the ideal type resulted from the "one-sided exaggeration of one or several aspects" of a phenomenon or from the combination of single phenomena "that can be accommodated to the one-sidedly emphasised aspects" to produce a unified mental construct (Rehmann 2013, 263, paraphrasing Weber 1988). In *Economy and Society*, Weber uses the term to describe even the concepts and "laws" of pure economic theory, for they

> state what course a given type of human action would take if it were strictly rational, unaffected by errors or emotional factors and if, furthermore, it were completely and unequivocally directed to a

44 | The Postdevelopmental State

single end, the maximization of economic advantage. In reality, action takes exactly this course only in unusual cases, as sometimes on the stock exchange; and even then there is usually only an approximation to the ideal type. (Weber 1978, 9)

In other words, the ideal type construes a "conceptually pure type of rational action" by reference to which the "irrational" and "affectually determined" complexes of meaning at work in people's behavior can be represented as "deviations" (Rehmann 2013, 263). Even the irrational is thought of as ideal type in itself, such as in the case of Weber's understanding of charisma and charismatic leadership as ideal types of authority.

The one-sidedness of the ideal type, however, raises a problem. It allows scholars to easily deflect criticism and evade responsibility for prescriptions based on their ideal types with the excuse that their concept was never intended to capture reality to begin with (Rehmann 2013, 291), obscuring their own situated standpoint within society.[9] As Jan Rehmann points out in his magisterial study and Gramscian reinterpretation of Weber's thought and politics, Weber invokes the authority of Immanuel Kant to justify this approach, and, by extension, to reject every relation of representation between concept and reality, insisting instead on the "discursive nature of our cognition" (Rehmann 2013, 264, citing Weber 1988, 195, 208). As such, for Weber, "it is not the *'objective'* relations of *'things'* but the *ideal* relations of *problems* that underlie the areas of operation proper to the sciences" (Weber 1988, 166, as cited in Rehmann 2013, 264). In my opinion, this austere separation between subject and object—what Weber (1975, 85) himself refers to as an "irrational hiatus" (*hiatus irratio-*

---

9. While Evans regards the developmental state as an ideal type, some neo-Weberian scholars such as Skocpol regarded their understanding of state autonomy not as an ideal type per se, but, rather, as a concept inferred through a process of analytical induction. In this context, there is a stronger claim being made as to the law-determined or causal nature of the phenomenon than in Weber's use of the ideal type, which, as discussed below is based on positing an irrational gap between concept and reality. Analytical induction also has its origins in the "type" method, but is regarded as a method that is able to generalize on the basis of its abstractions. For Znanieki (1934), who coined the phrase, the historical sciences are objective (but not sensory) for they deal with objectively determined values (Hinkle 1994, 57). To my knowledge few developmental state theorists have embraced this view. While Evans was one of the cowriters of the conclusion to *Bringing the State Back In* (Evans et al. 1985), which embraces this method, he nowhere notes the contradictions between analytical induction and the ideal type method. Regardless of these differences on the type method, however, both Skocpol and Evans equate the state with its internal structure and organization.

The Democratic Deficit of Developmental State Theory | 45

nalis) between concept and reality—obscures more than it can elucidate. Ultimately, it results in one big tautology whereby a concept's success in grasping a phenomenon and the criteria for evaluating such success rest ultimately upon ideas that can have no basis in empirical reality.[10]

---

10. The origins of this approach lay in Weber's engagement with neo-Kantianism, and especially with thinkers such as Wilhelm Windelbrand, Heinrich Rickert, and Emil Lask, also known as the Southwest school (and sometimes as the Baden or Heidelberg school) of neo-Kantianism. Reacting against what it saw as a deterministic approach to culture and society based on the model of the natural sciences, this school of neo-Kantianism became known for its distinction between the historical (ideographic) and natural (nomothetic) sciences, a distinction between a conception of law-determined nature and value-determined culture that rests in part on a radical separation between subject and object (cf. Arato 1974). As Rose (1981) discusses, these thinkers considered the concrete world and the intellect to be starkly opposed to one another in a manner that belied Kant's formal presentation of the "thing in itself" in the *Critique of Pure Reason* and his understanding of the synthetic unity of apperception as operating in connection with sense experience. Instead, they embraced an antipsychological understanding of the subject that was focused on the transcendental logic of values (or, for the Marburg school of neo-Kantianism, of *validity*) to the debasement of spatiotemporal reality (Rose 1981, 9). For the Southwest neo-Kantians, critical scrutiny of the faculty of cognition was replaced by a view emphasizing the irrational and inscrutable nature of reality, of which all we might know is the discursive meanings that individuals assign to its endless, meaningless flux (Rehmann 2013, 185). The cognitive subject, in short, was seen primarily as a valuating or value-oriented one.

It's important not to understate the aspatial, ahistorical nature, and anticognitive basis of this understanding. Values were not seen as the result of historical practice in the sense of a sensuous engagement between subject and object. But, rather, the values that subjects oriented their activity toward were considered transcendental; that is, they are "set off both from the real objects they are attached to and the valuations and aims of the subjects involved, forming an autonomous realm beyond the subject and the object" (Rehmann 2013, 228). History is, in this sense, oriented by the philosophy of values rather than seen as a process generative of values on its own. The role of the scientist is to grasp the timelessly valid or "ideal" values within empirical detectible values by nature of his or her being "value-affected" and thus aware of the "value-relatedness" of human thought. In other words, the scientist recognizes empirical value-orientations by being susceptible to values. What makes their thought *objective* is not the discovery of any particular law or tendency based on interaction with the material world (such is not the purview of the historical sciences), but, rather, the suspension of any final value judgment: in other words, through conformity with what is taken to be the valid system of values of scientific culture. The Southwest neo-Kantians, and not Weber per se, are the origin of the "value-free science" he is often associated with.

Weber innovated upon the neo-Kantian understanding of the value relation and concept formation by considering specific values to be not transcendental but historically mutable according to culture and personality. Even though Weber dismissed the neo-Kantian idea of a transcendental realm of values, he retained a transcendental under-

46 | The Postdevelopmental State

Consequently, Weber's arguments remain circular: the ideal type can only be determined by reference to its "success with regard to the cognition of concrete cultural phenomena," but the criteria of success turn out to be dependent on "our" attribution of meaning (Rehmann 2013, 266, paraphrasing Weber 1988, 193–94): that is, the ability of the researcher to posit and detect value-orientations. For values can have no strict or causal basis in empirical reality. As Rehmann (2013) argues, this radically subjectivist approach lacks a critical understanding of its own social standpoint. The ability of a social scientist to grasp his or her object (the values of a particular time and place) is simply regarded as a matter of an elective affinity between their thought and the empirical orientation of the practical values under consideration. There is nothing here to prevent the scientist from projecting their own value-related standpoint—their own unstated value judgments about a particular course of action—back into history and "recognizing" it in its values (either as identical or as different) while dismissing rival approaches that contain explicit value judgments as unscientific (Rehmann 2013, 228). Moreover, Weber's illusion of value-freedom—the idea that social science requires suspension of value judgment, itself seen as an ideal "value" of scientific culture—provides ideological cover for a standpoint that is, in fact, guided by judgments about specific courses of action, and that tailors itself to particular social standpoints in reality. As Rehmann (2013) notes, for Weber this action included a political alliance between the bourgeois and the labor aristocracy posited through a shared ethic; for neo-Weberians, it is oriented toward tacit support for the developmentalist mentalité they saw as shared between growth-oriented state planners, bureaucrats, and other development professionals.

The obscuring of ideological values has been noted in the critical literature on Weberian thought. Weber himself has been criticized for reducing social and structural differences to a series of individual/national values and personalities based on his own value judgments and prejudices. As Farris (2013) points out, for instance, Weber saw the issue of personality in Asia as defined by a "lack" of qualities, especially rationality, that he attributed to a putatively "Occidental" personality. This representation, which Farris (2013, 203–7) argues is particularly prevalent in the last chap-

---

standing of the value-orientation. In essence, he substituted historically variable cultural values in place of transcendental values, seeing value-orientation itself as the transcendental factor. Hence, he retained the distinction between subject-independent objectivity and culturally conditioned, value-guided cognition: a gap between the subjective and the objective world that leads to a radical subjectivism in theory.

ter of Weber's *The Religion of India*—"The General Character of Asiatic Religion"—depicted Asia in an orientalist manner as a homogenous and immobile whole, where individuals were found lacking in psychological autonomy from ascribed meanings, that is, lacking in the sense of personality in the sense that Weber found in the Occident.

> Weber argued that the striving for inner clarity and consistency that he evocatively depicts as the attempt "to take the self by the forelock and pull it out of the mud" was unthinkable in Asia. The individualities nurtured by Asiatic thought were, therefore, by (Weber's) definition, incoherent constellations of inarticulate traits that could not develop into proper personalities. (Farris 2013, 206, citing Weber 1958, 342)[11]

Farris makes the compelling argument that this depiction plays a performative role in Weber's advocacy for a political union between the Puritan personality and the German bourgeoisie. Here, the Asiatic personality becomes a stand-in for the personality-less bureaucracy—one lacking a passionate devotion to a cause—that Weber felt needed to be counterpoised by the charismatic politician imbued with a Puritan-like attitude that he found central to the capitalist mind (Farris 2013, 208–9).

What is interesting about the neo-Weberian theory of the developmental state is how the value judgments of Weber's orientalist framework are inverted. Instead of a personality-less passivity, the neo-Weberians found among the bureaucratic corps a passionate devotion to a plan: the pursuit of rapid industrial development. This value-orientation was assumed to be shared among a staff whose cohesion has been shaped by meritocratic recruitment and long-term career rewards. In this manner, it

---

11. When it comes to the study of personality, Weber was interested in the study of historically specific individuals who stood out for him as markers of culture, and thus bearers of value ideas. The personality was understood as constituted by value-decisions, ultimate standards of values that determine action and give meaning to life, and thus translate into teleological-rational ends (Rehmann 2013, 239). In an elitist twist inspired by Friedrich Nietzsche, Weber further asserted that this ability to institute *meaning* delimits the mental life of a person of culture from other individuals. And by and large, his ideal types of personality concentrate on unique, historical individuals that he sees as bearers of the cultural value ideas that constitute his ideal types: for instance, the (ironically) non-Puritan Benjamin Franklin becomes seen as the representative of the Protestant ethic of thrift and frugality. In other words, the personality served as an ideal type that reflected the internalized values of a wider culture: a part that stood for a whole and that could be used to facilitate cross-cultural comparison.

48 | The Postdevelopmental State

represents something of an affirmative stereotype that performs an important explanatory function for the role of the state in studies of East Asian development much like the discourse of Asian values does in the popular imagination of it that is circulated by politicians and media pundits: the sense of a collective value-orientation that works for the greater good, respects authority, and exercises thrift. But this value-oriented narrative comes at too high of a cost: that of overstating the autonomy of the bureaucracy in a manner that externalizes it from civil society, assumes it to be rational, depoliticizes its activity, and identifies its "personality" with the state.[12] The result is praise for pro-growth politics using examples that may run against the grain of neoliberal accounts but do little to scrutinize the experience and political projects of those affected by the experience of rapid development; as such, it helps perpetuate conservative stereotypes about East Asian development and misses out on important sources of change and transition.[13]

In contrast to Weber's ideal type method, which rests on an epistemology that separates concepts and reality, Gramsci embraces a more concrete understanding of ideas as "conceptions of the world" that are *practically* tied together with reality (Wainwright 2010). Theory, for Gramsci, coincides and identifies itself with elements of practice, it renders practice more coherent and develops its potential, and, vice versa, practice renders theory more rational and realistic. Mental constructs are not seen as the result of attributing values to an irrational, external, empirical reality. Instead, concepts must be seen as bound up with reality itself in a situated,

---

12. This idea of personality might also be contrasted to Gramsci's idea of the person, or *la persona*, as Gramsci preferred to name it. This is a category that Thomas (2009, 398) describes as "less focused upon the interiority of a consciousness as constitutive of identity, than with the imposition (and passive or active acceptance) of an 'exterior' network of social relations that create the terrain of social action and therefore social identity." The personality is not seen as an ideal type of bearer of culture per se, but rather as "an interpenetration and concentration of social relations in a determinate, particular individual" (Thomas, 2009, 435), a historical bloc "of purely individual and subjective elements and of mass and objective or material elements with which the individual is in an active relationship" (Gramsci 1971, 360).

13. The neo-Weberian view shares an awkward affinity with Park apologists such as the controversial conservative sociologist Lew Seok-choon, son of Park's secretary of political affairs Lew Hyuck-in (Ryu Hyŏkin). Lew (2013) approvingly affirms the arguments of developmental state theorists concerning bureaucratic rationality and capacity and argues that Confucian values and associated "affective networks" are what provided state officials and the wider populace with strong "moral" cohesion under the ethical leadership of Park Chung-hee. See Miller J (2021) for an interesting account of the affirmative reception of Asian values discourse by neoconservative thinkers.

The Democratic Deficit of Developmental State Theory | 49

sensuous manner that resists such dualistic thinking (Doucette 2020b; Ekers and Loftus 2020; Kipfer 2012). Peter Thomas (2009, 97n34) names this understanding of ideas a "politico-gnoseology," a term he contrasts to "epistemology." He associates the latter with the problem of the production of knowledge, and the former with the effective reality of human relations of knowledge as a social practice. Paraphrasing Gramsci, Thomas (2009, 228) notes that insofar "as a hegemonic apparatus intervenes on and modifies the relations of force in the superstructures or ideologies, 'the theoretical-practical principle of hegemony,' Gramsci argues, 'also has a gnoseological significance [*portata*].'" Thomas (2009, 123, 228) argues that this view does not reduce knowledge to politics; rather, it shows how knowledge arises within determinate political constellations in a manner that contributes to the transformation of human relations and practices.

Recognition of such situated knowledge, of concepts and ideas as something to be struggled over, to use the terminology of feminist standpoint theory, provides a means for a more critical and reflexive approach to that reality: one that can allow analysis to *reflexively* situate itself within the relations that shape the analyzed and the analyst in a process that might be best described as "interested interaction" (Pels 2004, 286). In short, research is shaped not by *separation* from the world and a *withholding*, or disguising, of judgment. Rather it is shaped by an ethic of *alignment* and *interaction* with actors in the world. This is a strategy that requires critical engagement with practical, real-world political struggles, and the ideas and imaginaries that shape their activity. Such engagement informs this book's strategy of examining the project of economic democratization from the perspective of the integral state, in order to grasp the dilemmas involved in its realization, and to use such challenges as a means for reorienting research on so-called developmental states. Here the task of the researcher becomes something closer to a work of *translation* between difficult political conjunctures and broader social theories in a spirit of revision and recontextualization that can aid social transformation (Ekers et al. 2020; Hart 2018). As such it provides a basis for a postcolonial reconstruction of political economy by overcoming unhelpful ideal types based on orientalist "personalities" and instead aligns itself more critically with the projects of progressive movements. Such alignment, however, does not equate to uncritical praise for specific courses of action and visions of reform. For as feminist standpoint theorists have discussed (Harding 2004), to recognize that knowledge is partial and situated in social reality does not mean reducing analysis to a form of essentialism that reifies identity (e.g., that of specific movements or a "people") outside of the historical experience under study. Rather, it is something more tactical, based on identifying the dilemmas and contradictions in a shared project of transformation. In short, it is a model of *solidaristic* scholarly practice.

This approach to conjuncture-sensitive concept formation is directly inspired by an intervention made long ago by another Gramscian thinker, Stuart Hall, into debates about "authoritarian populism." Hall used the term to describe a form of politics associated with Thatcherism, garnering criticism from Marxian thinkers of a more structuralist variety for lacking a general and global explanation of Thatcherism (Gallas 2016, 11–25). While in no way defending an ideographic approach, Hall (1985, 118) responded that his interest was to self-consciously foreground the political-ideological dimension of what he saw as a "deliberately contradictory" phenomenon: a movement toward a "dominative and 'authoritarian' form of democratic class politics" that was rooted, paradoxically, in elements of populist discontent. (Likewise, the strategic problem of the postdevelopmental state discussed in this book can be seen as an outcome of an attempt to mobilize popular discontent for a project that seeks to reregulate features of developmentalism and neoliberalism rather than pursue a more substantial break with them of either an explicitly social democratic inflection or something beyond.) Reflecting on his approach, Hall contended that his concept was situated in *conjunctural* analysis, constructed during historical events, and thus necessarily more descriptive—a claim he makes for many of Gramsci's concepts—than a purely abstract and theoretical idea that "can be transferred directly into the analysis of concrete historical conjunctures" (Hall 1985, 118). Hall also responded to a second, related critique that is useful to review here for it is germane for the analysis of economic democracy as a reform imaginary: that of "ideologism," or the idea that he was supposedly ignoring economic activity in favor of "the modalities of political and ideological relationships between the ruling bloc, the state and the dominated classes." Hall notes that such a focus does not, in fact, exclude economic-corporate relationships, for "in order really to dominate and restructure a social formation, political, moral and intellectual leadership must be coupled to economic dominance" (119). Rather, his *relative* emphasis on the political-ideological stems in part from its neglect or reductive treatment by economistic accounts. The same motivation animates my account here, especially in chapters 3–5, which can be said to take the form of a *political* economy in the sense that it is precisely such political-ideological practices of popular movements that have been neglected in dominant accounts of the developmental state.

Conclusion

The theory of the developmental state once provided a powerful, practical intervention into the field of East Asian political economy by describing some, but not all, of the key institutions associated with rapid development. However, it neglected the experiences of actors affected by rapid growth and lacked a critical understanding of how political and civil society have shaped and contested state policy, meaning that it missed out on key sources of change and transformation. Addressing this democratic deficit, I argue, requires both an empirical and conceptual reframing of how research on the geographical political economy of development and democratization is carried out, reorienting it toward the socioeconomic contours of inequality—as is done in the next chapter—and the political strategies undertaken to address it, the task of the chapters that follow. As this chapter has shown, this reframing also involves a humbler role for the researcher, shifting their role from a deliberation of an "ideal" type of state to a more strategic, solidaristic intervention sensitive to the projects of pro-democratic actors and aligned with their concerns about social and economic justice. This standpoint of "interested interaction," I believe, should appeal not only to scholars and intellectuals interested in the transformation of Korean and East Asian political economy, but also to those interested in the challenges encountered by pro-democratic actors, democracy movements, and socially engaged civil society organizations in articulating an alternative to developmentalism and neoliberalism elsewhere.

This broader application of this book's approach is discussed further in the concluding chapter, but I add here that it is particularly relevant for places beyond Korea where pressures for democratization and neoliberalization have intersected in complex fashion as they have in contexts as diverse as South Africa, Ethiopia, Ecuador, Brazil, and Taiwan: places where the idea of the developmental state has also recently been revived in an often depoliticizing and contradictory manner. In these places and others, the feeling of having accomplished a historic task, an enormous feat of collective will, only to encounter the potential of the moment seemingly limited by the political and economic constraints of a changing world economy and the process through which reform projects have been imagined is not unique. Rather, it is a condition strongly associated with the experience of the third wave of democratization in diverse locales, for these are places where democratization movements near the end of the Cold War helped to dislodge anticommunist, authoritarian, and developmentalist modes of politics but were also quickly confronted by strong pressures for neoliberalization. This challenge is often described in the language of a condition of postdevelopment in a manner that resonates with the understanding of the postdevelopmental state advanced in this book. In these contexts, the term often signifies, economically, that economic growth has been already achieved, stalled, or even reversed, and denotes efforts to escape or to find alternatives to the various productivist, extractivist, colonial, and market-oriented models of economic development that are often used to construct and govern the Global South or Third World as objects for expertise (Escobar 1995). In many of these cases, the solution to the economic problem of postdevelopment cannot simply be found in simply more growth, narrowly construed, but rather some kind of alternative to it. For some the form this often takes is in the shape of either an idealized "local" or traditional alternative to capitalism that can be equally problematic, for others it involves a radical reimagining of development itself in a more radically democratic vein that aligns it with plural and egalitarian aims and demands in a cognate manner to some of the efforts explored in this book.

Ultimately, understanding the fortunes of such movements requires sensitivity to both structural forces and social standpoints that shape them in the spirit of solidaristic learning and translation provided by the Gramscian approach discussed above. Intellectually, this means that studying efforts to find new alternatives to developmentalist forms of political economy does not proceed deductively: that is, through the selection of an alternative theory and model. Rather it must be grasped through the real or *actual* practices that seek to institute such alternatives. As the discussion of Gramsci has shown in this chapter, his ideas do not provide "the answer" to the question of what an alternative may be, but, rather, a means to locate such practices and ideas that seek to realize one. Likewise, in what follows economic democracy is not seen as a model to be pulled down from the shelf and used to judge initiatives as simply right or wrong. Rather, it is project understood in relation to the terminology and practices that shape it, along with relational comparisons with other cases in the spirit of overcoming the democratic deficit of developmental state theory. This is the task to which the remaining chapters now turn.

2

The Political Economy of the Postdevelopmental State

To better understand the economic *rationale* for the project of economic democratization, in other words the structural conditions toward which it addressed itself, this chapter examines the transformation of Korea's political economy over the last 25 years. For the changes that have shaped Korea's political economy within this period have raised important strategic questions about both the nature of the economy and the priorities of reform. One event stands out in any account of the contemporary period: the Asian financial crisis of 1997–98, or the IMF Crisis as it is known in Korea. For this event corresponded to the inauguration of the first liberal administration to emerge from the pro-democratic bloc following Kim Dae-jung's victory for the Democratic Party in the 1997 presidential elections. This conjunction is topical, for Kim's administration accepted the unenvious task of finding a solution to the crisis while also seeking to institute reforms that would satisfy long-standing demands for political and economic democratization. It was at this moment, and with this task in mind, that the *integral state*—the dense connections and nexus between political and civil society—began to become particularly operative within the pro-democratic bloc as a source of policy ideas and as a mechanism of legitimation for liberal administrations. As argued in the previous chapter, grasping the dynamics of the integral state requires a reorientation of developmental state research. Instead of *idealizing* the state as a coherent, cohesive, autonomous entity, a standpoint sensitive to the activity of the pro-democratic bloc and the liberal administrations that have emerged from it is required. But this shift also requires a change in economic metrics. Instead of the usual focus on the dynamics of rapid growth, a broader range of indicators concerning socioeconomic inequality is necessary in order to situate the political and ideological dynamics of progressive economic and legal reform explored in the following chapters.

For this reason, the present chapter focuses on the broad economic contours of this postcrisis period and highlights some of the persistent problems of inequality and enduring power relations that progressives have sought to tackle. As discussed below, the crisis led to the rapid extension of an already nascent neoliberal model of economic governance to wider spheres of the economy and crystallized a pattern of growing economic inequality that continues to be felt to the present day. And yet despite neoliberal restructuring, relations from Korea's developmentalist past continue to inform the present: the power of the largest chaebol has grown considerably; elite ministries and a resilient conservative bloc continue to frustrate liberal and progressive forces; and labor remains relatively marginalized. Grasping this condition, of what we might call the economic contours of the postdevelopmental state, requires a framework sensitive to both continuity and change. Unfortunately, neither the state nor market-led approaches that have long dominated Korean political economy are very helpful in these regards. Both tend toward a parsimony that is unhelpful for grasping its contradictory dynamics. Moreover, despite the polemical exchange between these two approaches—based on attributing "success" to either the market or the state—about the period of rapid growth (Stiglitz 2002; Weiss 1998), neither has had much to say about the dynamics of the last three decades, a period of slower growth in which neither the "rationality" of the state nor the market is readily apparent.[1]

Likewise, the economic complexity of the contemporary period, and its unique contours of expanding inequality and resilient corporate power, represent a challenge for other, more critical perspectives that have been used to analyze the contemporary global political economy, such as the broad literature on financialization. This concept has also been used by Korean scholars to understand the transformation of the Korean economy (for a review, see Park HJ and Doucette 2016) and has shaped domestic debates about the priorities of economic reform, as explored in chapter 3. But while the idea has some utility for analyzing some of the causes of crisis and the expansion of financial activities such as speculative invest-

---

1. Nonetheless, there are a few who view this period as proof of resilient "developmental" coordination (Evans 2014; Kim KM 2020; Thurbon 2016).

The Political Economy of the Postdevelopmental State | 55

ment in credit, stocks, and real estate since then, it also has its own limits for grasping the place-specific processes that have shaped economic reform in Korea. For example, the explosion of household debt and its absorption into speculative financial activities is one area where financialization can be seen, but when it comes to the chaebol the evidence is to the contrary, as discussed below. For the chaebol that survived the crisis have reduced their dependency on external finance by shrinking their debt burdens and have retained managerial control over their conglomerates *despite* reforms aimed at improving shareholder value and markets for corporate control. Furthermore, financial reforms alone do not account for the broader growth in inequality since the financial crisis. Much of it can be directly related to the growth of the nonstandard employment relations (or "irregular work" in Korean terminology) that has occurred since then. While the financial crisis may have provided a rationale for labor restructuring, the expansion of precarious labor relations since the crisis should not be reduced to it. As explored below and in chapter 4, liberal administrations since the crisis have continued to institutionalize a dual labor market model that includes stark differences in pay and benefits between regular and nonregular workers. And despite efforts to expand social protection for nonstandard workers and social welfare in general, these have grown at a relatively slow pace that many argue has not been able to address the inequality caused by both the long-standing subordination of labor and the neoliberal restructuring of the labor market.

Although I use the term "postdevelopmental state" to primarily grasp the strategic dilemmas encountered by progressive forces within political and civil society, it can also help to grasp the structural complexity of this conjuncture and its contradictory dynamics. In an economic register, the term helps to describe a predicament that defies parsimonious either/or description, for it combines elements of both developmentalism and neoliberalism. It can be used to capture how financial reform has mingled with deepening dependence on export-led economic growth; how neoliberal labor market reform has deepened, in many ways, the developmentalist exclusion of labor; and how despite the explosion of household debt alongside other speculative activities, the largest chaebol have become stronger and more powerful. Nonetheless, the term's utility for capturing the contradictory nature of these structural changes does not mean it should be regarded as an *ideal type* or merely a structural description. Rather, it is useful because it helps to grasp both a problem and attempts at its solution. In other words, it shows that the developmentalist legacy of the past continues to shape the neoliberal present and suggests that the contradictions produced by them have yet to be overcome despite the political project of economic democratization. To better understand this dilemma, this chapter provides a roughly *quantitative* account of structural changes that have shaped inequality in a manner that sets the stage for the relatively more *qualitative* interpretation in the chapters that follow of how reformers have tried to address them through the project of economic democracy and its cognate initiatives of creating income-led growth and a "society that respects labor."

To do so, the chapter starts by examining financial reforms that occurred before and after the crisis that help capture both the changing dynamics of corporate and household debt in the economy and the continued power of the largest chaebol. It first revisits some of the literature on Korea's "high-debt" model to see what has changed and, consequently, paints a picture of state-business relations that is more contested and contradictory than has been emphasized in classic work on the developmental state. These two areas are salient for discussion for they help reveal both new and old sources of inequalities of wealth and power in the economy. They also reveal how the dynamics of debt and savings that animate the Korean economy have raised worries of further financial and livelihood crises under liberal and conservative administrations alike. The chapter then moves on to discuss concerns about income inequality, welfare expansion, and irregular work. These topics are salient for understanding the challenge of the postdevelopmental state in a more granular fashion, for they reveal several key dimensions of the problem of socioeconomic inequality that reformers have tried to address in their efforts to extend democratization. The final section returns to the broader macroeconomic picture of the Korean economy in which these dimensions are located. It argues for greater attention to how financialization and other political economic processes unfold in a place-specific and geographical variegated manner. Instead of seeking to capture these processes through a one-size-fits-all understanding of developmentalism, neoliberalism, or financialization, what is necessary, I argue, is a reflexive approach to conceptual development and application, particularly in export-oriented contexts such as South Korea. The chapter concludes with some final thoughts about how the macroeconomic context it has explored helps to grasp the perceived necessity for economic democratization and the various imaginaries, policy initiatives, and relations of force as explored in the chapters that follow.

The Politics of Debt

The period since the 1997–98 Asian financial crisis has been animated by a dynamic of continuity and change that is difficult to capture using the pro-growth rubrics of either developmental state theory or mainstream neoliberal wisdom concerning free markets. Nonetheless, grasping the dynamics of this period is essential for understanding the challenges encountered by the project of economic democratization. For their part, scholars associated with both perspectives have tried to understand the crisis itself, and while they disagree on the causes—some see it as the result of "crony capitalism" of collusive state-chaebol relations (Kang D 2002) while others see it as the effect of premature liberalization (Chang HJ et al. 1998)—both recognize the profound effect it had on the dynamics of debt and finance within the Korean economy. The shifting dynamics of debt and finance are thus a good place to begin to understand the effects of the crisis, for the transformation it induced is particularly visible when it comes to both corporate and household debt. Whatever take one may have on the vices or virtues of the high-debt model, it is clear that the pre-crisis system of industrial expansion using policy loans—a system considered to be a key feature of Korea's developmental state—has been drastically reformed (Doucette 2016). The highly leveraged chaebol have been forced to considerably reduce their debt burdens following the crisis. As figure 1 shows, the debt levels of large manufacturing firms reached dramatic highs shortly before the crisis from what had already been a high level for decades. The debt-to-equity ratios of manufacturing firms reached close to 500 percent in the late 1970s and early 1980s, but rapidly declined following the crisis. In its wake, policymakers placed strict limits on corporate borrowing to keep debt ratios under 100 percent to bolster investor confidence that firms had the assets needed to pay back their borrowings should there be a problem. While this shift led to the collapse of numerous chaebol firms, it also benefited the largest chaebol, who seem to have not only survived but thrived from this transformation. In parallel, however, Korean households quickly transitioned from a high rate of savings to become more indebted than ever, raising concerns about the exact nature of the postcrisis transition and its consequences for the economy.

To better understand this transformation, the sources of Korea's highly indebted conglomerates need to be understood. In this case, they can be found in the Korean state's efforts to support the expansion of the economy through various financial means that benefited the chaebol, includ-

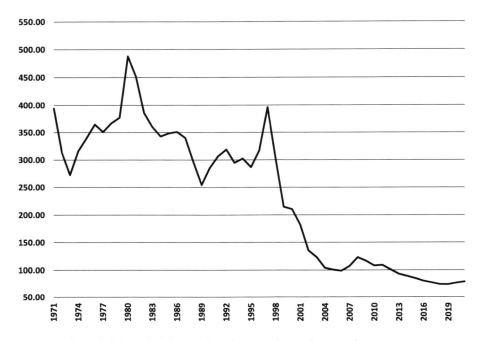

Fig. 1. The end of the high debt model? Debt ratio of manufacturing firms, 1970–2021 (%). (Data from Bank of Korea.)

ing export subsidies, policy-driven loans geared toward industrial upgrading and export expansion, and tight regulation of import and export licenses (Amsden 1989; Wade 1990; Woo 1991). To support the expanding chaebol, the state channeled household savings into industrial development and recycled foreign exchange earnings through its control and direction of the banking system. As Glassman (2018, 10–11) notes, this topic area (state control of finance and the funneling of surplus toward industrial expansion) is one of the more persuasive features of the high-debt model described by the developmental state approach. Nonetheless, the ability of the Korean state to do so did not purely derive from its internal structure and organization (its autonomy or externalization from society) but needs to be situated in its socio-spatial context. In short, Glassman argues that the ability to allocate finance to industry was complemented by capital provided through foreign aid, and especially by wartime overseas procurement contracts provided by the US during the Vietnam War, and, later, by lucrative construction contracts awarded to Korean firms for overseas infrastructure projects (Glassman 2018). Economic expansion was both a product of domestic industrial policy *and* the participation of

The Political Economy of the Postdevelopmental State | 59

the state and business groups in the broader Pax Americana.[2] During the Cold War, this context was supportive of rapid industrialization policies that benefited the chaebol, leaving them both highly diversified and highly indebted. After the end of the Cold War, with the fall of the Soviet Union and growing détente with China, it was less so. In these regards, the choice between a neoliberal and developmentalist approach to economic policy is not simply an ideational one chosen by state policymakers in a vacuum but also was influenced by a broader regional and international context. Nonetheless, this context does not mean that the sources of the eventual restructuring of Korea's high-debt model were simply "external" to the Korean economy.

In general, the debt-fueled expansion of the Korean chaebol was paralleled by strong GDP growth (fig. 2) for several decades. But the political and economic risks of this high-debt model and the growing power of the chaebol within it were immense. And yet they were often understated in literature that idealized the state's rationality in managing the economy, neglecting the complexity of state-chaebol relations. These risks were apparent even during the peak of the developmentalist dictatorship under Park Chung-hee, when the control and discipline of the economy by the state was assumed to be at its highest. Even during this period, state planners became so concerned about the growing power of the chaebol that some sought to use constitutional amendments to limit their power (Kim YT 1999). Consequently, several forms of legislation were eventually introduced during this period to address the growing power of the chaebol. These included the Capital Market Promotion Act of 1968 and Initial Public Offering Inducement Act of 1972 that sought to disperse the ownership of chaebol firms (creating a market for corporate control) and provided ministers with means to target specific firms and to restrict lending and other assistance (Kim JB 2013, 14). This legislation was followed by the introduction of a credit management system in 1974 that required banks and financial intermediaries to monitor lending to groups of affiliated firms (Kim JB 2013, 15). This system was later followed by the Monopoly

---

2. As a number of Marxist and world-systems scholars have shown (Glassman 2018; Chibber 2003; Song HY 2019b; Burkett and Hart-Landsberg 2000) this participation shaped the differential power of both the state and the chaebol in a manner that involved extensive geographical relations of collaboration and contestation that are hard to grasp using Weberian ideal types. At times, the state was able to discipline the chaebol groups, at other times the chaebol's own capacities and international networks allowed it to take the lead in shaping important decisions about regional economic development and urbanization (Choi and Glassman 2018).

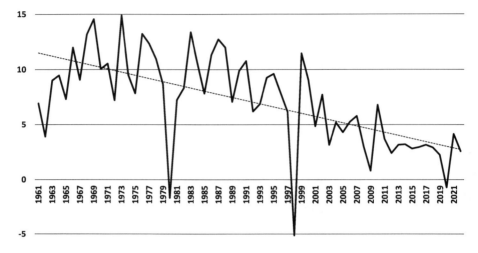

Fig. 2. Growth rates of Korean GDP (annual %), 1961–2022. (Data from World Bank.)

Regulation and Fair Trade Act of 1980 and revised Fair Trade Act in 1986, which continued to target reciprocal shareholding by the chaebol. Nonetheless, many of these initiatives were unsuccessful, as the chaebol used various forms of collusion and cross-shareholding to evade restrictions on credit management. Furthermore, such practices were often tolerated if conglomerates met performance-based targets aimed at expanding their productive capacity and exports to foreign markets. Nonetheless, these regulations reveal that the state-chaebol nexus was much less solid, and much more internally contested, than is often depicted (cf. Kim EM 1997). They also provide a hint of neoliberal reforms that would both precede and follow the financial crisis.

The high-debt system did not only pose economic risks, however. The growing economic power of the chaebol, which it in part created, also made ruling party politicians conscious that the conglomerates might become political rivals—a fear that was borne out during the Roh Tae-woo administration when the chaebol decided to engage in political competition with the Conservative Party. During the 1992 presidential elections, Hyundai's Chung Ju-yung, Daewoo's Kim Woo-chung, and the former president of the Pohang Iron and Steel Company, Pak Tae-joon,

The Political Economy of the Postdevelopmental State | 61

signaled interest in running for the presidency. Chung ultimately ran as a candidate for the Unification National Party, a party created after he signaled his intention to run and that campaigned on reunification and economic deregulation. Though unsuccessful in securing the presidency, the episode revealed that the chaebol were a potential political threat to the ruling party. Perhaps as a response, market-led financial reforms grew considerably in the period after the election. They accelerated with the announcement of President Kim Young-sam's "Globalization" (*segyehwa*) reforms in 1993. Kim sought to phase out policy loans and liberalize external borrowing to encourage stronger market competition. But this policy amplified the risks of the high-debt model. For while Kim's financial reforms intended to strengthen competition by promoting competitive financial markets, they also weakened the ability of the Korean government to regulate and supervise the investments made by the conglomerates. For the chaebol, this opportunity provided them with a chance to finance new investments using resources from financial intermediaries known as nonbank financial institutions (NBFIs). These institutions, often investment arms of the chaebol themselves, borrowed extensively on foreign short-term credit markets. Some used this money to invest in sectors under excessive competition in the mid-1990s, dragging down profits. Samsung's investment in automobiles and Daewoo's investment in semiconductors (neither of which were areas of their core competency at the time) is a prime example of this trend toward deregulated investment (cf. Shin JS and Chang HJ 2003). In 1993, the 30 largest chaebol raised 53 percent of their borrowed funds from the commercial banks and 46 percent from NBFIs for a combined total of 30 trillion won. By 1997 they were borrowing nearly 68 percent of their funds from NBFIs and only 32 percent from the commercial banks for a combined total of 110 trillion won (see Jeong SI 2004, 59, table 3.6, based on data from the Ministry of Finance and Economy). Korea's external liabilities more than doubled between 1992 and 1997 (Shin JS and Chang HJ 2003, 62). Consequently, during the Asian financial crisis 90 percent of Korea's $120 billion external debt was from the private sector (Kim YT 1999, 453).

The Great Debt Swap

When the Asian financial crisis erupted with the collapse of the Thai baht in 1997, international lenders began to call in the short-term credit they had advanced to Korean firms and financial institutions. NBFIs became rapidly insolvent, leading to a run on the Korean won. Cheap credit dried up and debts were rapidly called in. Consequently, the crisis rapidly spread across the economy as it was put under structural adjustment and austerity induced by the International Monetary Fund (IMF). The restructuring that resulted is by now a well-known story, one that often emphasizes the gains made by foreign capital that bought up considerable assets during the crisis and the rapid institutionalization of neoliberalism in the domestic economy. Citing the chaebol's overinvestment and high debt levels as a moral hazard, and ignoring the deregulation that facilitated it, the IMF helped engineer a solution that saw recapitalized banks privatized and distressed industrial assets sold off. Shares in banks and manufacturing firms were purchased by foreign funds in many cases. As a result, the crisis itself has often been represented as an example of financial imperialism, especially in left-nationalist circles (Jeong SJ and Shin JY 1999; Medley 2000; Wade and Veneroso 1998). Nonetheless, the influence of foreign capital should not distract from the fact that many domestic officials, such as Kim Dae-jung's chief economic advisor You Jong Keun and Bank of Korea governor Chon Chol-hwan, warmly embraced IMF prescriptions and carried out supplementary reforms aimed at increasing market transparency and expanding foreign ownership of Korean firms. Meanwhile, others saw it as a pretense for implementing drastic neoliberal restructuring to the labor market. Despite some friction between Korea and the IMF on what methods to use to dispose of nonperforming loans (Park YC 2006, 80–81), reformers in subsequent liberal administrations would come to regard the embrace of "market fundamentalism" as not simply a matter of IMF pressure but in part initiated by the top economic bureaucrats from the Kim administration.[3]

Regardless of its sources, economic restructuring in the wake of the crisis radically altered the debt dynamics of the Korean economy discussed above. Limits were placed on domestic lending to the industrial sector to lower debt to equity ratios. As can be seen above in figure 1, debt levels were drastically reduced following the crisis alongside new regula-

---

3. As one of Roh Moo-hyun's chief economic policy advisors put it to me in an interview during my doctoral fieldwork in early 2007: "The biggest issue is neoliberalism or as I call it market fundamentalism. It has a history of about 10 years because the DJ [Kim Dae-jung] government introduced it partly by the pressure of the IMF and partly on their own initiative. . . . That movement was initiated by the top economic bureaucrats who came from the Honam government . . . they are the forerunners of the market fundamentalism movement." Honam refers to the area corresponding to Korea's older southwestern Jŏlla Province.

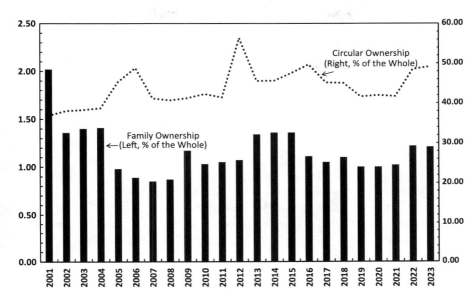

Fig. 3. The continuation of circular ownership: the structure of the Samsung group. (Data from Fair Trade Commission.)

tions on cross-shareholding, succession, and diversification (see Kim KW 2004 for an account of corporate governance reforms in particular). The debt ratios of manufacturing firms have mostly remained under 100 percent ever since, amid declining rates of GDP growth. Ironically, this transformation has benefited the largest chaebol, for they were essentially bailed out by the government and, in many cases, allowed to acquire the assets of their distressed competitors. Consequently, the chaebol became *less* dependent on external finance in the form of bank and NBFI loans. Interest payments on their now reduced debt declined rather rapidly after the crisis. As foreign ownership of chaebol shares increased, however, concerns arose about the chaebol succumbing to a shareholder value-based form of governance that would lead to asset stripping and hostile mergers and acquisition by foreign capital. This dimension of financialization has proven to be overstated despite these concerns, although they are certainly not unfounded as is discussed in chapter 3 (Park HJ and Doucette 2016; Van der Zwan 2014). Instead, most ruling families of the largest conglomerates have remained quite solidly in control of their firms *despite* increased restrictions targeting cross-shareholding and strengthening minority shareholder rights.

As figure 3 shows, using the case of the Samsung group, circular and cross-shareholding remains resilient even as, in some cases, direct ownership by the ruling family has decreased. In many cases, cross-shareholding has allowed for family control to be enhanced. This system of management allows effective control by the ruling family with very little directly owned stock and is discussed in more detail in chapter 3 (see fig. 11 for more detail), but it is prudent to mention here to signal that the chaebol remains a strong and dominant actor in the economy. Since the crisis the largest chaebol have grown to the extent that as of 2020 the revenue of the top 64 chaebol was equivalent to a whopping 84 percent of Korea's GDP, with Samsung's revenues alone sitting at near 20 percent of GDP (Song CK 2020). As Hyeng-joon Park (2013) argues, when discussing these financial changes that followed IMF restructuring, a more nuanced approach is required than simply one that assumes domination by external forces and the dominance of (foreign) financial capital over industrial capital. While it is tempting to depict this period as one that pitted foreign against domestic capital, finance against industry, what has in fact been brought about is a stronger fusion between domestic and international capital, including the rise, Park argues, of the chaebol as a powerful form of transnational capital in their own right—one that plays a dominant role in the Korean economy. In short, while stock ownership by "foreign" financial capital has increased, it generally seems quite happy to profit from ruling families' managerial control of the conglomerates. In other words, these fractions of capital seem to have found a form of harmony within the existing cross-shareholding system.

Regardless of how one interprets the decline of the high corporate debt ratios of the developmentalist period, it is strikingly clear the crisis shifted debt creation from corporations to households. And it is here that many aspects of financialization can be seen within the Korean economy, for this expansion has helped to increase stock market capitalization, and has shaped speculative bubbles in consumer credit, project finance, and real estate (cf. Crotty and Lee 2009; Doucette and Seo 2011). In effect, the Asian financial crisis engineered a historically significant debt swap (cf. Park CJ 2014). Instead of funneling household savings into industrial expansion by a highly leveraged corporate sector through bank credit and policy loans, in its place mortgage and consumer credit markets were expanded. As such, this transformation moved Korea from an economy with high to low household savings, as is detailed in figure 4. The household savings rate remained consistently high before the crisis and low after it, recovering briefly during the COVID-19 pandemic in line with global trends as consumer demand was restrained due to lockdowns and public health measures then declining again as pandemic measures receded. Figure 4

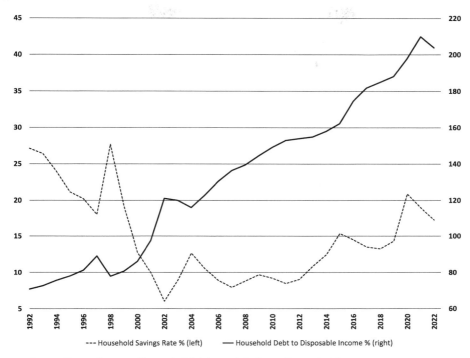

Fig. 4. The explosion of household debt and decline of household savings, 1992–2022. (Data from Bank of Korea.)

also shows the rise in household debt relative to disposable income, which has continued to grow since the financial crisis. By 2020 this ratio had reached 200 percent, witnessing the fastest growth in the OECD, and long surpassing ratios reached during the US subprime crisis that hit as high as 130 percent (Kim YS 2021). Similar to Japan's bubble economy of the 1990s, household lending has spurred real estate bubbles, residential construction booms, and speculative forms of urban development. The latter have led to periodic crises for smaller financial institutions, such as the collapse of the project finance bubble in the early 2010s. But more importantly, such investment has also aided growing income and wealth inequality (Shin HB and Kim SH 2016; cf. Park HJ and Doucette 2016). While successive governments have introduced taxes to cool overheating property markets, they have had little effect, raising questions about whether the economy might face its own Japanese-style bubble collapse.[4]

---

4. The profound effects of this transformation seems to have been registered in the cultural sphere perhaps long before its political significance was recognized by economists. For instance, Joseph Jonghyun Jeon (2019) makes a striking observation that

Inequality and Irregular Work

It is certainly clear from the discussion above that the IMF crisis brought changes to the Korean economy that have raised concerns about slowed economic growth, growing debt and speculation, and the resilient power of the chaebol. While these are all concerns that have frustrated long-held democratic demands for social-economic equality and aspirations for a stronger welfare state, the marked increase in inequality that has been brought about by the crisis has been the most concerning for progressive actors. Such inequality can be seen quite clearly using data from the World Inequality Database. As figure 5 shows, the income share of the top 10 percent of income earners rose to close to 50 percent after the crisis, while the income shares of bottom 50 percent and the middle 40 percent (the range between the bottom 50 percent and top 10 percent) have fallen parallel to one another. But why has this been so? The reasons cannot simply be found in financial changes alone, such as the growth of speculative investment fueled by household debt. Income inequality has also been reinforced by labor restructuring in the wake of 1997 that expanded insecure jobs and nonregular forms of employment from an already high baseline. The result has been the intensified exploitation of working people, a phenomenon that Jeong GH and Jeong SJ (2020) document using the Marxian rate of surplus value (s/v)—the ratio between the amount of surplus value appropriated by capital relative to the amount invested in the purchase of labor power—a rate that, they argue, has risen significantly since the crisis (2020, 268; cf. Jeong 2010). In short, workers have found themselves working relatively harder and longer for their share of compensation. This direct exploitation, in the Marxian sense, has been further complemented by the *indirect* exploitation of workers in the financial sphere in the form of debt and credit. In other words, rising rent and house prices, along with increased household debt, have created an extra degree of compulsion for workers to engage in precarious employment.

The inequality documented in figure 5 is directly related to the expansion of flexible or nonstandard forms of employment commonly known in Korea as "irregular work" (*pijŏngyujik*). The term is used to describe forms of casual, contract, and contingent labor such as part-time work, temporary or dispatch work, subcontract work, home-based and day laborers. While the meaning of the cognate terms "nonregular" and

---

Korean cinema since the IMF crisis has been preoccupied by the logic of debt and indebtedness and explores how the fears and anxieties that surround it at the personal, urban, and national scale have been represented in film.

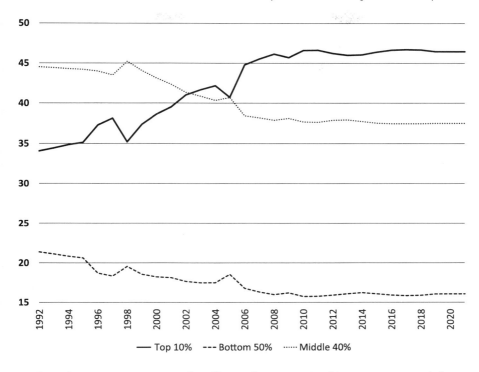

Fig. 5. Increasing income inequality: Shares of pre-tax national income, 1992–2021 (%). (Data from World Inequality Database.)

"irregular worker" are fluid and subject to change, they can be used in an expansive, informal sense to include other precarious forms of work such as disguised subcontracting, self-employment, and even migrant labor. Many of these irregular forms of work, which were already at high levels before the Asian financial crisis, increased considerably after it and have been a persistent political problem for liberal administrations. For the labor movement, they are a sign of democratization delayed or reversed (Song HY 2013). The expansion of temporary and day work after the crisis is shown in figure 6, revealing its rapid expansion after the crisis from an already high baseline. The category of temporary and day work, however, does not capture all forms of nonstandard employment relations. In fact, the very definition and measurement of nonregular work has been contested and has undergone changes since the early 2000s. In 2002 the Korean Tripartite Commission and Ministry of Labor developed a definition of nonregular employment that includes temporary, day work, and other forms of atypical employment, including part-time work, special

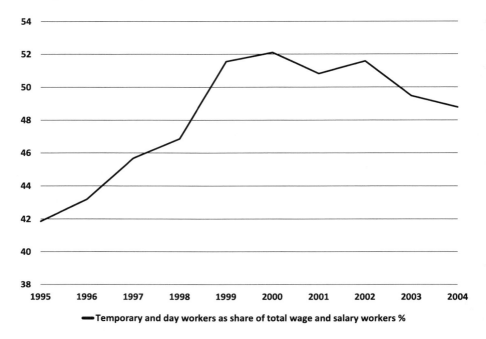

Fig. 6. The increase of irregular workers following the IMF crisis. (Data from Korean Statistical Information Service.)

work, dispatched labor, and home-based work (see Grubb et al. 2007, 75–76, for a discussion). Figure 7 shows that nonregular work has remained high since the early 2000s. Moreover, it also reveals that nonregular work is distinctly gendered, with close to half of female wage workers in nonregular employment, and generally less than 30 percent of male workers in nonregular positions (Lee JH 2004). Consequently, as Lee and Kim (2020) note, the higher incidence of irregular work among female workers helps to shape income inequality not only due to the precarious and temporary nature of the employment contract but also through the denial of wage benefits that accrue to regular workers under seniority-based wage systems at large firms.

Figure 7 also shows that the number of nonregular workers begins to decrease from the mid to late 2010s as the government encouraged "regularization" of nonregular workers through direct hiring and the use of indefinite term contracts (*mugi kyeyakjik*). However, as discussed in more detail in chapter 4, the latter are a form of contract that risks hiding the problem of unequal wages, benefits, and terms of employment under a status that technically counts as regular employment but doesn't quite

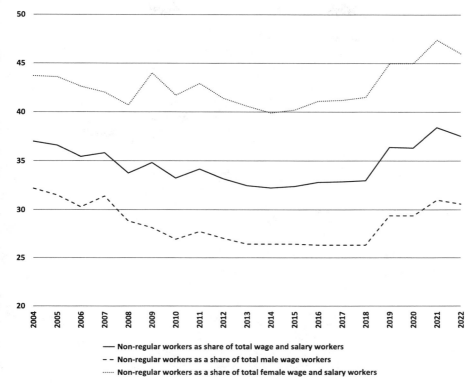

Fig. 7. The high incidence of nonregular work (total and by gender, 2004–2022). (Data from Korea Labor Institute Statistical Archive; Korean Statistical Information Service.)

measure up in terms of status, job tenure, and benefits. Curiously, figure 7 also highlights that the number of nonregular workers has expanded again since 2018 during the very implementation of the Moon administration's income-led growth and labor-respecting society initiatives. Again, here, it is important to keep in mind the contested nature of statistical classification. The Moon administration's response to reports of this rise, and to conservative criticism of his labor policy, were to point out that it is due to the adoption of the International Labour Organization's revised categorization method for work relationships. The revision sought to better capture workers who are "dependent contractors"—a status similar to "disguised subcontracting" that describes workers who work to produce goods and services for a company that is not their employer—and those who work for short employment periods despite having "regular" contracts (personal communication, Korean Confederation of Trade Unions official, November 2019; Park JH 2019). Nonetheless, changes to official statistical calculations alone did not capture all of the increasing incidence of irregular work, which also grew again following the start of the COVID-19 pandemic. Furthermore, the Korean Confederation of Trade Unions and labor scholars have long argued for a broader definition of nonregular work that considers factors such as employment type, status, contract duration, and insurance coverage that, they argue, would put the number even higher, and this is without considering phenomenon such as the self-employed, unpaid family workers, and many migrant workers (Eun SM 2010). In short, even by cautious statistical classification such as ILO and OECD standards, the numbers already put Korea at close to the highest incidence of nonstandard work in the OECD.

The effect of such duality in the labor market means that the wages and benefits workers enjoy are uneven. Successive liberal administrations have tried to remedy this problem by expanding social protection, but such efforts have largely benefited regular workers. For instance, figure 8 depicts social insurance coverage of nonregular workers compared to regular workers as of 2022. It details how nonregular workers are much less likely to be covered by health and employment insurance and the national pension. At a glance, this situation is much improved since the early 2000s, when only around a quarter of irregular workers were enrolled in employment and health insurance and the national pension (Jang 2007, 43), and this earlier figure was itself an improvement on the decade before it because the employment insurance system only dates to 1995. Nonetheless, the disparity in coverage reveals the bifurcated nature of the labor market and the uneven nature of social protection. As nonregular workers are less likely to earn significant benefits under the system, which is compulsory but suffers from poor enforcement, the expansion of social protection has predominantly benefited male and regular workers employed at large enterprises who enjoy job stability and strong bargaining power rather than casualized, day, and self-employed workers. As such, scholars have cautioned against an overoptimistic reception of the Korean government's welfare policies, for despite their expansion Korea's social expenditure remains among the lowest in the OECD. Consequently, labor scholars such as Gray (2009) argue that the welfare expansion introduced by the Kim Dae-jung administration following the Asian financial crisis established not a redistributive welfare state, as some argued, but a minimalist, means-tested "workfare" state (cf. Kwon HJ 2006, 732; cf. Yang JJ 2017). Likewise, Lee JH (2017) argues that the expansion of social protection since the crisis has hardly been gender neutral, as sex segregation in employment and the fact that women are more likely to perform nonstan-

The Political Economy of the Postdevelopmental State | 71

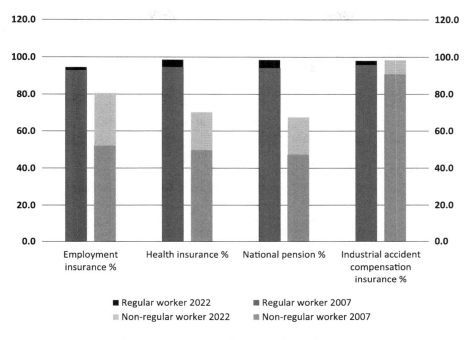

Fig. 8. Uneven social protection among workers: Social insurance coverage, 2022 vs. 2007. (*Note:* nonregular worker category excludes independent contractors. Data from Ministry of Employment and Labor.)

dard work prevent them from fully benefiting from expanded social protections that favor male, regular workers.[5]

For pro-democratic reformers from the labor movement and progressive civil society organizations, the high level of nonstandard employment, and the uneven system of social protection and welfare that surrounds it, remains a trenchant political problem. For it is a sign of the unevenness of democratization and the deferral of core democratic aspirations of equality—signs that are even more frustrating because they

---

5. As Song (2009) has noted, the uneven protections that rolled out since the crisis have put social movements and civil society organizations in an awkward position. Examining those that participated in Kim's welfare initiatives, such as his Minimum Living Standard Guarantee, Song describes how civil society organizations found themselves having to decide which subjects were "worthy" of the welfare they were enrolled to administer. Many felt that this position undermined their prior advocacy for a socially just and universal welfare system and raised questions about the participation of CSOs within the state in a manner similar to the dynamics examined in chapter 4.

72 | The Postdevelopmental State

remain problems *despite* the inclusion of progressive reformers inside of the state. The expansion of irregular work and the policies that seek to remedy it thus reveal some of the broader contradictions of the democratization process. On the one hand, the election of Kim Dae-jung facilitated a shift from authoritarian-era restrictions on the pro-democratic trade unions and confederations. On the other, the restructuring of employment relations made it difficult for irregular workers in both small and large firms to collectively bargain and lawfully pursue industrial action (Doucette and Kang 2018) as is discussed further in chapters 4 and 5. While regular workers at large firms enjoy high union density, high wages, and social protection (they enjoy corporatist arrangements shared by workers in other advanced economies), irregular workers lack such protections. As of late 2022, only 0.2 percent of nonregular workers were union members, compared to 13 percent of regular workers who work predominantly in large enterprises (see Korea Labor Institute 2022). Consequently, since the late 2000s the struggles of irregular workers over employment status have become a persistent feature of the labor movement. In many cases, workers have resorted to difficult and even traumatic tactics such as factory occupations, high altitude protests (actions such as climbing construction cranes, transmission towers, or billboards), *sambo ilbae* ("three steps one bow," an arduous form of protest march in which participants prostrate themselves every three steps), protest-suicides, and "Hope Bus" campaigns (a tactic that involves busing supporters to workplace sit-ins and aerial occupations such as Kim Jin-sook's heroic Hanjin Heavy Industries protest) to bring attention to the problem of irregular workers (see Nam H 2021; Lee Y 2015; Doucette 2013b). Nonetheless, this predicament should not be cause for a nostalgic treatment of the developmentalist era as one of fair and secure employment. Even in that period, political repression and exploitation at work was intense, and there was always a high degree of workers in precarious employment such as day and temp workers. Neoliberal labor market restructuring has simply exacerbated inequalities that already existed, largely to the benefit of the chaebol. It has allowed the latter to squeeze the profit margins of their myriad suppliers and subcontractors and to weaken the associational power of workers within their workplaces.

The Persistence of the Export-Led Economy

From the section above, it is clear that the position of work and employment is central to a critical understanding of the political economy of the postdevelopmental state. Fulfilling the democracy movement's demands

The Political Economy of the Postdevelopmental State | 73

for greater equality has been hampered by the growth of inequality facilitated through the expansion of irregular work, increased financial speculation, slowed GDP growth, and growing household debt. And while it is tempting for some to write off this problem as solely one of neoliberal reform induced by foreign speculative capital (see Park HJ and Doucette 2016 for a discussion), institutions associated with the developmentalist period persist in a residual fashion. The chaebol have grown to be the dominant player in the economy, labor remains marginalized, and spending on social welfare remains *relatively* low despite some increase. Meanwhile, after the Asian financial crisis, the economy became more dependent on exports than ever. Figure 9 grasps this tendency in relation to the components of Korea's GDP. The figure shows that exports have significantly grown as a source of demand since the crisis while private (household) consumption has continued to shrink. Such export dependence has raised concerns for policymakers due to the vulnerability to external shocks that it produces. For instance, recent events such as US-China tensions, Northeast Asian trade frictions, and the COVID-19 pandemic have all led to declines in exports and swelled the ranks of irregular workers as some firms shed production. As such, they also provide an economic rationale for income-led growth strategies to offset export dependence, besides the obvious political rationale for such policies in terms of satisfying demands for improving job quality, employment, and compensation. Nonetheless, the past weighs on the present in such a way that it remains to be seen how effectively household and government spending can be used to offset Korea's export orientation, for social expenditure remains low despite a modest increase, and expanding household debt has raised concerns about the sustainability of current rates of household spending. Moreover, the conservative bloc has sought to capitalize on the employment pressures faced during export downturns to place the blame on pro-labor policy itself (such as the raising of the minimum wage and reduction of work hours) rather than on the broader features of Korea's exportist economic model.

As discussed above, it is difficult to understand these changes using the state vs. market frameworks that have often dominated discussions of East Asian political economy. For the place-specific context of economic restructuring in Korea has led to a "model" with features of developmentalism, neoliberalism, financialization, and exportism that are hard to capture in parsimonious terms.[6] Korean intellectuals have made cognate

---

6. This last point is salient not only for the political problems described in this book but also for the broader political economic literature. While it is beyond the scope of this

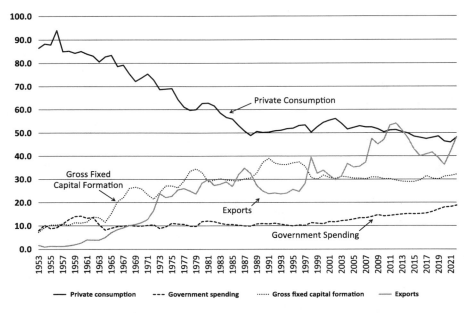

Fig. 9. Deepening export dependency? GDP spending structure, 1953–2022 (%). (Data from Bank of Korea.)

criticisms. For instance, Marxist scholars such as Jeong (2010) argue that instead of witnessing a transition to a "finance-led regime of accumulation regime" during the period of neoliberal globalization, the Korean economy has been caught in a state of limbo in which "the old statist accumulation regime" became defunct "without its replacement by a new one" (Jeong 2010, 157–58). As such, Korea does not fit the profile of a "finance-led" structure of accumulation, a system where the expansion of financial

---

chapter to review this literature here (but see Doucette 2018 for a discussion), as this chapter has shown financial transformation is a geographically uneven process. It does not have the same actors, drivers, and effects in all economies. This contrast is particularly clear when it comes to understanding the dynamics of financial transformation in export-oriented economies and in locations outside of the core economies of the North Atlantic. To some extent, early work by scholars such as Mikuni and Murphy (2003) and Metzler (2013) has tried to account for some of these differential dynamics, and, recently, an emergent literature on "subordinate financialization" has also responded to the need for more critical and geographically varied understandings of financial transformation (see Alami et al. 2023; Bortz and Kaltenbrunner 2018; Choi CL 2020; Kalinowski 2013, 2015). But there is certainly more work to be done. Topics such as subhegemonic relations among exporting countries, their role in extending financial activities across global value chains (see Sial and Doucette 2020), and their effects on labor relations all deserve further inquiry.

The Political Economy of the Postdevelopmental State | 75

Fig. 10. Uneven consumption dynamics: Final consumption expenditure, 1970–2022 (% of GDP). (Data from World Bank [data for the US ends at 2021].)

activities leads to a significant increase in domestic consumption as a driver of GDP (Boyer 2000; Stockhammer 2008). Jeong is correct here in pointing out that financial transformation in Korea has not boosted consumption as it has in the US and the UK where consumption grew in tandem with expanding financial activities until the subprime crises of 2007 and 2008. As figure 10 describes, the final consumption expenditure (the sum of household and general government consumption) for Korea strongly contrasts to that of the US and the UK. The already high level and slight rise in consumption in the US and UK from the 1990s to the subprime crisis is contrasted with the gradual, secular decline of consumption as a source of demand in South Korea. In the latter case, financial transformation, and the growth of household debt that has accompanied it, has not driven accumulation. Instead, export industries continue to drive the economy but in the context of slower GDP growth, raising the need for a political strategy that can address the unique contours of Korea's financial transformation as it has been experienced.

Jeong's argument about the nature of the transformation resonates with this book's understanding of the postdevelopmental state as being

76 | The Postdevelopmental State

both a structural predicament and a political dilemma—one that is difficult to capture using simplistic either/or categories. At the same time, the argument in this book departs somewhat from Jeong GH and Jeong SJ's (2020) recent arguments about the effects of income-led growth strategies within this broader context of financial transformation. These strategies are bound to fail, they argue (277–79), because reformers fail to understand that it is accumulation that drives income distribution and not vice versa. It is here that the strategic and relational understanding of the postdevelopmental state articulated in this book departs from Jeong and Jeong's characterization of the present moment. As discussed further in chapter 4, the existence of such constraints should not be used to write off such strategies, per se. The problem with income-led growth, part of Moon's broader "society that respects labor" reforms, was that it was primarily understood in a largely technical sense, in terms of wage policy and employment status, and not as a broader political project developed in tandem with the labor movement that might address unbalanced class relations. The development of income-based strategies does not necessarily need to exclude the question of a progressive approach that emphasizes investment and accumulation, as well as other measures related to taxation, ownership, and redistribution. The problem is that they haven't been used as such. In sum, the predicament of the postdevelopmental state should not be understood in a deterministic manner driven solely by accumulation, in the sense of external limits that constrain progressive strategy tout court. Rather, it should be seen as place-specific dilemma that is relationally conditioned by political struggle—the forms of coordination and conflict that go into developing reform strategy, and that decide what areas of policy are activated—as much as it is through the wider structural contours of the global political economy that its politics helps to navigate. And, in fact, the chapters that follow in many ways privilege a reading of the postdevelopmental state as very much a politico-ideological problem over a reading of it as merely determined by economic structure.

Conclusion

In this chapter, the transformation of Korea's political economy following the Asian financial crisis has been explored so that the structural contours that the project of economic democratization has been tasked with addressing can be better understood. As discussed above, the financial transforma-

The Political Economy of the Postdevelopmental State | 77

tion that has resulted is particularly important for grasping the politics of economic reform. For the dynamics of the high-debt model has been shifted from firms to households, resulting in an explosion of household debt that has contributed to income and wealth inequality and speculative investment in real estate and other financial products. Meanwhile, the largest chaebol emerged from the crisis larger than ever and, in many cases, with their managerial control intact if not enhanced. The economy also remains even more dependent on exports than in the period before the crisis. On its own, however, financial transformation is not a sufficient explanation for the forms of inequality that reformers have been tasked with solving. The restructuring of the labor market and the expansion of irregular work, itself a highly gendered phenomena, have significantly contributed to inequality. And while enhanced social protection has sought to correct for inequality and precarity, it has expanded relatively slowly.

The political economy of the postdevelopmental state explored in this chapter speaks to the urgency of the project of economic democratization and its associated initiatives concerning work and employment. But as the following chapters document, progressives within the pro-democratic bloc have continued to struggle with reform strategy. Efforts to reform the chaebol remain ambivalent and poorly coordinated with labor, while efforts to improve labor relations have floundered without effective union participation. Moreover, the very imaginary of economic democracy has increasingly narrowed toward a simplistic pro- or antichaebol register that neglects a broader understanding of justice. As discussed in chapter 3, the problem of parsimony that animates scholarship on the developmental state has also influenced political practice as various strategies of economic democratization come to rest on assumptions that dynamics witnessed in other economies can be or are being replicated in Korea: in particular, that the emphasis on shareholder value will somehow lead to the decline of the chaebol or that protecting the chaebol will facilitate the transition to a welfare state. As Jayasuriya (2005, 382) warned in the wake of the Asian financial crisis, these views risk what he calls "institutional fetishism," a view that blinds scholars to the broad constellation of social relations that constitute states and markets. Thus, it is to that broader interaction between social forces within the integral state that the following chapters now turn so that the political-strategic dynamics of the postdevelopmental state, including the imaginaries and the reform challenges that have shaped political economic reform, can be grasped in more concrete detail.

3

Debating Economic Democracy

How have progressive reformers sought to address the political economy of the postdevelopmental state? For the structural contours of inequality and financial transformation it represents have created a rationale for greater socioeconomic equality. It has also shaped the imaginary seen as essential for realizing this demand: the vision of economic democracy. The Moon Jae-in administration (2017–22) embraced this project as a key task for realizing its vision of Candlelight Democracy, as a solution to the problem of expanding inequality, speculative investment based on record household debt, the proliferation of irregular work, and the growing power of the "super-chaebol" (Lee BC and Jeong JH 2014). But the project did not emerge out of thin air. Rather it arose from a set of ideas that animated Moon's previous presidential campaign and that had long been promoted by progressive reformers in both political and civil society: that is, within the integral state. For these reformers, the project of economic democratization (*kyŏngje minjujuŭi*) was seen as an alternative to both neoliberalism and developmentalism. To implement this project, Moon appointed several progressive intellectuals and civil society organization (CSO) activists to prominent positions in his administration: from Blue House secretaries to elite appointments such as presidential chief of policy planning, chairman of the Fair Trade Commission, and chief executive officer of the Korean Development Bank, among others. And yet Moon's economic democracy initiatives largely met with disappointment, particularly when it came to the chaebol.

As this chapter details, one of the reasons for this disappointing result concerns the various imaginaries of economic democracy that have been embraced by progressive reformers in the integral state and how their associated meanings have changed over the last 25 years. As discussed below, these visions of economic democracy have become increasingly oriented toward a simplistic pro- and antichaebol register, departing from their more radical origins within the democracy movement. What was once a more comprehensive strategy of social justice and transformation has gradually become a relatively narrow set of policy ideas that revolve around corporate governance. To better understand this transformation, this chapter begins by examining the heated debates over the idea of economic democracy that took place in advance of the 2012 presidential election, for this moment provides a window into the evolution of the concept over time and revealed its important political stakes. Moreover, the term itself witnessed perhaps its widest circulation as a political idea during the election and was subject to vitriolic debate that crystallized what were once a more fluid set of positions that have remained more rigid since then. Hence, to understand the changing imaginaries of economic democracy, this chapter focuses on the development of two main progressive camps in the debate that have each played a role in the integral state: one camp based around the project of chaebol reform as synonymous with the meaning of economic democracy, and another seeking to protect the chaebol by articulating economic democracy as a part of project aimed at the creation of a "welfare state." Despite the passion of these debates, the visions of economic democracy embraced by both camps became strategically problematic for the broader egalitarian goals of the democracy movement, for their imaginaries came to revolve around capital-centric and market-based visions of reform and offered little in the way of a substantive overcoming of neoliberalism and developmentalism. As such, during the 2012 elections in particular, progressives were unable to significantly challenge the policies proposed by the moderate conservatives who led Park Geun-hye's campaign to victory by appropriating their progressive-sounding slogans and terminology. And after electoral success in 2017, the policies that were introduced under this rubric left much to be desired, resulting in criticisms of a wasted mandate and lack of a vision for policies that might appease the demands of the Candlelight protests.

In what follows, this chapter situates the debates over economic democracy within the broader development of the pro-democratic bloc and its nexus with civil society. In doing so, it shows how the question of addressing economic power has changed, practically and ideologically, since the 1990s, leading to the eventual development of these two camps and a more narrow, technocratic understanding of chaebol reform. The chapter ends by noting how these two dominant imaginaries have continued to shape progressive strategy with little modification since Park's appropriation and quick abandonment of economic democracy in 2012. After this event, the Moon administration's promises to finally implement economic democracy to satisfy the demands of the Candlelight Revolution led to disappointing results. The reforms to the chaebol he embraced under its banner focused largely on corporate governance and lacked substantive coordination with labor. In sum, this chapter explores how chaebol reform has become seen as the resolution of *intra*-class conflicts among stockholders (ruling families vs. minority shareholders), rather than as an *inter*-class strategy that involves important aspects of social and economic justice. And yet in an age where abuses of power (*gapchil*) by chaebol families garnered wide attention—often in the form of scandals, such as the "nut rage" incident involving Korean Air vice president Cho Hyun-a, and Samsung's Lee Jae-yong's alleged bribe to Park to cement his managerial control over the conglomerate—the relatively tame nature of the pro-democratic bloc's imaginaries of chaebol reform raises questions about the nature of the alternative progressives might offer. If the progressive imaginary of economic democracy could not satisfy long-held demands for social and economic justice, if it could not address the legacy of injustices created in the developmentalist period and amplified in neoliberal times, then what might? What other alternatives might help address the problem of the postdevelopmental state?

Situating the 2012 Elections

South Korea's 2012 presidential elections provide an excellent entry point into the project of economic democracy, for it provided a moment that allows the reader to work both backwards and forwards to see how this imaginary has been operationalized over time. During this election, both ruling conservative and liberal opposition parties fought their campaigns using it as a slogan. Under the banner "economic democratization," they promised to address social polarization by tackling the enormous concentration of wealth in the hands of the chaebol, expanding social welfare, and creating thousands of new, high-quality jobs. The urgent need for such seemed apparent to all. Kim Jong-in, the architect of Park Geun-hye's economic policy campaign (and an important historical figure we will turn to later), declared that "no matter who becomes president, if they do not effectively push economic democracy and chaebol reform, they will end up an early lame duck and the administration will be short lived"

(Kwak 2012b). Moon Jae-in, then the presidential candidate for the Democratic Party, similarly announced that "the task of the next government is to realize economic democracy. . . . Without chaebol reform, economic democracy cannot take place" (Son 2012). Even to conservative observers, this emphasis on welfare and economic democratization, with chaebol reform at its center, appeared to be significant departure from the status quo (Kang, Leheny, and Cha 2013).

Despite the transition to democratic elections in 1987, conservative politicians have rarely ceased using Cold War rhetoric to demonize the opposition and have frequently labeled even moderate liberal economic reformers as "reds" or "pro-North Leftists."[1] During the previous presidential election in 2007, conservatives promoted a growth-first rhetoric that faulted the "leftist" policies of previous liberal administrations for slowing Korea's growth momentum and undermining its national identity. This sudden enthusiasm for welfare expansion and for curbing corporate power surprised politicians in both the ruling and opposition parties, who quickly found themselves musing about the Korean people's newfound "passion for welfare" (Chung TI 2012). Moon Jae-in himself enthused that during the Roh Moo-hyun administration (2003–8), "advocating economic democracy would have had you labeled as a leftist. Today, however, the entire public supports economic democracy" (Lee TH 2012). Kim Sang-jo, the prominent reform economist and civil society activist, voiced a similar sentiment: "Economic democratization is the spirit of the times now, but just one year ago the opposition camp pointed a finger at me calling me an extremist, red-leftist about my opinions" (Kwak 2012a).

For conservatives to suddenly emphasize economic democracy appeared to be a complete U-turn.[2] Previously, the winner of the 2007

---

1. Both the military dictatorships that ruled until 1987 and conservative governments that succeeded them have repressed concepts and ideas associated with social democracy. After his 1961 military coup, for instance, President Park Chung-hee curtailed the activities of social democratic parties and arrested their leaders under the National Security Law. Socialists fared even worse (see Roh 2002, 312–13).

2. This departure should be treated with a grain of caution, however. For despite the fact that the Conservative Party fought its official campaign in the center, Cold War discourse still played an active if underground role in the presidential election, especially in its later stages. After Park Geun-hye's victory, it was discovered that conservative state agencies had organized their own covert social media campaign to discredit the liberal-left opposition parties as "*chongbuk chwap'a*" (a term translated as "pro-North leftists" that has connotations of being slavish to or followers of North Korea), and, of course, her administration quickly fell back on a Cold War footing following her

82 | The Postdevelopmental State

election, Lee Myung-bak (2008–13), claimed that he would usher in an era of high growth and "national advancement" (*sŏnjinhwa*) beyond democratization and industrialization.[3] Lee eased regulations on the chaebol established by previous liberal administrations—such as the equity investment ceiling that limited cross-investment among chaebol affiliates—and relaxed laws on the separation of finance and industry. In the midst of Korea's slowdown following the global financial crisis of 2008, however, Lee failed to deliver on his "747" plan (a promise to achieve 7 percent in annual GDP growth, $40,000 in per capita income, and make Korea the world's seventh largest economy). By 2012, conservatives could not ignore the effects of widening socioeconomic polarization, rising levels of household debt, and a banking crisis related to Korea's poorly regulated project finance market. The unpopularity of Lee Myung-bak's pro-chaebol policies and his corruption-prone and ecologically destructive infrastructure projects such as the Four Rivers Project combined with these factors to make talk of *sŏnjinhwa* sound anachronistic, even to commentators in the popular conservative press. For example, Lee Jin-seok (2010), an economics reporter for the conservative *Chosun* newspaper, asked, "Is it reasonable for the Korean people to repeatedly deplore their backwardness and cry for national advancement"?

To distinguish herself from her predecessor, Park would need an alternative to Lee's pro-chaebol policies that might assuage popular concerns about inequality and social welfare. "Economic democratization," a slogan traditionally associated with the left, seemed fit for the purpose. To promote a moderate image, the Conservative Party appointed Kim Jong-in, a former advisor of Park's father, to lead her economic campaign. Kim has been described as the "father of economic democracy" for his role in amending the Constitution during Korea's June Democratic Uprising of 1987 and makes for an interesting object of study in his own right. For Kim's career speaks to the fluid nature of the nexus between intellectuals, elite bureaucracies, and political parties. The son-in-law of Kim Chung-yum (Park Chung-hee's former secretary of state who, along with Oh Won-Chul, was one of his leading economic technocrats), Kim began his career as a professor of economics at Sogang University, home to the growth-first Sogang school of economists. He later advised Park's govern-

---

inauguration. As Lee N (2022, 140) notes, the origins of this term concern factional conflict with the Korean Democratic Labor Party. See also Bae (2010) for a discussion of that conflict.

3. For a sustained analysis of the discourse of *sŏnjin'guk*, see Kim JT 2011, 2012.

ment on national health insurance policies before running for the National Assembly following Park's dictatorial Yushin regime. As a National Assembly member for the ruling Democratic Justice Party (a predecessor of today's Conservative Party), Kim drafted Article 119, item 2—the famous "economic democracy clause"—of the revised Constitution of the Republic of Korea (1987), which reads:

> The State may regulate and coordinate economic affairs in order to maintain the balanced growth and stability of the national economy, to ensure proper distribution of income, to prevent the domination of the market and the abuse of economic power, and to democratize the economy through harmony among the economic agents.

This clause provided a constitutional basis for economic reform. It authorized the state to intervene in the market to take on powerful groups such as the chaebol, whose economic power Kim had become reticent about.

In early 2012, Kim Jong-in (2012) released a book entitled *Why Economic Democracy Now?* in which he identified the subcontracting, cross-shareholding, and the illegal succession practices of chaebol families as targets for reform. Kim's willingness to criticize established interests, including those within his own party, helped shift the frontiers of official debate beyond Lee Myung-bak's conservative discourse of *sŏnjinhwa*. Because of his antichaebol stance, however, Kim's role was not universally welcomed on the right. The Federation of Korean Industries complained that economic democracy was populist politics. More conservative advisors to Park tried to dilute Kim's calls for chaebol reform by arguing that Park's earlier 2007 "*chulp'use*" platform—short for *churigo* ("reduce"), *p'ulgo* ("relax"), and *seugo* ("set right")—on which she had run, unsuccessfully, for the Conservative Party's nomination had embodied the ideal of economic democratization. In response, Kim Jong-in dismissed Park's earlier approach as obsolete and openly criticized his own party for lacking the political will needed to resolve the chaebol problem. Following Park Geun-hye's election and abandonment of her economic democracy pledges, he would later leave the Conservative Party in protest and join the Democratic Party as interim leader in a move that demonstrated his ability to negotiate the terrain of the party system with unusual political tact.

While Kim and other moderate conservatives helped to enable the popularity of economic democracy as a political slogan during the 2012 elections, the appeal of the slogan should not be reduced to his initiative.

84 | The Postdevelopmental State

Rather, it is an idea that has long been fought for by Korea's progressive economic-reform-oriented CSOs. Both the Democratic Party and independent presidential candidate Ahn Chul-soo enlisted the help of prominent activists from CSOs, such as Peoples Solidarity for Participatory Democracy (PSPD) and the Citizens Committee for Economic Justice (CCEJ), among other groups, to craft their economic democratization campaigns. Ahn recruited the liberal economist and prominent minority shareholder activist Jang Ha-sung as his economic advisor (for an excellent profile of Jang, see Hamlin 2001). Meanwhile, the Moon campaign enlisted the help of left-liberal economists Yoo Jong-il and Lee Joung-woo to draw up its economic democratization plans. Their inclusion signaled a shift away from the policies of previous liberal administrations, at least on the surface. Both men had advised former liberal president Roh Moo-hyun during his first two years in office but had broken ties with his administration over its neoliberal economic policies such as the Korea-US Free Trade Agreement. Like other civic activists, they considered the trade, labor, and financial policies instituted by previous liberal administrations to be the reason behind rising inequality since 1997. The party's failure to combat inequality had led to the renewed appeal of developmentalist, pro-growth politics and, ultimately, the Conservative Party's victory in the 2007 presidential elections. What the Democratic Party needed now was to put "people first" by resolving social polarization and the concentration of wealth and power within Korean society. As Moon Jae-in declared as he accepted his party's candidacy, "The spirit and mindset to lead the next five years is to correct this imbalance of 1 percent to 99 percent in our society" (Moon as quoted in Son 2012).

The chaebol's interlinked cross-shareholding practices, illegal intergenerational transfers of wealth, abuse of subcontractors and irregular workers, and expansion into traditional small business sectors such as neighbourhood shops and bakeries were targeted as the source of inequality by both parties. But despite a political climate that favored strong and assertive proposals for egalitarian reform and the construction of a welfare state, the discourse of economic democracy embraced in the campaigns of both parties remained surprisingly narrow, and mostly concentrated on the corporate governance of the chaebol. To tackle the chaebol's enormous strength, the Democratic Party promised to force the chaebol to abandon existing cross-shareholding arrangements between affiliates (the source of the ruling family's control over the entire group of firms) within three years. Meanwhile, the Conservative Party pledged to ban new cases of cross-shareholding and to vigorously enforce the Monopoly Regulation and Fair Trade Act, as well as introduce measures to protect small- and mid-sized business from unfair trading practices. The intense focus put upon the conglomerates' misdeeds, however, left little room for substantive proposals on the development of a welfare state even though both parties stated their intentions to work toward this goal. The task of chaebol reform itself became *synonymous* with the concept of economic democracy to the degree that progressive reformers struggled to remind the public that economic democratization includes both chaebol reform *and* the task of resolving social polarization (see Kim Sang-jo 2012b). Without a comprehensive strategy for achieving a welfare state, the promises both parties made appeared unrealistic. In the words of the eminent scholar of Korean democratization, Choi Jang-jip (2012b, 4–5), "the electoral campaign . . . degenerated into a competition of rhetoric rather than substance."

Debating Economic Democracy

The intense focus by the ruling and opposition parties on the task of chaebol reform in the lead up to the elections spurred a heated debate among liberal-left intellectuals associated with Korea's civil society movements. The debate was provoked by an intervention from the globally recognized development economist Ha-joon Chang who in a rather iconoclastic manner waded into the fray in support of the chaebol rather than against it. He complained that politicians had mistakenly embraced economic democratization as a process of "weakening the strong," adding that "economic democratization isn't such a thing that simply promotes small stockholders' rights or prevents cross-investment between subsidiaries" (Chang, as quoted in Lee Sang-eon 2012, 74). In opposition to weakening and dissolving conglomerate power, Chang and his close associates (some of whom were members of the very CSOs that supported chaebol reform) argued that the large conglomerates should play a vital role in the establishment of a Korean welfare state (Chang et al. 2012c). This critique hit a nerve and provoked a heated series of exchanges that became known as the "debate on the nature of the Korean economy" (see Choi BC 2012).

The publication of a book of conversations between Ha-joon Chang, institutional economist Jeong Seung-il, and economics reporter Lee Jong-tae (2012a) entitled *The Choices We Have to Make* catalyzed these exchanges. In it, they advocated for a transition to a welfare state and criticized the strategies of chaebol reformers. This book was published roughly

86 | The Postdevelopmental State

at the same time as another by Kim Sang-jo (2012a) entitled *The Korean Economy Inside Out: Escaping the Trap of the Chaebol and MOFia*.[4] Reviews of both led to a vitriolic back and forth published by the progressive internet-based magazine *Pressian* that spilled over into other progressive online and offline publications such the *Hankyoreh*, *Citizens and the World*, and *Redian*, among others. The debate quickly became about much more than just the chaebol, however. At its heart, it concerned the long-term legacy of progressive movements and their strategies for social transformation. For many participants in the debate had come to political maturity in the democracy and student movements and had participated in various factions of the peoples' movements that would eventually form contemporary CSOs. As such, the debate restaged earlier tensions and grievances between progressive camps, as discussed below.

On one side of the debate, Ha-joon Chang and his associates—a group that I shall call the welfare state camp (WSC) for short—argued that Korean reformers faced a choice between neoliberalism and "productive welfare" (Chang HJ et al. 2012a).[5] They objected to what they saw as the chaebol reformers' two-step strategy of separate agenda items: first pursuing chaebol reform and then establishing a welfare state. They claimed that weakening the chaebol (e.g., by restricting cross-investment) would only amplify shareholder pressure on firms, and make progressive labor and welfare policies difficult to implement. Instead of neoliberal chaebol reform (breaking up the chaebol to make them more responsive to shareholders), the WSC urged progressives to focus on the "positive aspects" of Korea's past developmentalist regimes, such as industrial policy and control of speculative capital, and seek to bargain with the chaebol in line with the principles of a welfare state. As the owners of capital would have to be taxed and domestic investment increased to advance toward this goal, they recommended that an agreement be made with the chaebol that protected their management rights in order to win their consent for a social compromise. In their opinion, the chaebol needed protection from speculative markets to concentrate on productive investment. They thus described their conflict with reformers such as Kim Sang-jo and others as one between "chaebol reform according to the principle of shareholder

---

4. "MOFia" is a slang term for the Ministry of Strategy and Finance, offspring of the Economic Planning Board, the nodal ministry once praised by developmental state scholars.

5. Coincidentally, Ha-joon Chang is the cousin of reform economist, minority shareholder activist, and (later) Chief of Policy Planning (under President Moon Jae-in) Jang Ha-sung, which added the element of a family feud to the debates.

Debating Economic Democracy | 87

capitalism" and "chaebol reform according to the principle of the welfare state" (Chang et al. 2012c; cf. Kim JC 2012).

To better understand the WSC's argument, it is important to grasp the phenomenon known as cross-shareholding or "circular equity investment," which was briefly discussed in chapter 2. This arrangement is known in Korean as *sanghoch'ulcha*, a term that is loosely translated as reciprocal or mutual equity investment. Chaebol families use this system to maintain control over the whole group. In many cases, the family might only own a sliver (e.g., 2–3 percent) of an affiliate firm but are able to retain control over it because of elaborate cross-shareholding arrangements that give another subsidiary considerable voice over its decisions. Figure 11 provides a simplified representation of what this system looks like (but see fig. 3 as well). As figure 11 shows, the ruling family owns a large quantity of shares belonging to Firm A, which owns a high percentage of shares belonging to Firm B, which owns shares belonging to Firms C, E, and F, and so on. In the case of chaebol such as Samsung and many other chaebol, this structure is multiplied over some 50 more affiliated firms, creating dense interconnected webs through which ruling families are able maintain managerial control over the whole group (see Kim JB 2013 for a discussion). While this system allows chaebol heads to retain control, it also raises big challenges for passing down shares within the family without facing a significant inheritance tax. As a result, there have been several controversies surrounding the transfer of shares within chaebol firms, and allegations of corruption, collusion, undervaluation, illegal transfer of ownership, and other improper activities. By protecting the chaebol's management rights, the WSC felt that they might agree to the increased domestic investment and taxation to spur job creation and fund the necessary expansion in social security needed to establish a welfare state.

On the other side of the debate, intellectuals associated with the Democratic Party and progressive CSOs greeted this proposal with swift and severe criticism. They labeled Chang's camp "pro-chaebol*ists*" and charged them with being apologists for Park Chung-hee whose regime had nurtured the chaebol into the large conglomerate firms they are today (Lee BC 2012a). They argued that protection of the chaebol's management rights under the existing system was a reckless way to achieve a welfare state and accused the WSC of overexaggerating the threat posed by foreign capital. For instance, Chung Tae-in—public intellectual and former economic advisor to President Roh Moo-hyun—criticized the WSC for naïvely thinking that the chaebol would agree to such a proposal. After all, Chung (2012) argued, the largest chaebol that survived the Asian financial

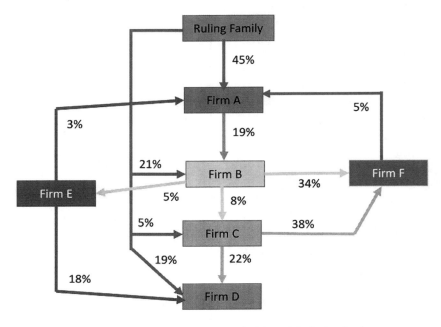

Fig. 11. Cross-shareholding structure of the chaebol (simplified). (Author's own drawing based in part on a diagram of the Samsung group by Back 2014.)

crisis "do not feel particularly threatened," having retained managerial control despite several administrations' attempts to reform them. Enhancing the chaebol's managerial control risked giving away the goods, reducing their incentive to follow through on a social compromise. This opinion was echoed by Kim Sang-jo, who, along with Jang Ha-sung, was considered the leader of Korea's minority shareholder movement (MSM). Kim argued that instead of offering the chaebol the "carrot" of guaranteed management rights, progressives should push for legislative policies to enforce transparency and punish economic crimes. This "stick" would discipline the chaebol into a social compromise and help to create a "fair market economy" (see Kim SJ 2012a).

It was not only liberal economists such as Kim Sang-jo and Jang Ha-sung, however, that promoted chaebol reform during this debate. For instance, Lee Byeong-cheon (2012b), a public intellectual and "post-Marxist" economist (see Jeong SJ 2013), argued that chaebol reform might provide a gateway to a "symbiosis" in which independent businesses flourish in every corner of society and high-quality jobs increase. Seeking to mediate between the concerns of liberal chaebol reformers in the MSM and those of the WSC, Lee advocated that both internal and external capital holders should be strictly regulated and criticized Chang's camp for ignoring the syncretic nature of the chaebol and transnational capital (see also Park HJ 2013). As Park GS and Kim KP (2008, 68) have previously pointed out, foreign investors have learned to reap greater profits from the conglomerate structure of the chaebol as a whole and have "become timid toward promoting transparency" in the management of individual subsidiaries. Lee argued that the WSC had thus misrepresented the threat to the chaebol, which, he added, has also advocated for neoliberal financial and labor market reforms that suit their interests. Moreover, Lee added, the protection of the chaebol's management rights risked condoning *historical* crimes and injustices the chaebol heads had committed, including the illegal means–political slush funds, illegal transfers of stock, and tax evasion, which they have used to maintain managerial control. The collusive nature of the chaebol, Lee (2012b) claimed, had its origins in the policies of the Park Chung-hee regime, which allowed them to grow into the mammoth organizations they are today not only through strategic industrial policies but also by labor repression, graft, and corruption. Hence, chaebol reform should not be regarded as merely a technical problem of governance, but a historical one concerning social justice. As such, the WSC's proposal to preserve the chaebol's management rights risked not standing up to the chaebol and, by extension, leaving the historical injustices of past regimes unresolved.

While the exchanges between both camps were vitriolic and antagonistic, their passion conceals their similarities. For the main contours of the debate focused narrowly on intraclass relations among capital holders. In other words, their proposals were largely oriented toward supporting the interests of either ruling families or minority shareholders. As such, both perspectives failed to prioritize the interclass relationships between labor and capital in their visions of economic democracy. Neither the chaebol reformer's stricture that firms abide by the principles of shareholder value, nor, conversely, the welfare state camp's championing of "national" firms against "international" finance challenged the social relations upon which the market sits. This fact was noted by other progressive intellectuals on the periphery of both camps. For instance, in his open letter to Ha-joon Chang, the late progressive reformer and economist Chung Tae-in (2012) pointed out that both the WSC and the MSM tend to view the chaebol in terms of competition between capitals. Addressing Chang directly, Chung noted that "the difference is that you consider the chaebol as victims suffering from the competition with foreign capital, but Prof. Kim Sang-jo sees the chaebol as a group that exploits minority shareholders." Likewise,

90 | The Postdevelopmental State

the pro-welfare CSO activist Choi Byung-cheon pointed out in another important intervention that this narrow focus leads both camps to propose strategies that neglect the overall balance of power in the Korean economy:

> The problem in contemporary Korean society is short-term profit optimization caused by shareholder capitalism *and* the exercise of mighty political-economic-social power by chaebol heads. . . . Given this situation, for the discourse surrounding the character of the Korean economy to advance in a progressive direction, it is imperative that both camps (those who champion chaebol reform, on one side, and those who champion defeat of shareholder capitalism, on the other) demonstrate how the political-economic-social "authority" and the "balance of power" in the hands of workers-ordinary people-citizens can be strengthened. (Choi BC 2012; author's translation)

Choi urged both sides to be more sensitive to the appropriate checks and balances needed to limit the power of capital in general and create an effective balance of power between socioeconomic classes.

Hyeng-joon Park (2013) uses the felicitous phrase "progressive critiques, conservative solutions" to describe the antagonism between these two dominant economic reform camps. While one side unpacks uncritical assumptions about the market economy and the other criticizes the abuse of monopoly power, their understanding of Korea's political economy rests on either an idealized view of the state planning of the Park Chung-hee economy—and by extension the role of the chaebol within it—or, conversely, the assumption that markets are rational means of distributing economic resources. As such, these narrow perspectives confine the strategies of both camps to solutions that are commensurate with those of conservative forces. The demand that the chaebol respect shareholder value resonates with moderate conservatives, such as Kim Jong-in, who see the chaebol's concentration of economic power as a moral hazard and obstruction of "fair competition." Meanwhile, the preservation of the management rights of the chaebol because of their role as productive industrial capital accords with the pro-growth vision of national champions that traditional conservative forces advocate. And yet both camps emerged from progressive civil society organizations and see their strategies as oriented toward greater democratization. To better understand the disjuncture between their progressive critiques and conservative solutions, then, the

Debating Economic Democracy | 91

trajectories of both camps need to be examined in closer detail to understand their strategies and their limitations. Two factors stand out that are examined in the following two sections: the evolution of economic reform CSOs that followed the transition to electoral democracy and the effects of the 1997–98 Asian financial crisis on the Korean economy.

From Equality to Efficiency

The intense rivalry between chaebol reformers and their critics builds on a central ideological tension on the Korean left between a strategy of emancipation that targets the structures of monopoly capitalism and another that prioritizes nationalism. This tension, already present in the peoples' movements of the 1970s and early 1980s, crystallized in the social formation debates of the late 1980s and early 1990s.[6] These debates, which aimed to revive and develop Marxism in South Korea, led to the theoretical clarification of rival "people's democracy" and "national liberation" camps. These became colloquially known by the acronyms PD and NL, which are still used in a loose sense to distinguish among left-nationalist and egalitarian political factions. In the words of Marxist economist Jeong Seong-jin, "people's democracy conceived Korea as embodying neocolonial state monopoly capitalism, requiring an anti-imperial and anti-monopoly-capital people's democratic revolution." In contrast, "national liberation argued for the anti-imperial and anti-semi-feudal people's democratic revolution to overthrow a colonial semi-feudal Korea" (Jeong SJ 2010, 199–200). While some intellectuals attempted to form a synthesis or advocate alternative frameworks in these debates, NL and PD emerged as the dominant positions (cf. Park M 2008). For instance, Lee Byeong-cheon, mentioned above, participated in the 1980s' social formation debate as a Marxist theoretician of PD (see Lee BC and Yoon SY 1988) and played a mediating role in earlier debates between rival economic policy camps within both Peoples' Solidarity for Participatory Democracy and the Alternatives Network (Taean Yŏndae). The demise of the Soviet Union spurred many to reject the orthodox Marxism of these debates, for as Jeong SJ (2013, 223) puts it, both tendencies shared "fatal theoretical

---

6. The social formation debate has been collected and published in four volumes edited by Park Hyun-chae and Cho Hee-Yeon (1989–92). Cho, a progressive sociologist, was a cofounder of PSPD, Sungkonghoe University professor, and since 2014 education superintendent for Seoul.

defects, such as economic determinism, catastrophism and stagism."[7] Nonetheless, the antimonopoly and nationalist understandings of the Korean economy articulated in the debates continued to inform the priorities of the civil society groups and alternative academic communities that developed out of the democracy and student movements of the late 1980s and early 1990s (Kim W 2011). Movements for economic reform retained the frameworks of the debates but, in many cases, substituted anticapitalist perspectives for an idealized understanding of state and market relations.

After the 1987 June Democratic Uprising and transition to free elections, the antimonopoly tendency of the Korean left strongly influenced new economic reform movements such as the CCEJ, founded in 1989, and PSPD, founded in 1994. The CCEJ explicitly targeted the "chaebol monopoly system" for bringing "undeserved suffering" to the citizens who produced Korea's economic miracle (Citizens Committee for Economic Justice n.d.). The CCEJ's activism concentrated on issuing public statements critical of both government policy and specific chaebol firms and holding public hearings and press conferences to make their criticisms of the chaebol heard. These efforts were later strengthened with the formation of PSPD, which sought to bridge the gap between popular social movements and middle-class groups like CCEJ. PSPD had a greater diversity of voices within its ranks, including liberal lawyers and economists, as well as Marxian thinkers and many former student, democracy, and labor movement activists.

Within PSPD, the idea of using shareholder activism to pursue chaebol reform was first discussed in its Economic Democratization Committee before the organization decided to form its Participatory Economy Committee. The Participatory Economy Committee launched Korea's first and most prominent minority shareholders movement to take on the concentration of economic power in the hands of the chaebol. Several high-profile cases of corporate crime and malpractice—such as the collapse of the Sŏngsu Bridge in 1995—and amendment of the Korean Securities and Exchange Act strengthening minority shareholder's rights made this strategy possible (Rho 2004, 12–15). These reforms gave minority shareholders considerable legal leverage with which to challenge managerial decisions at individual affiliates of chaebol firms. By mobilizing minority shareholders, PSPD was able to move beyond the CCEJ's modus operandi of public forums and policy statements and directly challenge the chaebol as capital

---

7. For a discussion of stage-theoretical debates in Korean Marxism, see Miller (2010).

Debating Economic Democracy | 93

holders. Using their legal right to monitor corporate data, they were able to raise issues that management of the chaebol affected: from the exploitation of minority shareholders' self-interest by controlling families to the tunneling of funds between affiliates to support "nonviable" investments and strengthen family control over the group. In addition to traditional shareholder concerns, PSPD documented other abuses of corporate power—such as illegal political donations—and advocated for stakeholders ignored by management.

Given PSPD's primary mission to work toward social justice, shareholder activism did not appeal to everyone in the organization at the start. As Rho Han-kyun points out, for some of the Marxian intellectuals involved in PSPD,

> capitalist actors like shareholders or boards of directors had never been acceptable allies. Furthermore, most PSPD members doubted whether minority shareholder rights would work well for checking corporate mischief. One member predicted that shareholder activism would not be so effective, that it could only draw media attention at best. (Rho 2004, 16)

Once launched, however, the movement was more successful than originally anticipated. During the 1997–98 economic crisis, which many blamed on the chaebol, PSPD launched and won the first derivative suit in Korean history against Korea First Bank. The suit charged that Korea First Bank's directors had failed to investigate the risks involved in a large loan to Hanbo Steel, which declared bankruptcy shortly after it received the loan. This case and other high-profile victories raised public awareness of the MSM's efforts. In some cases, the MSM actively coordinated their actions with major overseas shareholders. In the case of SK Telecom, an affiliate of the SK chaebol, it allied with foreign investors to get outside board members elected, create an auditing committee, and force the firm to repay funds it used to prop up other troubled affiliates. Tiger Management, which allied with the MSM in this case, remarked that because of the MSM's successful campaign "international investors should eventually be more willing to invest in Korean companies" (Julian Robertson of Tiger Management, quoted in Hamlin 2001). While some members of PSPD remained uncomfortable appealing to shareholder interests, others—such as the liberal economists and lawyers who made up the bulk of the Participatory Economy Committee—were content to frame their demands around shareholder interests and market-oriented

94 | The Postdevelopmental State

conceptions of monopoly power but took care to position their campaigns in the public interest.

Most of the prominent liberal economists who participated in the Participatory Economy Committee had trained in mainstream economics at US universities or, locally, in the "reformative Keynesianism" of Cho Soon and Chung Un-chan, prominent professors of economics at Seoul National University. Their reformative Keynesianism bore an affinity to Paul Samuelson's "neoclassical synthesis" of microeconomics with Keynesian macroeconomics. Chung was associated with the Hak'yŏn school around dissident economist and Seoul National University professor Byun Hyung-Yoon, who, along with Cho, were seen as prominent critics of the economic policies of Park Chung-hee during the dictatorship and provided critical support for pro-democratic activism. The "distribution-oriented" Hak'yŏn school was the rival, pro-democratic critic of the "pro-growth" chaebol-oriented policies of the Sogang school (Park SJ 2013, 8 n2) and included Keynesian, institutionalist, and Marxian economists, among other intellectuals. Despite their antagonism, there was some connection between both schools. For instance, Kim Jong-in and Chung Un-chan shared a decades-long friendship dating from the dictatorship, under which Kim intervened to protect Chung from dismissal. Despite being courted by the Democratic Party as a potential presidential candidate, Chung would later be appointed as prime minister by conservative president Lee Myung-bak to help find a balance between big business and small firms as a means of deflecting criticism from Lee's pro-business policies. Likewise, Kim Jong-in would later become seen as a more diplomatic and moderate member of the Sogang school in his concern with monopoly power and income distribution. Besides his role in shaping the Conservative Party's economic democracy campaign, Kim Jong-in would later come to lead the Democratic Party as interim leader before switching back again to the Conservative Party.[8]

Chung Un-chan believed that the state had a strong role to play in creating market infrastructure through "micro-economic and structural

---

8. While the nexus between the Sogang school, the dictatorship, and subsequent conservative regimes, and the Hak'yŏn school, progressive civil society, and liberal administrations is well known, the careers of economists such as Kim and Chung reveal that rival political blocs are not simply organized along lines of the antagonism that often dominates political discourse but have demonstrated some fluidity, even during past regimes. While it often appears that it is a logic of enmity and confrontation that animates relations between them, there are moments of passive revolution, appropriation, and mobility between them that are also important to recognize.

intervention" (see Chung 1999, 24–25). He saw the concentration of economic power among the family-led, conglomerate structure as an obstacle to fair market competition and the professionalization of corporate management. He went so far as to describe the chaebol as "dinosaur-like" monsters that "took the whole economy hostage" (Chung 1997, 18). Reflecting a drift away from the radical demands of the democracy movement, the understanding of the "concentration of economic power" Chung and members of PSPD and CCEJ embraced had less to do with the balance of power between classes than with understandings of monopoly predominant in mainstream economics. The government-funded Korea Development Institute—the former think-tank arm of the Economic Planning Board—introduced the concept of the concentration of economic power into public policy in the 1980s to express concerns about the distortion of the market caused by the chaebol (Rho 2004, 9). Prominent Korea Development Institute economists, such as Kim Woochan and Yoo Jong-il, have participated in the MSM and liberal administrations.[9] Rather than interclass relations, the Korea Development Institute's use of the concept drew attention to issues of monopoly power such as ownership concentration and succession, diversification, inter-affiliate support, and the ruling family's influence on management (Rho 2004, 9). In order to regulate the chaebol's concentration of economic power in these areas, the government prohibited holding companies in 1986 under the Monopoly Regulation and Fair Trade Act (Jang, Kim, and Han 2010). Nonetheless, through circular shareholding and cross-investment, the ruling families retained managerial control over their affiliates. Hence, concerns about the concentration of economic power remained saliant and were validated by the 1997–98 economic crisis when, as individual chaebol affiliates became bankrupt, the chaebol's elaborate cross-shareholdings and cross-loan guarantees began to pull down other members of the group and much of the economy with them.

The liberal economic reformers who participated in PSPD's MSM, such as Chung's former pupil and leading chaebol reformer Kim Sang-jo, believed that the chaebol's concentration of economic power and "inefficient" corporate governance had contributed significantly to the financial

---

9. The diversity of voices within the Korea Development Institute speaks to both the complex legacy of economic expertise and the fact that the economic ministries were not necessarily united around a pro-chaebol orientation, belying the stereotype of a rational bureaucracy with a shared mentalité. In reality, there are many intra- and interministerial tensions and alliances that extend beyond the state itself and that are difficult to unpack using neo-Weberian ideas about the state.

crisis. Jang Ha-sung, chair of PSPD's Participatory Economy Committee at the time, wrote that "many blame the flight of foreign capital for the crisis, but while such capital may have been a carrier, it was certainly not the virus itself." Rather, the virus was the risk from the "inadequate" and "poor corporate governance" of the chaebol (Jang 2001, 73). Likewise, Chung Un-chan (1999, 28–29) declared that chaebol reform should now move beyond its previous grounding in the "egalitarian viewpoint" because with "efficiency considerations brought into the argument, the chaebol system has now lost whatever remaining justification [it had]." In the midst of the crisis, Chung declared that "if such a great opportunity is squandered, we may not see another chance for a long time" (29).

As the citizen's movement had helped create pressure for chaebol reform, Kim Dae-jung's "5 + 3" principles for the chaebol restructuring—implemented in January 1998 and August 1999—largely adhered to their concerns about the concentration of economic power. The first "5" principles sought to combat the concentration of economic power in the hands of the chaebol by enhancing transparency in corporate management; eliminating intragroup debt guarantees; improving the capital structure of independent firms; promoting concentration on core competencies; and increasing the accountability of controlling shareholders and management. To these were added an additional "3" supplementary items in August 1999: restrictions on industry's control of finance; suppression of circular investment and unfair transactions among affiliates; and prevention of illegal and improper bequests to chaebol heirs (Kim KW 2004, 8–9). Some MSM members complained that the president's reforms had not gone far enough toward improving corporate governance, as Kim's administration had banned hostile mergers and acquisitions. Kim Sang-jo (2002, 71), for instance, complained that the postcrisis reforms had not produced the "big bang" (a term with Thatcherite connotations) needed to develop "competitive domestic financial capital" independent of the chaebol and, by extension, to professionalize corporate governance. While Kim, Chung, and other liberal economists sought to restructure the corporate governance of the chaebol, this does mean that they were uncritical of the neoliberal restructuring of the Korean economy. Chung and others were particularly frustrated by the high interest rates mandated by Korea's IMF-supported workout plan. Nonetheless, most of the IMF's prescriptions for economic restructuring were willingly endorsed by economic advisors to Kim Dae-jung, despite leading to numerous bankruptcies, mass layoffs, and retrenchment. As such, pro-industrial-policy critics came to resent the hubris of both Kim's advisors and civil society activists.

Debating Economic Democracy | 97

Nonetheless, it was only after the crisis that such clear lines of tension between the MSM and its critics emerged within the progressive camp.

Defending the Developmental State

In the backlash against the IMF reforms and the continuing attempts to restructure the corporate sector during the administrations of Kim Dae-jung (1998–2003) and Roh Moo-hyun (2003–2008), the antimonopoly perspective of the MSM and other liberal economists became associated with the damage that the Asian financial crisis had caused. Liberal and progressive economists from PSPD and the MSM began to face bitter criticism from other intellectuals, including development economists and industrial policy advocates, who were associated with a loose network called the Alternatives Network (Taean Yŏndae) that had emerged from PSPD and other CSOs. The long-standing debate among these reformers is sometimes referred to as the debate on the "97-regime" inasmuch as it often revolves around the consequences of the Asian financial crisis. Some of these intellectuals later formed the faction around Ha-joon Chang described above. Chang and his colleagues Jeong Seung-il and Shin Jang-sup, in particular, went beyond blaming the negative effects of the crisis on the neoliberal policies of the IMF and Wall Street and criticized their colleagues in the civic movement for undermining Korea's political economy. They accused chaebol reformers of selling out the country by promoting the speculative, stock market model of corporate governance favored by foreign financial capital—the same capital that bought up undervalued Korean assets during the restructuring process and sold them again for a handsome profit (Park BG 2012). For while chaebol reformers saw the conglomerate structure of the chaebol as a moral hazard and the cause of the crisis, Chang and his associates blamed the Asian financial crisis primarily on the liberalization of the Korean state's capital controls and industrial policies, which led to extensive foreign borrowing in short-term debt. They argued that the chaebol's buildup of large nonperforming loans during the crisis resulted not from "the inherent inefficiencies of the Korean corporate sector," but because of "an abrupt change in financial environment in a way that excessively punished high debt" (Shin and Chang 2003, 88). They argued that neither the high levels of debt taken on by the chaebol nor their interlinked corporate governance structures had led to a crisis before the liberalization of external finance.

Instead of following a market-oriented path of development, the WSC

98 | The Postdevelopmental State

that evolved from Chang's criticisms has argued that the Korean state's cultivation of the highly diversified but also highly indebted chaebol—through policy loans, product licensing, and export-promotion targets—was an integral component of Korea's "successful" developmental state model. They saw the pro-chaebol industrial policies of the Park Chung-hee regime as a model oriented toward innovation, competitive export performance, and patient capital (e.g., capital that is oriented toward long-term investments that lead to substantial gains in the future). External control by the stock market and minority shareholders (the interests of which are often oriented to short-term gains) was not the only way to create market efficiency. In opposition to the MSM, Ha-joon Chang and his colleagues justified cross-shareholding and insider control as a mechanism with positive implications for innovation and development. "If a capital market is underdeveloped it may be more efficient to rely on intra-group mobilisation of capital than to rely on capital markets. If a business group has financial institutions as its member firms, the intra-group capital market can be even more effective" (Shin and Chang 2003, 27). In their view, chaebol subsidiaries benefit from intrafirm exchanges such as direct subsidies, loan guarantees, shared expertise, and indirect financial support—the very same practices that chaebol reformers saw as market distortions.[10] From what would become WSC's point of view, the Anglo-American–style shareholder capitalism chaebol reformers were promoting was the wrong direction. For them, the attempt to break up the chaebol by changing the financial system toward one where the stock market acts as a market for corporate control had been the cause of the slower growth that heightened the social polarization that followed in the wake of the Asian financial crisis (Chang HJ and Park HJ 2004). Korean firms were timid to invest, they argued, because their management rights were under threat and in need of protection. Chang warned that if shareholder pressure continues, "professional CEOs would be too afraid of stockholders to make reinvestments. They would have no choice but to recruit as many non-regular workers as possible and attempt to make do without employee training simply to seek short-term profits" (Chang, quoted in Lee SE 2012). As discussed in the previous chapter, this is a largely hyperbolic assessment of the threat of foreign finance against the chaebol.

Revealing that the debate on the Korean economy was not simply a debate about the Korean economy but about the wider orientation of

---

10. Jeong Seung-il, Chang's coauthor in the WSC, advances a similar argument in Jeong SI 2004. See also Chang HJ et al. 2012b.

Debating Economic Democracy | 99

democratization, the WSC would eventually reference the social formation debates of the 1980s in their condemnation of their rivals. They asserted that chaebol reformers had become misguided by their naïve belief in "progressive liberalism," a philosophy, they claimed, that had its origins in the Korean democracy movement. The WSC argued that this philosophy caused progressives to see "Korean capitalism represented by a Park Chung-hee–type state-controlled economy and the chaebol group system as 'abnormal' capitalism," as something to be replaced by importing institutions from other countries (Chang et al. 2012c). They identified their opponents among liberal-left chaebol reformers as the source of this perspective:

> It is most commonly known as "pariah" capitalism (Kim Sang-jo). It has been described as "semi-colonial" capitalism . . . or "new colonial state monopoly" capitalism (Lee Byeong-cheon was the representative proponent in the past) as well. The reason these adjectives are used is because Korea's capitalism has grown in a way that distorts the meaning of capitalism as understood in advanced countries, and in an immoral fashion. So it is said that without coming to terms with such a past, Korea's capitalism will not develop into "normal" capitalism. (Chang et al. 2012c, author's translation, parentheses in original)

The association drawn with the people's democracy tendency of the social formation debates and "progressive liberalism" (a tendency associated with Choi Jang-jip and other prominent intellectuals such as Choi Tae-wook, see Park SJ 2016) is a leap, and the latter is misrepresented here. For the term progressive liberalism only became widely used among reformers following a series of debates and forums in 2010 (see Lee GS et al 2011). Prior to this it had been promoted by a number of senior intellectuals who had served in the Democratic Party and under Kim Dae-jung such as Sohn Hak-yu (2000) and Lee Geun-shik (2006). Lee, who served as Kim's minister for government and home affairs, argued in these forums that political and social liberalism needed to be distinguished or separated from economic liberalism, which is a threat to economic equality. The government needed to help manage economic distribution and promote a mixed economy to ensure equality (Lee GS 2010).[11]

---

11. Interestingly enough, this criticism of progressive liberalism occurred in the context of the birth of Ahn Cheol-soo's party, whose think tank Choi Jang-jip momentarily chaired. The use of the term by Ahn's party created criticism of appropriation by Demo-

100 | The Postdevelopmental State

Nonetheless, the WSC make the correct point that there is no one set of market rules that are universally applicable to all economies, and that indeed such rules are rarely followed by hegemonic powers: "If you scrutinize the history of American and European capitalism, you will realize that they developed through underhanded and abnormal means with rampant corruption, anti-democracy, and pariah and government intervention" (Chang HJ et al. 2012c). Breaking a taboo that many on the liberal-left felt should not be broken, they also argued that Park Chung-hee regime's economic policies had many positive features—"such as control over foreign finances, control of shareholder capitalism, and the aggressive fostering of industry"—that could help establish a welfare state. The negative aspects of Park's regime, such as labor oppression, could simply be disregarded, they believed (Chang HJ et al. 2012c).

In their rush to condemn the market-based strategies of their rivals, the WSC committed many of the errors of parsimony and simplification for which they faulted their opponents. They did so by exaggerating the threat of shareholder capitalism against the chaebol (see Park HJ and Doucette 2016), and by idealizing the nonliberal or "good" financial policies of Park Chung-hee by abstracting them from the "bad" labor repression.

> Our point is extremely common-sensical: we should make use of the positive elements but disregard the negative elements (labor oppression) of Park Chung-hee's economic system. . . . We should wholeheartedly accept the positive legacy of the Park Chung-hee regime, such as control over foreign exchange, control of shareholder capitalism, and the aggressive fostering of industry. (Chang et al. 2012d, author's translation)

The problem with this standpoint, one that corresponds to the democratic deficit explored in chapter 1, is that it idealizes the state as a cohesive, even virtuous actor and largely ignores the social relations upon which the industrial policies of developmental states and even market economies rest, such as the dominance of private property relations, the exploitation of wage labor, and the subordination of social reproduction to the market.

---

cratic Party candidate Moon Jaein, who argued, "Progressive liberalism is not something (Ahn) can monopolize. The People's Government and the Participatory Government can also be described as having been of a progressive liberal position" (Moon as cited in Choi HS 2013). Moon's comments at the time were echoed by Seoul National University's professor and his later minister of justice, Cho Kuk, who had previously mediated between Ahn and Moon's campaigns in the 2012 elections.

Debating Economic Democracy | 101

The only way to separate the "shadows" from the "light" of the Park Chung-hee model in this case is to create an ideal type that valorizes institutions that do not conform to the standard prescriptions of laissez-faire economics, but at the cost of ignoring oppression, injustice, and exploitation.

The proposition that Korea's "developmental state" and the chaebol might together constitute desirable economic institutions has long sounded absurd to many pro-democracy activists. Nonetheless, in the wake of the Asian financial crisis, this criticism of chaebol reform began to gain attention. For it resonated with a nationalist register that interpreted the crisis as one *primarily* caused by external forces. By the mid-2000s, amid an increasing backlash against foreign speculative funds and growing social polarization due to the expansion of irregular work, the WSC's proposals that progressives should protect the management rights of the chaebol began to be more seriously entertained. Several high-profile cases of predatory behavior by foreign funds influenced the development of this proposal such as the hostile takeover attempt of the SK Corporation by the Sovereign Group in the early 2000s; the "assault" on the formerly state-owned Korean Tobacco & Ginseng Corporation by activist investor Carl Icahn—who forced it to sell off assets in order to increase its share price—in 2006; and criminal investigations against the Texas-based Lone Star Fund for stock price manipulation related to its acquisition of Korea Exchange Bank. In this context, liberal economists from the MSM voiced support for hostile mergers and acquisitions. For instance, Kim Sang-jo (2006) argued:

> A public backlash against overseas capital is not desirable. When takeover attempts are made, share prices of the targeted corporations rise in most cases. Increases in share prices indicate that external interference in corporate management is an effective means of enhancing corporate efficiency. Could the enhancement of efficiency be realized automatically without external interference? The answer is negative.

For the WSC, this attitude made it clear that chaebol reformers were more interested in crafting a neoliberal financial model than in defending the institutions that, from their point of view, had been so essential to Korean development. And while these cases of hostile attempts belied the facts that the chaebol had been gradually increasing their managerial control at this time (as discussed in chapter 2), they exposed the perils of the idealization of the market by many chaebol reformers.

The conflict between chaebol reformers and their critics eventually struck a nerve within progressive CSOs, leading to the formation of new organizations and reform factions that would participate in the economic democracy debates of 2012–13. The pro-chaebol theorists that became the WSC helped to form Taean Yŏndae while the MSM left PSPD in 2006 and its liberal economists such as Kim Sang-jo helped to form two new organizations. These were Solidarity for Economic Reform, which continued with shareholder activism, and the Center for Good Corporate Governance, which provided financial advice to the newly established Korean Good Corporate Governance Fund overseen by former PSPD director Jang Ha-sung. Established in 2006, the fund was managed by Wall Street's Lazard Asset Management and aimed to invest only in firms with good corporate governance. While the fund attracted several large, foreign institutional investors such as the California Public Employees Retirement System, it was shut down in 2012 after several years of significant losses (see Park GS and Kim KP 2008 for a fuller discussion of the MSM). In contrast to the MSM, the activities of proto-WSC activists at this time such as Jeong Seung-il went in the opposite direction. Jeong proposed that instead of trying to weaken the chaebol through limits on cross-shareholding, reformers should protect them from speculative capital by allowing the chaebol to create (tax-free) public foundations and appoint their heirs as directors (See Jeong SI 2006). The public foundation would then play the role of the majority shareholder, stabilizing corporate governance, and eliminate the need for illegal succession practices to pass control of the firm down to future generations. Critics of this approach pointed out that Samsung had previously used public trusts as a vehicle for transferring ownership directly to the next generation under the pretense of dispersing ownership. In short, instead of merely maintaining group integration, public foundations could easily be manipulated to enhance family control. The Democratic Party entertained a version of this proposal in late 2006, near the end of President Roh Moo-hyun's tenure. Party chair Kim Geun-tae proposed a New Deal Policy whereby the chaebol would promote jobs and investment in exchange for the removal of restrictions on cross-investment, protection of management rights, and pardons for several business leaders. But both the chaebol and their critics were skeptical about this strategy, and it quickly fell apart. Dissenting party members argued that the pledge was "designed to revive the economy not for the working class, but for the wealthy (or chaebol)" (Dong-a Ilbo 12 Aug 2006). In practice, however, the WSC replied to such criticism with the response that their critics were not able to separate the "useful-

Debating Economic Democracy | 103

ness and legitimacy" of the conglomerate structure as a nonliberal market institution (an ideal type) from the "selfish interests and desires" of the ruling families (Chang et al. 2012a). But since preserving management rights is a de facto offer to preserve the rights of ruling families, how can these be separated in reality?

The Politics of Reform Imaginaries

The economic democracy debate during the 2012 elections, and its precursors within liberal and left debates about the nature of Korean capitalism, reveal what might be called a parallel idealization of the market and the state by its two main camps, the MSM and the WSC. Consequently, this idealization raises important questions about the coherence of the progressive bloc's economic reform strategies and the ability of such strategies to articulate an alternative to neoliberalism and developmentalism that might satisfy demands for social and economic justice. The MSM's idealization of Anglo-American corporate governance based on shareholder value and open markets for corporate control ignores the diversity of actually existing capitalist institutions. In contrast, the WSC's argument that features of the Park Chung-hee model can be used to establish a Scandinavian-style welfare state appears, on the surface, to represent a more historically grounded approach. It tends to avoid fetishizing the idea of the market as a self-regulating institution and regards nonmarket institutions as salient drivers of economic development. But the WSC's emphasis on preserving the management rights of the chaebol represents, for many, a difficult strategic choice, as it risks condoning past injustices. The WSC's rationale for such an agreement is not grounded on a fundamental criticism of the commodification and exploitation of labor by capital, but on praise for the developmental merits of elite-driven industrial policy and the chaebol's family-led corporate governance. Without a strong countervailing force to capital, it is difficult to see how the strategies of either camp could lead to the development of an egalitarian Korean welfare state. For the strategies of both camps risk naturalizing the private property rights of dominant interests and neglecting interclass relationships, and even condoning the illegal activities through which chaebol heads and their offspring have maintained managerial control.

During the 2012 debates, it was often intellectuals associated with smaller economic reform CSOs who sought to point out the critical errors in the imaginaries of both camps. For instance, in one exchange, the WSC borrowed a phrase coined by the Swedish democratic socialist Ernst Wigforss to claim that their strategy was guided by the principles of the welfare state as a "provisional utopia" (Chang et al. 2012c). This phrase was popularized in a book by Hong Gibin (2011) entitled *Wigforss: Welfare State and Provisional Utopia* that he wrote to introduce a more critical and egalitarian understanding of Swedish social democracy into Korean debates surrounding the welfare state. In it, Hong describes how Wigforss came to represent the welfare state as a "provisional utopia" because there was no grand design or scientific route to socialism. The appropriation of the phrase by the WSC, however, departed significantly from Wigforss's understanding. As Hong critically points out, Wigforss based his critique of capitalism on how it has rendered the working class propertyless and placed them in a dependent condition that creates insecurity and competition. It was a situation that could be remedied only by the active participation of the working class in the organization of production and greater public control over the organization of the market (Tilton 1979). Despite Wigforss's pragmatic terminology, he remained guided by an ethical injunction to widen the field of participation and confront the issue of property relations in a manner that belied the WSC's more narrow usage of his term in relation to preserving the chaebol's management rights.

Unfortunately, the plans of both the MSM and WSC lacked any substantive role for workers and their organizations. While both recognized the empirical fact that organized labor played an important role in the establishment of Scandinavian welfare states, they remained ambivalent about the role that the Korean labor movement should play in the establishment of a Korean welfare state. In contrast to Wigforss's radical vision of participation, for instance, the WSC presented their version of a welfare state as one based on the logic of welfare as "group purchase." They advocated for an expansion of social spending through a compromise between the state and the chaebol to increase investment and taxation in return for preserving the chaebol's management rights, but *without* making strong demands for codetermination, co-ownership, or industrial democracy that were an integral part of the Scandinavian model as a precondition.[12] And indeed, some WSC members have a record of arguing against labor participation. For example, in the aftermath of the 1997–98 Asian financial crisis, Ha-joon Chang endorsed a Dutch-style system of "flexicurity" as a

---

12. Some WSC members later suggested that progressive groups such as the (now dissolved) United Progressive Party and trade union movement might embrace these preconditions. See Lee JT and Jeong SI 2014.

possible response to the crisis. Chang mused that "making redundancy easier by changing the labor laws may actually be desirable," if combined with the right institutional mix of social security and active labor market measures (Chang HJ 1998, 1560, cited in Hart-Landsberg 2001, 422).[13] As Hart-Landsberg (2001, 422) pointed out at the time, this response resonated with neoliberal responses to the crisis that asked the working class to bear the costs of profitability and competitiveness. This is not to say that Hong's intervention based on Wigforss's idea was to simply show that reformers got their model of Swedish social democracy wrong, or to endorse the view that reform strategies should be based on simply importing institutions from the "national" models of other countries. The manner in which I interpret it is to show that the relational foundations of such models should be taken into account if they are to be used as sources of inspiration (or "relational comparisons," see Hart 2018) for progressive strategy. In other words, a social democratic strategy for achieving economic democracy does not necessarily have to copy the same form of institutions, but its approach should consider the egalitarian principles they represent and try to apply them within whatever pragmatic and necessarily provisional strategy is assembled.

For Hyun-Ok Park (2015, 62–65) this symptom points to a broader stalemate among progressive forces. She notes that earlier progressive debates about overcoming the '87 regime were consciously based on the formation of a broad-based coalition between the masses (or *minjung*) and the middle class to complete the tasks of democratization (including overcoming the division system that maintains a divided Korean peninsula). But such a project contrasts with the more limited confines of what

---

13. Likewise, many of Chang's former collaborators, such as National University of Singapore–based economist Shin Jang-sup, have explicitly embraced pro-business positions, which in the case of Shin have devolved into nationalist hagiography of chaebol founders such as Daewoo's Kim Woo-chung. For example, as Samsung CEO Lee Kun-hee's health declined in the summer of 2014, Ha-joon Chang and his colleagues in the WSC proposed that the National Assembly draft a special law to allow the third generation of the Lee family to maintain its management rights in Samsung, with the caveat that the government could take over if the firm was not managed productively. Critics correctly replied that such a strategy risked perpetuating the notion that Samsung deserves special treatment and it did nothing to reconcile the historical injustices and antilabor policies Samsung had long embraced (Kwak 2014). Moreover, the proposal was not so different from what eventually happened during the Park administration, when Samsung heir Lee Jae-yong allegedly paid Park a bribe for the approval by the National Pension Service of a merger deal that would cement his control over the conglomerate.

106 | The Postdevelopmental State

has become known as economic democracy. As Park notes, the debate about the nature of the '97 regime, of which the 2012 debate on economic democracy can be regarded as a part, specifically lacks this form of mass politics and radical democracy. She notes that if the '87 regime understood the problem of economic democracy to be one of struggle between labor and capital, the '97 regime has come to see it as one that primarily involves financial regulation and corporate governance or a social compromise initiative between the state and business. Compared to the social formation debates of the 1980s, and despite their heated and often orthodox nature, what is missing is a broader, more comprehensive project of social transformation. The 2012 elections remain an excellent point to grasp this stalemate, and to see it as a moment, perhaps, of the exhaustion of progressive strategy. In Hyun-ok Park's terminology, it is a moment of repetition of earlier tensions in debates about the nature of Korean capitalism, but one that lacks a coherent alternative to neoliberalism and developmentalism inasmuch as the emphasis is placed on either the market or state-business compromise to fulfill the project of economic democracy.

Limits of Economic Democracy

Unfortunately, in the 2012 debates, this exhaustion became clear as neither the market-based vision of mainstream chaebol reformers nor the capital-centric proposals of the WSC addressed the social relations upon which the market sits. Instead, economic democracy became treated merely as a technocratic problem. Consequently, it was difficult for the liberal-left to distinguish itself from both moderate and traditional conservatives, aiding Park's attempt to portray herself as reformist conservative. While this image helped her win the election, it was quickly abandoned afterward, and, as chapter 5 discusses, she quickly returned to traditional anticommunist, public security politics.[14] After her inauguration, Park Geun-hye quickly introduced several bills aimed at modestly expanding old age pensions and childcare, restricting some cross-shareholding among conglomerate firms (under particular conditions), and protecting the rights of small franchise-

---

14. It was later revealed that such politics covertly influenced the election via a misinformation campaign by prominent prosecutors and advisors, as discussed in chapter 5. But this doesn't change the point that a moderate, reformist image helped Park to win the election.

store owners against their corporate suppliers. In a sudden about-face, the Ministry of Strategy and Finance declared that it would relax the rules on additional shareholding and funneling for companies that were facing insolvency. By late August 2013, Park promised to delay enforcement of the new laws and to revise her plans to amend the Commercial Code, which would have strengthened the power of minority shareholders. Her promises to increase pension and childcare benefits were also changed to a paltry, largely means-tested system instead of a substantial, universal one. After introducing these bills, Park stated that the task of economic democratization was complete and that now she would shift to fostering a "creative economy" and reducing "cancerous" regulations that impeded economic growth (see Oh 2013). Her administration dropped all mention of economic democratization, much to the dismay of moderate conservatives such as Kim Jong-in, who publicly lamented the cosmetic nature of Park's policies. As mentioned above, Kim would later apologize for his role in her campaign and switched over to the opposition, taking the helm of the Democratic Party as its emergency leader.

After the Park administration, the tension between camps continued to animate efforts by reformers. However, in the time since that debate, the strategies of both camps changed little, even as their protagonists came to play instrumental roles formulating the policies of the liberal Moon administration. For instance, Moon appointed veteran chaebol reformer, academic, and shareholder advocate Jang Ha-Sung as his initial chief presidential secretary. Likewise, Kim Sang-jo was appointed to lead the Fair Trade Commission, and later replaced Jang as Moon's policy chief. However, chaebol reform under Moon remained rather limited. While Moon's administration revised the Monopoly Regulation and Fair Trade Act to strengthen the regulation of cross-shareholding (lowering the limit at which share ownership is subject to regulation), and expand the definition of illegal acts that restrict competition to create a broader definition of collusion, there was no revolutionary change in terms of chaebol regulation.[15] More so, the early parole of Samsung's Lee Jae-yong out of concerns for the "national economic situation and the global economic environment," as Justice Minister Park Beom-kye put it (Kim Y and Baek B 2021),

---

15. In response to these reforms, Ha-joon Chang argued in the right-wing press in late 2018 that the Korean economy was facing a "state of emergency" as Moon began to roll out his economic policies (see Kim ST 2018). Receiving much criticism, Chang later qualified his remarks by saying he wished to see a more "left" or pro-welfare approach.

signaled to many that Moon was not serious about holding chaebol heads to account. Finally, disclosures that some of these prominent reformers themselves had benefited from real-estate speculation undermined their "progressive" credentials and with it Moon's image as reformer.

This lack of ambition for chaebol reform also created friction with reformers in the citizens' movement who singled out their former colleagues for criticism (Kwak 2019). They argued that the model of chaebol reform proposed by Kim Sangjo, Jang Ha-sung, and others remained superficial. Like previous participants in the 2012 debates, they argued that Kim overidealized the shareholder system of Anglo-American countries, a model, they claimed, that was not appropriate for the Korean context, as economist and CCEJ activist Park Sang-in (2019) explained:

> As far as I can see the problem of the chaebol is the concentration of economic power. Director Kim Sangjo and the Solidarity for Economic Reform have only focused on corporate governance. That is why the main task has become the introduction of the outside board members and the shareholders' lawsuit system. But between the US and Korea the ownership and governance structure is fundamentally different. That is why even if we adopt this system it will have no purpose and exist only in name. (author's translation)

In short, what frustrated Park and other reformers was how the model being considered (an idealized understanding of shareholder value) failed to address the structural relations on which the chaebol sits, particularly its monopoly power over subcontractors and exploitation of labor. By focusing too narrowly on corporate governance, the broader goals of economic democracy remain limited. Such a point resonated with an apt observation made by Cho Young-chol during earlier debate about chaebol reform. Cho (2006, 109) remarked that the strategies of both camps risk "minimizing the seriousness of the historical circumstances surrounding the chaebol and overlooking the foundation on which they are based, on the grounds that these are merely property issues between chaebol owners and minority shareholders." Cho proposed that any solution must be oriented toward social justice, toward those whose rights have been sacrificed for Korea's rapid development instead of merely being confined to the managerial prerogatives of one group of capital owners over another. Unfortunately, the vision of economic democracy as practiced has not yet been able to live up to this injunction.

Conclusion

The narrowing vision of economic democracy discussed in this chapter highlights a strategic challenge that has haunted the pro-democratic bloc: how to create a substantive alternative to neoliberalism *and* to developmentalism. As the discussion above details, the attempt to limit economic democracy to the question of corporate governance reform diminishes the ability of progressive reformers to act in a comprehensive manner, or to deal substantively with inequalities created by both the past and the present. The progressive sociologist, and cofounder of PSPD, Cho Heeyeon has made a similar argument (Cho 2012b, 24–30). Cho argues that Korean democratization can be consolidated only when a solution is found to the monopolization of power by socioeconomic groups such as the chaebol. However, Cho cautions, "de-monopolization" should not be thought of as economic liberalization or the retention of monopoly power through developmentalist compromise, but rather as a process of "socialization" and "equalization" that continues to consolidate democracy through the relative dis-integration of the power of socioeconomic monopolies in relation to the power of diverse subaltern groups, including labor and other social identities. Without egalitarian reform, the benefits of "peaceful coexistence" between left and right remains limited.

In the case of policies around chaebol reform, Cho's broad understanding of de-monopolization has not been adhered to. And as the next chapter details, it has been the role of labor that exposes this weak point. For while liberal administrations have recognized that labor rights are a fundamental part of democracy, the role of labor in pursuing economic reform has remained limited *despite* efforts to extend the state in a manner that increases labor's capacity for participation in policy-making. But this lack of a transformative project for economic democracy can be seen elsewhere. As Albert Park (2018, 173) has remarked, "far from being a transformative tool for creating fundamental changes in the economy and society as claimed by its supporters, the contemporary discourse on economic democracy has made it into a category with little power to question established paths of development and envision an alternative economic system." For Park, this narrow vision has shut out broader projects of economic democratization found in social movements, such as agricultural cooperatives like Hansalim and iCoop. In other words, the focus on corporate governance belies the diverse and alternative understandings of economic democracy in other social movements such as worker coopera-

110 | The Postdevelopmental State

tives, cohousing, and social economy movements that have sprung up over the last 20 years, not to mention the near complete absence of feminist concerns within these debates. Despite the heated debates and participation of charismatic figures from the citizens' movement that lent Moon's efforts considerable legitimacy, the absence of a substantive vision of economic democracy among the pro-democratic bloc became a significant contributing factor to the easy co-optation of that discourse in 2012, and a factor that helped lead to a loss of faith in the Candlelight Democracy of the Moon administration. Despite the inclusion of key activists within the integral state to help demonstrate Moon's alignment with the goals of pro-democratic CSOs, their visions failed to promote a clear alternative, and, ultimately, helped to perpetuate the cycle of enthusiasm and disappointment associated with the dynamics of conservative democratization.

4

Social Democracy without Labor?

The imaginaries of economic democratization have clear social democratic ambitions in that many of the reformers who promote them dream of establishing a Scandinavian-style welfare state. And yet over the last two decades the discourse of economic democracy gradually became more fixated on the corporate governance of the chaebol to the neglect of a more comprehensive strategy of social democratic transition. Unfortunately, neither the pro-chaebol policies favored by reformers nostalgic for the economic planning of the developmental dictatorship nor the shareholder value-based vision of the firm and management embraced by minority shareholder activists who came to occupy prominent positions within liberal administrations have provided much in the way of an egalitarian strategy for economic reform. This conundrum illustrates one of the strategic challenges of the postdevelopmental state as articulated in the introduction of this book: that the dominant reform imaginaries embraced by the pro-democratic bloc have served to limit their ability to find an alternative to the status quo, that is, to the intertwined legacies of neoliberalism and developmentalism. This problem is not confined to chaebol reform but also to other key policy areas related to the project of economic democracy such as work and employment, social protection, and prosecution reform: topics that are covered in the present and following chapter. As this chapter describes, the effort to *extend* the state to better recognize labor as a political actor and address its subordination under past regimes is where the challenges of constructing an alternative to the status quo can most keenly be felt. For while workers have been offered a place in the slogans of liberal presidents—including the "mass participatory economy" of Kim Dae-jung, the "participatory government" of Roh Moo-hyun, and the "society that respects labor" of Moon

Jae-in—the participation of the labor movement within them has rarely been transformative.

This chapter explores labor's participation in the integral state to better understand some of the reasons for this lack of substantive transformation. It examines how liberal administrations have sought to make space for labor's participation by developing social dialogue and social partnership policies to improve labor standards, while also seeking to use such bodies to institute or legitimize neoliberal reforms. It argues that despite the pro-labor slogans of multiple liberal administrations, and even the inclusion of progressive reformers and veteran labor leaders, these initiatives have largely failed to provide an alternative to either neoliberal flexibilization or developmentalist labor subordination. Ironically, this situation has come about *despite* efforts by the pro-democratic bloc to promote institutions associated with social democracy. Progressive intellectuals within the party talk openly about adopting Northern European forms of welfare and social partnership (Lee JW 2007), but, ironically, such institutions have been used by liberal administrations to promote Anglo-American models of labor market flexibility (Cho SJ 2016). Labor's periodic participation in social partnership and tripartite meetings between unions, employers, and government has merely served as a legitimation mechanism, one that allows liberal administrations to demonstrate their pro-democratic credentials, while disguising the lack of broader coordination when it comes to a vision of economic and industrial democracy. Consequently, social dialogue has not been seen by pro-democratic actors as a site for *social* democratic struggle: one that includes respect for agonistic and contentious forms of participation. Instead, it has served as an institution for governing labor as an unruly actor.

The result is a situation that I call "social democracy without content." In short, there is an institutional preference among liberal administrations for the *form* of institutions associated with social democracy but not the *content* of social democratic labor struggle.[1] This dilemma directly maps

---

1. There is an open question here about how sincerely the embrace of this form may have been as well as the degree to which members of the Democratic Party actively worked to subvert labor inclusion, thus warranting some qualification about the degree to which a social democratic vision was fully embodied in reality. In my opinion, such behavior does not detract from the fact that there has been a conscious effort to promote features of social democracy, thus warranting an account of how labor inclusion has been organized since it was embraced with enough coherence to be put forward as a cohesive project by the bloc. Likewise, the failure of such a project does not preclude the fact that some members of the bloc may have worked actively against it.

on narrowing visions of economic democracy explored in the previous chapter that accorded little room for labor in its vision of economic justice. The telos of reformer's strategies on both sides there too was also a welfare state, but the means were confined to either neoliberal restructuring or developmentalist compromise with the chaebol. A more egalitarian vision of social democratic labor organization, mixed economic model, or other alternatives remained a subordinate concern for pro- and antichaebol perspectives. The pursuit of social dialogue has witnessed a similar dynamic in that it has been treated in practice as a mechanism of *legitimation* for labor policies that are largely oriented toward creating flexible labor markets. Despite the inclusion of key labor reformers to execute social partnership policies, the actual social dialogue process itself has been dysfunctional, remaining incomplete (often in partnership with only the former pro-government trade union confederation) and breaking down for long periods of time. Furthermore, the *instrumental* use of social dialogue combined with punitive labor control policies to respond to economic crisis and to institutionalize nonstandard work has led to the reticence of the rank-and-file members of the democratic trade union movement to endorse the participation of union officials, even when conditions have seemed more favorable to labor inclusion. The result is a contradictory situation where the Democratic Party realizes it needs to include labor and livelihood issues to maintain legitimacy—and seeks to use the carrot of institutions modeled on social democracy to do so—but lacks a vision of what the progressive outcome of creating such institutions might be, much less respect for the views and opinions voiced by the labor movement on the desired form and content of such institutions.

To better understand this dilemma, one that ultimately came to undermine Moon's "society that respects labor" agenda that was part of his broader economic democratization drive, the social dialogue initiatives of liberal administrations are examined below in relation to processes of labor market restructuring and associated strategies of labor control since the Asian financial crisis. Grasping the two together enables the broader relations of coercion and consent that condition labor's participation to come into view and help to explain labor's reticence to fully participate within the integral state. As discussed below, this reticence runs deeper than simply the lack of a progressive vision of social democratic struggle within the Democratic Party. For even by the standards of the progressive liberalism embraced by many progressive reformers and politicians in the party—a view that recognizes that political participation and social rights have lagged behind the embrace of economic liberalism—the dialogue process has lacked substance. For fundamental labor rights concerning basic freedoms of association—axiomatic rights that from a liberal perspective should precede dialogue—have themselves been treated as a bargaining chip in the dialogue process. As such, the rigorous application of labor standards necessary for a transformative framework to be negotiated in a manner that accords proper respect and autonomy toward labor has remained subordinate to demands that labor make concessions that ultimately undermine its bargaining power. This subordination of labor rights resonates too closely with the anticommunist "developmental liberalism" of past conservative administrations (Chang KS 2019) that subordinated social rights to the market economy. Forcing labor to bargain over its fundamental rights betrays, in practice, the very principles of pluralism and freedom of association embraced by pro-democratic administrations. Ultimately, despite the participation of CSOs and veteran trade union officials in helping to encourage social dialogue, the efforts of liberal administrations to *legitimize* themselves through social dialogue with labor have repeatedly failed to produce progressive outcomes that secure hegemony for the pro-democratic bloc and broader support for the Democratic Party. Instead, it has prolonged the cyclical dynamics of enthusiasm-disillusionment of conservative democratization and the strategic impasse of the postdevelopmental state.

Labor after Democratization

Moon's promise to create a "society that respects labor" has its origins in the subordination of labor under Korea's developmentalist dictatorships, and demands for respect, dignity, and effective labor rights made through decades of labor organizing before and after formal democratization. Far from being a neutral arbiter of labor relations, autonomous from both the demands of labor and capital, the developmentalist dictatorships actively molded labor relations in a manner that benefited capital's pursuit of rapid industrial development. This shared goal included a great deal of political repression, including the suppression of independent trade unions and plural union representation at multiple scales, as well as restrictions on collective bargaining and political activism by labor. Throughout the dictatorship period, labor activists were targeted by anticommunist laws, regulations, and rhetoric, a practice that, unfortunately, survived well beyond the transition to free elections. The role of the state was not simply repressive, however; it was also productive of a waged labor force with differential access to social protection. During the 1970s, the state promoted the development of "industrial warriors" (primarily male workers in heavy industries with relatively higher earnings and benefits) through technical training and factory-based mobilization (Kim HA 2013). At the same time, the state actively positioned socially reproductive labor as the responsibility of the patriarchal family and devalued women's labor power through discriminatory training opportunities and often violent labor control (see Moon S 2005, 75–81).

The subordination of labor under dictatorship led to the fusion of labor mobilization with the democracy movement during the 1970s, sprouting the seeds of the mass politics that catalyzed the June Democratic Uprising and Great Workers' Struggle of 1987.[2] Since the return to free elections and expansion of trade union power produced by those struggles, both the labor movement and pro-democratic politicians have sought to improve labor conditions by reforming the role of the state in labor relations and expanding social welfare. In the 10-year period that followed 1987, workers successfully fostered independent unions and expanded union density and collective bargaining coverage. To do so, they often pursued a militant "strike-first-talk-later" approach to workplace bargaining. For example, during the Great Workers' Struggle of 1987, a period of intense labor conflict, only 5.9 percent of disputes were legal, and 94.1 percent occurred illegally (Chang DO 2009, 119). Due to the lack of legal recognition for independent, democratic unions during the dictatorship period (1961–87), the leadership of these strikes was often different from the existing, pro-company union leadership in workplaces where unions existed (Chang DO 2009, 119). The result of these struggles, which continued well into the mid-1990s, was that workers were able to regain control of many pro-company unions from the dictatorship era or establish new, independent unions, or both. Collective bargaining became a necessary procedure for the implementation of managerial decisions, especially at large firms, rather than a mere formality. Beyond individual workplaces, labor activists expanded their political participation in Korean society by seeking to create industrial unions, a national confederation of democratic trade unions, and a labor party, and to promote engagement in social dialogue. These activities extended beyond sectoral interests, as labor activists and

---

2. While a history of the democratic labor movement is beyond the task of the current chapter, it is pertinent to mention that the merging of the struggles of women workers in light industry with nascent democratic mobilization has been well documented and is an important part of this history (Chun S 2003; Lee N 2007; Nam H 2021)

labor-supported CSOs assisted a range of grassroots struggles and agitated for social reform; for example, labor and CSO activists played a key role in expanding universal health care through the integration of medical insurance societies into the National Health Insurance Service (see Lee CS 2016, 125–29).

The pressure to recognize the demands of the labor movement and to include it in decision-making within the state did not come solely from below. It was a multiscalar process bound up with the global expansion of the Korean economy and effected by Korea's participation in international organizations such as the International Labour Organization (ILO) and the OECD. In their own ways, these organizations became sites of labor conflict, as their influence could be used to put pressure upon the national state to upgrade labor standards. For instance, after Korea joined the International Labour Organization in 1991, the Korean Trade Union Congress (KTUC), predecessor of the Korean Confederation of Trade Unions (KCTU), began to use the ILO's Committee on Freedom of Association (CFA) to press for improved labor rights through a wide range of complaints, including concerns about the rights of public servants and teachers and issues such as trade union monopolies, arrests of trade unionists, and other forms of governmental harassment. Consequently, labor rights violations became a crucial subject of concern during Korea's OECD accession period in 1996. Ultimately, its membership was made conditional on labor-related reforms—the first labor-related OECD accession in the organization's history (Salzman 2000, 780). As a result of OECD pressure, the conservative Kim Young-sam administration (1993–98) attempted to implement social dialogue through his Presidential Commission on Labor-Management Relations Reform, which included representatives from both the Federation of Korean Trade Unions (FKTU) and the then illegal KCTU (multiple trade union federations were prohibited at this time). The commission spurred the government to draft legislation recognizing union pluralism that would have allowed for representation of workers by more than one union in a firm, and in many cases break the monopoly of the formerly pro-government FKTU in many workplaces. In an about-face, however, the bill was amended in favor of business, dramatically expanding the ability to lay off workers and postponing union pluralism. Controversially, the bill was passed in the National Assembly in the dead of night without the opposition present, but workers quickly launched a historic general strike in December 1996 that forced the government to walk back its legislation (see Im 2018, 97).

The Trauma of the Grand Social Compromise

By the eve of the Asian financial crisis, labor's demands for improved standards and inclusion in decision-making were difficult to ignore by the major parties. Consequently, the victory in the 1997 presidential election of veteran pro-democratic politician Kim Dae-jung, long regarded as a friend of labor, seemed to signal hope and optimism for a break with the past. As the Asian financial crisis expanded, however, Kim was quickly placed in the unenviable position of being forced to negotiate a rescue package from the IMF, while also satisfying the demands of his supporters for greater welfare and democracy. As a result, the labor reforms Kim pursued were both accommodative and coercive, conceding to some democratic demands while forcefully introducing neoliberal labor market restructuring. As the first liberal government to emerge from the democracy movement, Kim's labor policies necessarily departed from those of the conservative administrations that had dominated Korean politics since the June Uprising. Kim formed a social dialogue body, the Korea Tripartite Commission (KTC), to initiate reforms that recognized union pluralism at multiple scales, gave the KCTU legal status, created a schedule to provide teachers with union organizing rights, and allowed some forms of union-organized political activity. But at the same time, Kim impelled KCTU representatives to consent to much of the labor market restructuring against which they had earlier struck: legislation that eased layoffs and expanded the use of contract, temporary, and self-employed workers. This concession was exchanged for expansion of social welfare and expanded coverage of the national pension and social security systems. For many observers, however, the nominal expansion of social security did not make up for the greater insecurity and increasing inequality caused by the crisis (Baek and Ahn 2012). In fury, the agreement was internally rejected by the KCTU's rank and file membership. However, the Kim administration refused to reconsider the agreement, and signed the "Grand Social Compromise for Overcoming the Economic Crisis" into law. The KCTU subsequently withdrew from the KTC, leaving it as a less than fully representative body (with labor represented by only the pro-government FKTU).

To this day, KCTU officials speak of the compromise as a "trauma" that shapes their attitudes toward participation in social dialogue and social partnership, including up to Moon Jae-in's "society that respects labor" initiatives. And yet many institutionalist scholars have regarded it as a successful corporatist experiment. For instance, Kong (2004, 30) argues that the compromise restored international confidence in South Korea and allowed employment to rebound by promoting a "productivist conception of welfare" that can contain costs and offer "high labour flexibility and the employment-led (rather than redistribution-led) alleviation of poverty." Kong argued that this "crisis corporatism" is an alternative to shock therapy and represents something of a more inclusive neoliberalism that can be pursued without the exclusion of labor (cf. Kuruvilla and Liu 2010). Likewise, Im (2018) argues that it represented a form of "innovative" and "crisis" corporatism. It was innovative because of the lack of prior institution-building and because of the unprecedented nature of the crisis that produced societal pressure for policy coordination, and it was an example of "crisis corporatism" because workers shouldered much of the costs of restructuring (Im 2018, 103). From the standpoint of the democratic labor movement, however, the "Grand Social Compromise" did not provide the long-awaited experiment in social dialogue that labor activists had been hoping for. Instead, it was an aggressive humbling of the trade union movement through easing layoffs and encouraging the expansion of nonstandard work. From the standpoint of the labor movement, the "compromise" provided little in the way of innovation and ultimately undermined long-term trust in the dialogue body itself.[3]

The sources of the labor movement's "trauma" with the compromise concern not only the lack of rank-and-file consent for the agreement but also the coercion that followed as layoffs were eased and the ranks of unemployed and irregular workers expanded. As discussed in chapter 2, nonstandard employment relations grew rapidly after the crisis, following mass layoffs. As figures 6 and 7 (in chapter 2) document, Korea's already high share of temporary and daily workers increased by 20 percent between 1996 and 2000 (from 42 percent to 52 percent of total workers). Female workers found that in many cases they were the first to be fired or (re)hired under temporary contracts, and they continue to face a higher incidence of nonstandard employment status (cf. Chun JJ 2009, 538–41). The incidence of nonstandard work has remained high since the crisis, despite some periods of marginal improvement in relation to the promotion of "indefinite term" contracts as a way of "regularizing" employment without the benefits many other regular workers enjoy. Consequently, the

---

3. Compared to recent approaches to corporatism in Korea, Choi JJ's (1989) study of labor unions and the state pays much more granular attention to the ironies and contractions of labor's engagements with the state.

employment of nonstandard workers has become common across both small and large enterprises. In the latter, workers found themselves redeployed on nonstandard contracts alongside their colleagues on regular ones, in some cases doing the same jobs, creating tensions between workers in the same workplace and undermining labor solidarity. What Jennifer Jihye Chun (2009, 537) describes as the "legal liminality" of nonstandard employment status—"a state of institutional exception in which workers are neither fully protected by nor fully denied the rights of formal employment"—has become one of the main objects of labor struggles since the crisis. Again, Korea has always had a high rate of temporary employment (and thus it is important to avoid romanticizing the authoritarian past as an age of full employment and decent work), but since the crisis struggles over employment status have taken on a new urgency. In short, the status of one's employment is a key feature that distinguishes who has effective access to pension, employment, health, and accident insurance, collective bargaining rights, and effective union representation, and who does not.

The Limiting of Workers' Rights by Law

Alongside the expansion of layoffs and irregular work chronicled above, liberal administrations enforced these changes through a shift in strategies of labor control in the form of extraordinary civil suits against labor activism for obstruction of business. This strategy was represented as an alternative to direct intervention by the state into labor conflict and the exclusion of pro-democratic unions. Instead of banning unions, the new practice recognized them as legitimate actors but used damage claims to depict many usual trade union tactics as uncivil and unlawful threats to business activity. This new mode of control did not emerge overnight, however, but was an iterative process wrapped up in and entangled with the global context discussed above. Immediately after the crisis, the Kim administration relied on a carrot and stick approach of promoting social dialogue (at least with the pro-business FKTU) while using aggressive protest policing to enforce its new labor policies. Chang (2002) refers to this period as one marked by what he calls authoritarian flexibility: the government allowed structural adjustment to be discussed through tripartite means but treated collective action in the form of "political" strikes against it as illegal acts. As a result, during the strikes and protests of late

1997 and early 1998 (against the IMF bailout agreement and labor restructuring), the Korean government was criticized by unions and international organizations such as the ILO, among others, for its mass arrests of striking workers. Amnesty International (1999) reported that in 1998 distressingly high numbers of trade unionists were arrested for engaging in collective action.

The Korean government responded to criticism by the ILO and various CSOs by declaring that instead of physical repression and criminal charges and detention, it would encourage the use of civil suits for obstruction of business as an alternative. The Kim administration announced these changes in its response to the ILO's Committee on Freedom of Association by promising that it would take steps to minimize worker arrests in all but the most "extreme" cases and announced that it would encourage employers to seek compensation from workers involved in "illegal" strikes. These steps included:

- minimizing arrests of workers;
- applying fines to workers arrested rather than physically detaining them;
- encouraging the employers to take disciplinary measures against offenders at the enterprise level; and
- encouraging the employers to seek compensation for damages against the leading players in illegal strikes. (International Labor Organization, 2000, paragraph 502)

The Kim administration broadcast these changes as partially satisfying long-held demands for less state intervention (through arrests and compulsory arbitration) and for greater autonomy in labor-management relations. Nonetheless, it was obvious here that workers' freedom of association was being treated with an economistic logic that limited their ability to effect such freedoms. Consequently, the labor movement and the ILO Committee on Freedom of Association remained concerned about the ease with which collective action could be declared illegal and subjected to obstruction of business claims.

The use of damage claims thus raised the long-standing issue of the limited recognition of Korean workers' labor rights, a point highlighted by the fact that Korea had not yet ratified three of the ILO's core conventions: Freedom of Association and Protection of the Right to Organize Convention, 1948 (No. 87); the Right to Organize and Collective Bargaining Convention, 1949 (No. 98), and the Forced Labour Convention, 1930 (No. 29).

Moreover, the expansion of nonregular work raised new challenges for ensuring the limited protections that already existed as it blurred the lines around who is a lawful subject of labor struggle and who is not. Under Korea's Trade Union and Labor Relations Adjustment Act (TULRAA), adopted in 1997, there are only a limited range of "justifiable activities" for workers and trade unions that are protected (Jang SW 2004; KCTU 2005; Kwon 2015). Article 3 of TULRAA (Restriction on Claims for Damages) protects workers and trade unions from claims by employers for damages (protection of indemnity) arising from collective bargaining and industrial action. However, Article 1 (Purpose) and Article 4 (Justifiable Activities) limit justifiable activities to a narrow reading of workers' constitutional protections as found in section 33(1) of the Constitution of the Republic of Korea: "to enhance working conditions, workers shall have the right to independent association, collective bargaining and collective action" (Republic of Korea 2012). In practice, Korean authorities only recognize legitimate collective action as limited to "peaceful" activity of a recognized/legal union dealing with *working conditions*—such as wages and work hours—with a *direct* employer. Because of the limited range of justifiable activities for which collective action can be taken, collective action is easily punishable for obstruction of business under section 314 of the Criminal Act (Republic of Korea 2009). This charge is applicable to any person who interferes with the business of another by the method of injuring credit (by spreading false facts or by fraud) or by the threat of force. Korea's Supreme Court broadly interprets "threat of force" to mean "all forms of power which may curb or disturb freedom of one's will" (ILO 2000, paragraph 395). "Obstruction" is defined as acts of impeding work or causing a danger that may impede work: "a crime that forces others to do such a thing or not to do other things" (ILO 2004, paragraph 787).

This narrow reading of "justifiable activities" circumscribes the ability of workers to act on issues affecting nonstandard workers, particularly in situations where the status of employee and employer are ambiguous (such as in the case of subcontracted, self-employed, agency, and illegally dispatched workers), or on political issues such as privatization and deregulation, among others. For irregular workers, the threat of damage claims and nonstandard status combine to create a situation of double jeopardy. For they quickly find that it is often difficult to establish *direct* employment relations with their employer or "user-enterprise" despite performing their core employment with them. This is particularly the case of the large numbers of disguised or illegal "in-house" subcontracting workers that expanded after the crisis. These workers found themselves working for a parent company in ambiguous legal arrangements, for subcontracting remains restricted in direct manufacturing, with few rights to bargain with that employer. In the case of many in-house subcontract workers, they are hired by an external agency but are supervised by the parent company (or user-enterprise) similar to direct employees or directly engaged in manufacturing activities that warrant direct employment, or both. Nonetheless, even in such cases it is very difficult to establish their legal rights to take industrial action against their de facto "employers." Hence, the threat of damage claims is more pronounced for subcontractors disrupting business activities by exercising speech by stopping work, or protesting in the workplace, and remains so.

This blurring or informalization of employer-employee relations thus creates difficult strategic challenges and stark legal consequences for labor. Employers have frequently been able to deny that an employment relationship exists between them and their subcontract workers despite the hallmarks of one, such as high levels of integration and subordination between these workers, their agencies, and the using firm (Lee JW 2013; Yun A 2007). Likewise, many temporary employment agencies have been found to practice illegal forms of labor dispatch to begin with—for example, dispatching temporary workers to manufacturing positions, changing contracts or company names every six months to evade regularization—making it difficult for workers to effectively bargain over the nature of their contracts (Noh H 2016). If workers walk out, stop work, or sit-in at their workplace they are in effect obstructing business and subject to exorbitant claims and dismissal and can face retaliation (e.g., nonrenewal of contracts) from both user-enterprises and staffing agencies. In practice, companies often drop suits against employees who agree to withdraw from their union or desist from industrial action, or both (e.g., for regularization of their employment status in cases of disguised employment) (Kwon 2015, 8). As a result, the use of damage claims generates cycles of strife that tend to go on until a strike is won or defeated, or an agreement or amnesty is reached between businesses and their workers that allows claims to expire, or both. For many workers, damage claims deprive them not only of their hard-won labor rights but also of their rights to a livelihood, as illustrated in figure 12.

While the government announced its new strategy in 2000, the use of civil suits against workers only became common practice after spring 2002, following "political" strikes against privatization at Korea Electric Power Corporation (Jang 2004, 274–75; Gray 2009, 114–15). Prior to this strike, civil suits were normally directed at the union and its managing staff. After this strike, however, civil suits increasingly targeted individual workers themselves: a tactic that punished individuals for engaging in col-

Social Democracy without Labor? | 123

Fig. 12. Damage claims: constraining workers' rights
(Translation: *Boss:* You must pay for damages caused to my company. *Police Officer:* You must pay compensation for the use of my nightstick and shield. *Rocks (top to bottom):* Damage claims and provisional seizure; Dismissal and disciplinary action; Arrest. *Worker's Headband:* Strike!) (Video still from a video produced by *Sonjabgo*, a small NGO fighting the use of damage claims against workers. Used with permission. Video available at: https://www.youtube.com/watch?v=q6Ir1qbhAA0)

lective action. In the aftermath of the Korea Electric Power Corporation strike, the affected companies applied for provisional seizure of 14 billion won ($11.7 million) against union staff; 14.5 billion won ($12.1 million) against the union's general fund; and 18.2 billion won ($15.2 million) against 3,172 members (Jang 2004, 275). The company also made a preliminary claim of 9.1 billion won ($7.6 million) from union members and staff as compensation for damages caused by the strike (Jang 2004, 275). Korea Electric Power Corporation's aggressive tactics against its workers, a stance encouraged by the Kim administration's own harsh criticism of the strike, provided a green light to other companies and government agencies to pursue similar claims. By January 2003, outstanding damage claims and provisional seizure of assets reached a combined $US177 million against hundreds of workers and their unions from over 50 workplaces (Lee B 2007, 163), resulting in a rise of protest-suicides by affected workers (Doucette 2013b). Since 2003, damage claims continued to be

The Postdevelopmental State

applied under liberal and conservative administrations. Damage claims for obstruction of business charges have been sought not only for the physical destruction of property during strikes and occupations but also for minor acts of civil disobedience such as nonviolent sit-ins, walkouts, extraordinary union meetings, blockage of traffic, nonpermitted rallies, and even the collective refusal of overtime work (ILO 2004, 2007; KCTU 2005; Yun 2007; NHRC 2015). Because the legal definition of obstruction of business is so broad, the Committee on Freedom of Association has argued that it encompasses "practically all activities related to strikes" (ILO 2004, paragraph 834), providing a powerful tool in the government and employers' hands. Consequently, as table 1 demonstrates, the extraordinary amount of damages claimed against Korean workers (depicted here at perhaps its peak under the Park administration) is unique by international standards, and limits the ability of individuals to maintain a secure livelihood and of unions to cover operational costs. For while trade union liability varies in other OECD countries—some of which have used strategic lawsuits against public participation to delay, intimidate, and obstruct labor organizing efforts by nonstandard employees (see Hallet 2015)—such extraordinary compensation suits are rare because of the wider range of legal strike activity or the maximum legal limit put on such claims, or both.

The Politics of Partnership

As hegemony involves a mix of coercion and consent, it is possible to read the expansion of nonstandard work and coercive use of damage claims as recursively related to the politics of social dialogue and cooperation, albeit in the first instance as an attempt to institute a neoliberal model of labor relations instead of a more social democratic one. Damage claims have provided much of the "force" needed to institute policies seemingly "consented" to during the Grand Social Compromise. Likewise, the hardships they have created for workers has led to promises of a more conciliatory attitude toward labor under subsequent liberal administrations and efforts to restore social dialogue. Kim Dae-jung's successor, President Roh Moohyun, for instance, tried to reinvigorate the social dialogue process. For while Kim had upgraded the status of the KTC it had languished since the crisis. In May 1999 Kim formalized the KTC by passing the Tripartite Commission Law as up until that point it had been regulated by presidential decree. As Im (2018, 107) recounts, by making the KTC a body with

TABLE 1. Outstanding Damage Claims and Provisional Seizure of Worker Assets in KCTU-Affiliated Workplaces (March 2015)

Workplaces	Amount of Damage Claims	Provisional Seizure
Ssangyong Motor	30.2 billion ($USD 26.4 million)	2.89 billion ($USD 2.5 million)
KEC	30.0 billion ($USD 26.2 million)	50 million ($USD 44,000)
Hanjin Heavy Industries & Construction	15.81 billion ($USD 13.8 million)	
KORAIL	31.32 billion ($USD 27.4 million)	11.6 billion ($USD 10.1 million)
MBC	19.51 billion ($USD 17.1 million)	2.2 billion ($USD 1.9 million)
Yoosung Enterprise	5.75 billion ($USD 5 million)	
Hyundai Motor (Ulsan nonregular workers branch)	22.56 billion ($USD 19.7 million)	
Hyundai Motor (Asan internal subcontracting branch)	1.67 billion ($USD 1.5 million)	40 million ($USD 35,000)
Hyundai Motor (Jeonju nonregular workers branch)	2.56 billion ($USD 2.2 million)	50 million ($USD 44,000)
Star Chemical	0.2 billion ($USD 0.2 million)	
Valeo Mando	2.65 billion ($USD 2.3 million)	
Sangsin Brake	1 billion ($USD 0.9 million)	0.41 billion ($USD 0.4 million)
Mando	3 billion ($USD 2.6 million)	
DKC	2.6 billion ($USD 2.3 million)	1 billion ($USD 0.9 million)
Robert Bosch Korea Buyong	0.21 billion ($USD 0.2 million)	
Continental Automotive	30 million ($USD 26,000)	
Kia Motor	33 million ($USD 29,000)	
Total	**169.1 billion ($USD 148 million)**	**18.23 billion ($USD 16 million)**

Source: Data supplied by KCTU.

legal standing, the government sought to provide an incentive for the trade unions to return. However, only the formerly pro-government FKTU rejoined the KTC, leaving the commission with low societal support or what Im (2018, 108) describes as "immobile corporatism." The Roh administration tried to reverse this trend. During his presidential campaign several veteran labor activists and scholar-activists (e.g. former Korean Trade Union Congress activist Park Tae Ju and progressive scholar Kim Tae Hwan) joined his steering committee, and Roh appointed veteran labor movement scholar, and Korea Labour and Society Institute founding member and director, Kim Kum-soo, to head the KTC in March 2003. However, despite informal talks and preparatory meetings between presidential advisors, business, and labor, the social dialogue body was not successfully revived as a fully representative tripartite institution that included both the KCTU and FKTU. This was in part due to the feeling among labor unions that they were being asked to "participate and self-reflect"—that is, to abrogate their militant history of grassroots mobilization (Lee N 2011, 54)—rather than participate as a substantive partner. Their hesitancy was also due in part to the labor relations "road map" drawn up by Roh advisors that, they felt, threatened to further institutionalize nonstandard employment. To the KCTU it appeared as a déjà-vu of the IMF compromise.

The road map proposed three different bills on the protection and use of temporary workers, "dispatched" workers (workers hired as casual or contract workers through staffing agencies), and the mediation of labor-management conflicts. Essentially, the road map sought to respond to the proliferation of irregular work following the IMF crisis and the earlier Grand Social Compromise. Formally, this expansion was only legally permitted in a very few select sectors, but irregular workers were being employed across the economy. The road map sought to recognize this reality not by limiting the use of nonstandard contracts, but by removing restrictions on the sectors in which irregular workers could be employed. In return, the government hoped to better regulate irregular work by extending social protections to cover such workers, as discussed in chapter 2. Consequently, the unions saw participation in social dialogue as an attempt to legitimize nonstandard work rather than to create alternatives to it. In formal and informal preparatory meetings and events, the two union federations demanded that a strict definition be drafted that clearly articulates the circumstances under which fixed and short-term contract workers can be hired. In contrast, the employers' federations advocated for a largely business as usual approach and sought to prevent a strict time

Social Democracy without Labor? | 127

limit on the duration that workers can be employed on nonstandard contracts. The KCTU demanded recognition of the principle of equal pay for equal work, voiced its concern over employer practices that limit workers' freedom of association (such as terminating contracts as a punitive measure against trade union organizing), and pressed for the regularization of casual workers who have already been employed for a total of more than two years. Without a rigorous plan for regularization, they argued, workers would simply be fired and rehired.

While the KCTU did not formally rejoin the social dialogue, the Roh administration passed the policies that constituted its labor relations roadmap with the consent of the FKTU, who agreed to the bills in exchange for the delay of provisions on union pluralism and the payment of full-time union staff—policies that would have negatively affected the FKTU's "monopoly" over its workplaces. As such, the agreement was quickly criticized as an opportunistic agreement (a 2.5 agreement) that betrayed the very spirit of *tripartite* dialogue. Before the new laws came into effect in July 2007, companies across all sectors began to dismiss temporary staff that had been employed close to the two-year limit to avoid having to offer them regular contracts. The KCTU's criticism that social dialogue would be used to legitimize the government's neoliberal policy orientation toward workers seemed to be confirmed.

For labor movement activists who believed in strengthening institutions of social dialogue, this result was disappointing. They felt that participation in social dialogue offered a chance to clarify the obligations and entitlements that irregular workers suffering from discrimination can receive, but they were also aware that their participation could weaken the associational position of labor by expanding irregular work. They complained that the process itself did not take into account this dilemma, leading to the administration and the unions embracing starkly different perceptions about social dialogue. While liberal politicians viewed the unions as cohesive actors with a unified voice that could either support or oppose policy, the unions saw the process as one in which their participation in agreements was subject to internal bargaining with members and modification of agreements. They saw social dialogue as an exercise of both *external* social partnership and *internal* union democracy. As one union activist who had been involved in the KCTU's previous dialogue efforts put it at the time:

> One important aspect of social cooperation is that an organization must be able to bring its members along with an agreement. What

128 | The Postdevelopmental State

> Kim and Roh wanted out of unions was an organization that at a moment's decision could act in unison. That is not possible, so when some key disputes took place the government's patience broke and said it could not trust unions. It just gave up. If an organization is capable of just doing that, turning around on its members one day to accept a decision that has just been made, given the histories that organization has had, that organization would be a very undemocratic organization.[4]

In other words, the KCTU and some Korea Labour and Society Institute officials felt that the government did not see the unions as long-term partners. There seemed to be little respect for the KCTU's internal processes or effective accommodation for the unions to delay legislation and discuss alternatives with their members. Instead, the administration treated dialogue in an instrumental fashion rather than in an *agonistic* framework: a framework that respects conflict between actors, where contestation can be seen as creating a positive good (Mouffe 2000). As one veteran trade unionist from the KCTU put it, "a partner in such an arrangement is only a worthwhile partner because it is such a difficult partner, and you have to respect that difficulty."[5] But, alas, the KCTU's "difficult partnership" was not respected. This sentiment was shared by progressive economic advisors in the Roh administration who argued that labor was seen less as a partner and "more as an obstacle to reform."[6]

The "Society That Respects Labor"

Ultimately, the lack of an effective plan to incorporate labor in conflictual dialogue at various scales during the liberal administrations of Kim and

---

4. Interview, former KCTU strategist, March 2007. Some of these strategists went on to work for the ILO. Participants in Moon's Economic, Social, and Labor Council would come to voice similar sentiments.

5. Interview, former KCTU strategist, March 2007.

6. Interview, former presidential advisor on economic affairs, December 2006. Even civil servants in the Labor Ministry tasked with addressing the issue of nonregular work argued that the administration did not understand how to effectively apply the principles of social cooperation and would tend to subordinate the tripartite process to their own policy goals. Interview, former member of NonRegular Workers Policy Team, Ministry of Labor. In the words of the Democratic Labor Party officials at that time, the government had come to see labor as "a subject to be controlled rather than as a participant or partner in running society." February 2007 interview, international coordinator, Democratic Labor Party, July 2006.

Roh led to an approach that prioritized punitive measures to contain contestation surrounding the expansion of nonregular employment, such as the use of criminal charges and civil suits for obstruction of business. This coercive approach fatally undermined attempts at securing labor's consent for reform plans and contributed to broader legitimation problems for liberal administrations. Moreover, the conservative administrations that followed Kim and Roh felt emboldened to carry on with their use of these punitive measures and supplemented them with tactics such as the deregistration of unions and aggressive protest policing. For example, the military-like operation that supressed strikes over layoffs at Ssangyong Motors in 2009 (later dramatized in the television series *Squid Game*) was followed by hefty damage claims as shown in table 1. This confrontation contributed to the suicides of over 20 Ssangyong workers and family members following these events and symbolized for many the approach of conservative administrations toward labor (Lee Y 2021). Both the conservative Lee and Park administrations sought to weaken employment protections, particularly in the public sector. The Park administration went so far as to deregister, and hence render illegal, the country's largest teachers' union over the membership of a handful of unemployed workers in the union. Consequently, the trade unions came to strongly support the Candlelight Revolution of 2016–17 and provided protest infrastructure and logistics to help sustain the event.

The Moon administration was keenly aware of the abuse of damage claims under Lee and Park and recognized the demand for better labor relations in its pledge to institutionalize the spirit of the Candlelight Revolution and create a "society that respects labor." To do so, Moon introduced a range of policies around the regulation of employment contracts and work hours, and sought to revive the tripartite social dialogue, renaming the Economic and Social Development Commission—as the KTC had been called since 2007—the Economic, Social, and Labor Council (ESLC) to better incorporate labor's participation. To institute his society that respects labor reforms, the Moon administration took inspiration from several initiatives in which labor-oriented CSOs had been involved during the conservative administrations. Due to the conservative climate of national administrations at this time, most of these initiatives were at the urban level, and had been facilitated by the election of progressive mayors and governors in local and regional elections. Among these initiatives, Seoul's approach to social dialogue and its urban labor policy stood out. The election of PSPD cofounder Park Won Soon as mayor in 2011 to lead the Seoul Metropolitan Government (SMG) facilitated this policy experimentation. Park recruited CSO officials from organizations such as the

130 | The Postdevelopmental State

Korea Labour and Society Institute, among others, to create a Labour Policy Division. The Korea Labour and Society Institute provided research support and policy studies to help the city deliberate on how to upgrade employment relations. Ultimately, the SMG decided to do so by regularizing the nonstandard workers it directly and indirectly employs through employment agencies and subcontractors and expanding employee representation within both the metropolitan government and the companies it does business with.

The experience of social dialogue under Seoul's labor policy departed significantly from the acrimonious experience of dialogue under national administrations. At the heart of the initiative was its Labor Rights Protection Committee, a dialogue body that included labor unions, employer associations, youth, women, the central government, and academics. What was novel about this dialogue body was the inclusion of actors such as women's associations and the youth labor movement. Their participation contrasted with traditional tripartite social partnership policies that rarely include more than union federations, government, and private employers. In coordination, these actors helped to create the Labor Policy Master Plan in 2015. The plan declared Seoul as a "city that respects labor" (Seoul Metropolitan Government 2015) and included several ambitious initiatives such as setting up local councils to tackle issues faced by youth, women, and precarious workers, and recognizing the unique needs of "emotional laborers" such as the city's customer service and call center workers (Kim JJ 2017). The SMG also introduced a job seeker's allowance, set up central and district-based welfare support centers, and mandated a living wage ordinance for regular and nonregular workers employed by the city (Kim JJ 2017). While it lacked the expansive power of the national government to reshape the contours of the employment relation, it was able to use its capacity as a large metropolitan government to increase regular employment among city workers, cater to a variety of worker interests, and demonstrate that dialogue and partnership with labor could be used to improve jobs and livelihoods.

The lesson did not go unseen by the Democratic Party. The Moon administration's "society that respects labor" (*nodongja chonjung sahoe*) slogan seemed to be directly inspired, in fact, by Seoul's "city that respects labor" (*nodongja chonjung t'ŭkpyŏlshi*). There were other similarities as well. Moon's policy began by promoting the conversion of nonregular into regular workers in the public sector, accompanied by a large increase in the minimum wage. To further reshape labor relations, Moon relaunched the social dialogue process to negotiate the reduction of working hours and establish a 52-hour workweek, promote an employee representative system, and develop policy on labor issues such as health and safety, vocational training, and other concerns. To lead the ESLC, Moon appointed several progressive CSO researchers, former labor activists, and intellectuals. These included figures such as Moon Sung-hyun, a former leader of the Korean Democratic Labor Party, the labor scholar and former Roh advisor Park Tae-joo, and staff seconded from the Korea Labor Institute with wide knowledge of comparative labor relations. Similar to the SMG's labor policy, the ESLC included representatives of "public interests" including youth, women, nonstandard workers, and small and mid-sized enterprises.[7] Despite these innovations and the inclusion of several progressive figures in running the ESLC, the dialogue body and Moon's broader labor reforms quickly faced criticism.

First, Moon's policy of using the public sector to regularize irregular workers was implemented in a manner that lacked strong coordination with the labor movement. Moon needed to act quickly with his reforms, so this policy was not part of the wider deliberations scheduled for the ESLC. In addition, as discussed in chapter 2, the workers "regularized" by Moon in the public sector in most cases had their contracts converted into "indefinite term contracts" using newly created subsidiary companies for public corporations. While this conversion increased the number of "regular" employees, it created questions about just how substantive this new form of employment status might be. Subsequently, recalling Roh Moo Hyun's earlier attempt to bring the KCTU back into social partnership, the ESLC's preparatory discussions between labor leaders from both trade union federations, business, and ESLC officials yielded poor results. While initial discussions seemed positive, when put to a vote the rank-and-file members of the KCTU did not ratify the motion to formally participate in the ESLC, limiting its representative nature. The traumatic memory of the earlier grand social compromise remained. Moreover, activists in the KCTU felt that the warm connections (*inyŏn*) between ESLC officials and the KCTU might be a problem, by influencing the KCTU to legitimize

---

7. While the inclusion of diverse public interests in social dialogue was a highly innovative example of democratic experimentation here and had the potential to cover a wide range of labor issues faced by precarious workers, the voices of migrant workers were absent and provide a sense, perhaps, of the limits of the ESLC's innovations. Migrant labor issues have been represented, in part, by the Migrant Trade Union of the KCTU and potentially through industrial bargaining. However, without KCTU representation on the ESLC, as discussed below, it is difficult to raise migrant labor concerns through these channels.

government policy that went against workers' interests. In addition, no sooner had it passed its new 52-hour workweek legislation, the Moon administration began to push for an agreement on a flexible working hour system (Park KY and Lee JH 2018) that could be used to extend the working day, and limit overtime pay, by expanding the units (e.g., from three to six months) under which work hours can be spread out.[8]

Additionally, in perhaps its most fatal flaw, the Moon administration portrayed the agreement on a flexible working hour system as something to be exchanged for the long-awaited ratification of the ILO's core conventions. Despite promises to do so, Korea had never ratified the core conventions concerning forced labor and freedom of association mentioned above. The latter convention, Freedom of Association and Protection of the Right to Organize (No. 87), was seen as essential by many labor activists for resolving the question of inequality and exploitation of irregular workers, for their unions are often not legally recognized and their strikes are easily declared illegal (Ryu M 2019). This approach to asking labor to bargain for its fundamental rights strongly contrasted with Seoul's labor policy, and its Seoul Declaration on Decent Work City (Seoul Metropolitan Government 2017) that treated this convention as an a priori or axiomatic principle that preceded dialogue. As such, the Moon administration faced criticism from a variety of CSOs that it was "narrowing the gateway" for labor's participation and for substantive dialogue in ESLC before it was even formally launched (Park K and Lee 2018). In a response that amounted to something of a Gramscian "war of position" within the integral state, other actors in political and civil society such as PSPD, the National Human Rights Commission of Korea, the European Union's pressure under the EU-Korea free trade agreement, the UN's periodic review, and others argued that the conventions should simply be ratified promptly and without conditions. Such commentary lent its voice to the criticism that social dialogue should not be used in such an instrumental fashion, and that fundamental rights such as freedom of association should be a *precursor* to dialogue and not the basis for it. For instance, while it did not encourage the use of such claims, the fact that the Moon

---

8. The early stages of the COVID-19 pandemic witnessed a similar dynamic. KCTU chairman Kim Myeon-hwan called for an emergency dialogue at the ESLC to engage in discussions about protecting workers from dismissal and other measures to mitigate the crisis. An agreement was drafted, but KCTU delegates did not approve the agreement, which included language that the KCTU would work toward flexibility on working hours in exchange for business making efforts at job retention (see Seol 2021).

Social Democracy without Labor? | 133

administration did nothing to address outstanding damage claims against workers was seen as a sign of lack of concern about the poor protection of labor's freedom of association.

The Moon administration eventually passed its recommendations on flexible labor time through the ESLC with only the participation of the FKTU. Like earlier attempts to include labor in the state and promote social dialogue as a tool for creating alternatives to neoliberalism, the ESLC could not be seen as fully representative. It lacked the participation of the KCTU; moreover, the working time system revision was also objected to by the public interest representatives on the committee such as the youth, nonregular workers, and women workers (Chun HW 2019). The fact that the diverse public interest representatives involved in the ESLC to help address the subaltern position of irregular workers, women, and youth in the labor market themselves criticized the bills demonstrates that the innovative potential of its design was in many ways squandered. More concerning, the FKTU would later protest the government's labor policies, arguing that its revisions of TULRAA as part of the ILO ratification process betrayed the social agreement (see FKTU 2020a, 2020b). The government did so by implementing the flexible work hour system, but introducing restrictions on the activities of dismissed workers and full-time union officials, as well as restrictions on collective action on employer's premises, all of which betray the principles of freedom of association in the conventions.[9] In this regard, ESLC participants voiced worries that they were becoming merely "wallpaper" for the Moon Jae-in administration. In other words, they questioned whether or not their presence was merely to legitimize the policy directions of the Moon government rather than serve as a substantive platform for deliberating on a more socially inclusive model. This was a difficult position for reformers, for while they felt that the trade union movement had its own internal difficulties (such

---

9. Labor lawyers argue this revision is legally dubious, and that one test of future administrations will be how the ILO conventions are treated in law. Some feel that the conventions will be ignored, while others feel that the conditionalities put in TULRAA by the Moon administration will have to be thrown out. Meanwhile, civil society groups have campaigned for further revision of TULRAA (the "yellow envelope law") that would expand the protections for workers in indirect employment relations and for workers to take collective action on a broader set of issues regarding working conditions. While the Democratic Party supported this initiative following the election of Yoon Seok-yeol, why such a law wasn't endorsed sooner in Moon's tenure is an open question.

as rivalry between regular and irregular workers, and other problems related to enterprise-level bargaining) that the democratic experimentalism of such councils could address, they did not view the dialogue body merely as a site to rubber-stamp government policy but to overcome the internal difficulties of both the administration and the labor movement in advocating for working class interests.

Commenting on the internal divisions in the labor movement, veteran labor scholar and proponent of social dialogue Kim Kum-soo (2021) notes that both major federations lack a comprehensive vision for social change. The result is that they remained divided, particularly the pro-democratic confederation, the KCTU, despite its long-held demand that democratization benefits working people as a whole. But while it seeks to represent irregular workers' struggles, it has made little progress deepening industrial democracy. For despite its progressive history, regular workers at large enterprises within the union appear invested in maintaining enterprise-level bargaining. Industrial-level bargaining remains poorly developed beyond the health sector, which is a problem that even KCTU officials have noted. In addition, Kim complains that the KCTU has lacked a strong societal and political influence since the decline of the Democratic Labor Party. Ironically, it was the leaders of the latter that were enlisted by the Moon administration to launch the ESLC for they had strong relations with union leaders. Both ESLC officials and trade union officials I have interviewed regarded these connections as both a promise and a threat. It was a promise for policymakers in that these connections could help labor push the government to implement labor-friendly policies. But for trade unionists it was a potential threat in that these connections might drive the membership into accepting an agreement that was bad for them, which would repeat the trauma of the grand social compromise all over again. Nonetheless, the internal division in the labor movement between rank-and-file activists and more conservative workers at enterprise unions also made it difficult to effectively advocate for a comprehensive plan for national labor reform. Overcoming the Democratic Party's coordination problem with labor, it seems, also involves solving labor's own internal coordination dilemmas. But this dual task seems difficult within a broader pro-democratic bloc whose main political party has actively sought to subordinate labor rights to neoliberal labor reform, and where the voice of minority parties has been further dampened by recent negative changes to the proportionate representation system.

Labor without Labor

It was not only in the ESLC where the problems of Moon's "society that respects labor" reforms can be seen. While the ESLC was chosen as the desired place for coordination between labor, the administration, and business, other areas of labor reform prioritized as part of Moon's "pro-labor" policies similarly lacked effective coordination with the labor movement despite the role of veteran labor activists, intellectuals, and labor-oriented CSOs in policy formation. Noting this contradiction, by the second half of the Moon administration, progressive intellectuals within civil society began to offer an assessment of his policies. For instance, the progressive scholar-activist Cho Don-mun—known for his activism for labor rights and campaign to end the use of damage claims against workers—pointed out the lack of coordination with labor in pursuing regularization in the public sector. This task was entrusted to individual government institutions, leading to a high degree of variation in terms of the numbers of workers regularized and their treatment. In some cases, regular employees even protested the hiring of nonregular workers. As Cho (2021a) notes, there was a wasted opportunity here to engage in industrial-level bargaining with trade unions or to utilize a forum like the ESLC so that a comprehensive plan for regularization might have been developed. Nonetheless, Cho (2021c; see also 2021a, 2021b) notes that the Moon Jae-in administration did better than previous administrations in promoting regularization, but the process of using subsidiaries to hire workers and placing them on indefinite term contracts shows a disregard for stronger social protections and the collective bargaining potential of direct employment. It represented a form of labor policy without coordination with the labor movement. For union officials, it also set a bad example for private companies as a model for "regularization." Some chaebol requested that they too be able to use the subsidiary model as an alternative to illegal "in-house" subcontracting; that the two models are not so distinct in practice demonstrates the weakness of Moon's regularization plans.

A similar criticism was made concerning Moon's minimum wage policy. Again, there was much that was initially progressive about this policy, which lead to a 16 percent increase in the minimum wage. Moon had hired progressive economist Hong Jang-pyo to lead the minimum wage commission, and former PSPD activist Jang Ha-sung served as Moon's core economic advisor and policy planning secretary at the time. Despite their involvement, the wage increase led to criticism from both business

136 | The Postdevelopmental State

and CSO activists (You JS 2019). The increase took place in the context of the US-China trade war and trade frictions between Korea and Japan, both of which had affected the performance of the Korean economy. The shock of the raise on small and midsize enterprises and the self-employed created a public backlash against it due to job losses. The backlash against the wage increase subsequently led the Moon administration to backtrack by amending the Minimum Wage Act to include regular bonuses, benefits, and expenses in the calculation of the wage (effectively reducing the promised increase), leading labor to pledge to boycott further social dialogue. Critics and even some progressive CSO members who participated in the policy noted that the plan was poorly integrated into a broader vision for social and industrial democracy (Kim JH 2022; Cho DM 2021a). A broader set of redistributive policies and supports such as the extension of collective bargaining agreements to nonunionized workers, solidarity wages, and other policies coordinated with the labor movement might have created more support for the policy. More so, the administration's attempt to quickly reverse the wage increase demonstrated that it lacked a broader plan for achieving its "society that respects labor" and "income-led growth." Ironically, beyond the short-term, conjunctural shock of the wage increase, the policy did seem to have a positive impact on reducing inequality between the top and bottom 10 percent of wage earners (Kim JH 2022; cf. Cho DM 2021b). But as the later chair of the income-led growth committee and Korea Labour and Society Institute member Kim Yoo Seon pointed out, the government "fussed over short-term statistics" and backtracked from its pledges (quoted in Kim JH 2022).

These conundrums surrounding labor's participation, or lack of it, in Moon's "pro-labor" policies generated friction with progressive CSOs and reformers, such as progressive economist Lee Byeong-cheon (2019), who, along with Cho Don-mun, formed the Intellectuals Declaration Network (Chishigin Sŏnŏn Net'ŭwŏk'ŭ) after the Candlelight events to hold the Moon administration to its pledges for social and economic reform. Lee noted that the administration had simply interpreted that the minimum wage increase alone would suffice to produce income-led growth. As a result, Moon lacked a comprehensive plan for his slogan. The presence of key reform personalities on their own was not enough, both Lee and Cho lament.

> Hong Jang-pyo, former chief secretary for economy at the Blue House, Kim Sang-jo, Chairman of the Fair Trade Commission, and Jang Ha-sung, former head of policy at the Blue House were chosen

Social Democracy without Labor? | 137

to symbolize reform, but it was difficult for them to lead the reform by their abilities alone. (Cho DM as interviewed by Park SY and Cho SE 2021a)

Despite their inclusion within state policy, these progressive reformers were constrained by wider dynamics of the administration and the politics of the Democratic Party. Lee (2019) puts this down to a problem of the will of the administration itself. In other words, the Candlelight government itself was putting the candlelight out. But others have argued that the problem isn't simply one of the policy choices of the administration but also the specific visions of reform and of economic democracy embraced by some reformers themselves, imaginaries that accord little agency to role of labor as a broad, substantive partner.

Conclusion

The irony of the failure of Moon's society that respects labor reform is that on the surface it seemed destined for success. The nexus between political and civil society appeared strong and included progressive intellectuals, CSO activists, even former labor party officials, all with strong ties to or experience within the democratic trade union movement. And yet the ESLC broke down despite such embeddedness and cohesive networks between the administration, CSOs, and veteran reformers. Reflecting on the similar failure of labor policies under the Roh administration, the sociologist Lee Cheol Sung (2016) argues that one reason they failed may be that the unions lacked strong policy and deliberation channels with the incumbent Democratic Party, in part because of the trade union's efforts to support the then ascendent Korea Democratic Labor Party. During the Moon administration, the social dialogue process itself became led by former Democratic Labor Party activists who had built up cohesive networks with the labor movement. It was in *spite* of these networks and a favorable atmosphere for labor reform (of embeddedness and cohesiveness, to use Lee's terminology) that efforts to create a broadly representative dialogue body and to use it to introduce substantive policy changes failed. In my opinion, this result had less to do with the sociological categories of cohesiveness and embeddedness, and more with the politics of legitimation that the nexus was used for, a politics that speaks to broader dynamics within both the Democratic Party and the pro-democratic bloc.

For while the Democratic Party and progressive intellectuals prefer to

138 | The Postdevelopmental State

adopt the form of institutions associated with social democracy to legitimize themselves and appeal to workers, they have rarely used such institutions as a *site* of social democratic struggle. This result is due, in part, to the lack of broader coordination with the democratic labor movement outside of such tripartite bodies (beyond, for instance, the corporatist relations that exist between the FKTU and Democratic Party). As one progressive intellectual and proponent of economic democracy who has been involved in the CSO movement and the Blue House put it,[10] ruling party politicians have a lot of interest in social democratic policies around job creation and labor market protections that conform to their party's broad slogans, but they are not necessarily interested in the relations between societal actors that come with them. In his opinion, economic democracy has not been envisaged as social democracy or as industrial democracy. There is only room for policies associated with social democracies but not the politics of social democratic struggle. In this manner, such policies led to depoliticization, for the role of labor is treated merely as a technical issue. Moreover, most liberal administrations have tended to use such institutions to implement Anglo-American style labor market reform that expands nonstandard employment and eases dismissals. And despite the "progressive liberalism" of many reformers and Democratic Party politicians—a philosophy that seeks to broaden pluralism to better represent working class interests—liberal administrations have failed to treat labor rights as axiomatic—much less pass long-promised, comprehensive antidiscrimination legislation—leaving damage claims on the books and ratifying the ILO conventions "with conditions attached."

This problematic approach to labor inclusion then raises the question of how actors in the pro-democratic bloc might coordinate to better satisfy demands for comprehensive and egalitarian political economic reform. In other words, why hasn't it embraced a strong vision of social and industrial democracy in its project of economic democracy? This is a perennial challenge faced by progressives, especially those that have come to unwittingly play a legitimation role. To some the solution would simply be the creation of an explicit social democratic or labor party. Such is the role that the Korean Democratic Labor Party and later the Justice Party has sought to play. This strategy, however, is in part obstructed by the two major parties themselves, which have, at times, colluded to ensure that they dominate

---

10. Interview, October 2019.

Social Democracy without Labor? | 139

elections.[11] For instance, the creation of satellite parties by the major parties to manipulate the mixed-member proportionate representation system has limited the voice of minor parties and was seen by them as a betrayal (Shin GW 2020; Mosler 2023). But the problem involves more than simply the party system. It involves the broader relations between both the pro-democratic and conservative blocs themselves. For the resilience of the conservative bloc, as explored in the following chapter, produces, in several ways, the necessity for both liberal and progressive political forces to work together, to form a pro-democratic *bloc* to begin with. It is this necessity, in many ways, that creates the need for comprehensive visions of democratic reform among progressive forces. But the various interests that compose the bloc—its liberal, regional, progressive, party boss, neoliberal, and even moderate conservative elements—also serve to limit the coherence of those visions when in power. And while in some ways it might be preferable for the bloc to split and form more cohesive and independent political entities, the conservative bloc's own structure and unity serve to obstruct such reformation. The need for a bloc persists, in part, because of the conservative bloc's own "integral state" connecting the public security apparatus, conservative politicians and intellectuals, and the chaebol.

The next and final empirical chapter examines this "bloc politics" in more depth, by focusing on the challenges raised by the conservative bloc leading up to the Candlelight Revolution and the efforts to overcome them as part of the broader project of economic democracy afterward. These efforts focused on reforming the power of the prosecution service and other residual aspects of the Cold War state. This task is important, reformers have argued, for it is difficult to check the abuses of power by the chaebol or the aggressive policing of labor without it. However, in this area, too, the problems of reform imaginaries and politics of legitimation described above have also persisted, and eventually led to the denouement of the Moon administration's reform drives. In this case, this disillusionment involved not merely the reform visions or legitimation-though-inclusion role of progressive figures, but the contradictions involved in the very *personality* of specific reformers themselves. As the next chapter argues, the politics of personality that surrounded a few specific figures in the Moon administration obscured the wider meaning and tasks of legal reform, and distracted attention away from a critical discussion of the

---

11. For an excellent history of the structure of Korea's political parties and their periodic collusion in maintaining a two-party system, see Mobrand (2019).

positive and negative aspects of its prosecution reform plans to begin with. As a result of doubling down on and uncritically valorizing the personalities of key reformers as opposed to foregrounding the democratic rationale for important legal reforms, both the administration and many members of the pro-democratic bloc opened themselves up to criticisms that they had not lived up to the standards of fairness and equality they claimed to champion. A door was left open for the conservative bloc to revive its popularity by appropriating the discourse of fairness as part of its strategy to recover from the impeachment of Park Geun-hye, albeit in a distorted manner that posited the liberal-left as the "vested interests" to be overcome.

5

The Integral State of the Conservative Bloc

Early in his administration, President Moon Jae-in announced that a key task of building Candlelight Democracy would be to create a country that eliminates unfairness. This task included addressing inequality through labor and economic reform as much as it involved reforming the power of public security agencies inherited from the authoritarian era of the developmental state, including the Ministry of Justice, the National Intelligence Service, the police, and associated organizations. Key reformers agreed, noting that economic democracy could not be accomplished without reform of the prosecution and judicial apparatus so as to eliminate collusive relations and non-enforcement of laws and regulations governing corporate crimes (Park SI 2021). So far, the previous chapters have examined the project of economic democracy and the inclusion of labor primarily in relation to the internal dynamics to the pro-democratic bloc. The limits and contradictions of specific progressive imaginaries of economic democracy and social partnership have been explored, as has the politics of coordination and conflict that have stemmed from the inclusion of labor and other progressive actors to help legitimize the policies of liberal administrations. But the obstacles to resolving this dilemma are not limited to these internal dynamics alone. They also involve relations between both the pro-democratic and conservative blocs, that is to say, relations that might be considered relatively "external" but that help to constitute the necessity for the formation of a pro-democratic historical bloc to begin with. For the power of the conservative bloc itself and the cohesion of its own integral state (its nexus between political and civil society) provides a powerful obstacle to deepening democratization and is composed of alliances between right-wing politicians, state personnel, and conservative civil society. This nexus allows the conservative bloc to

142 | The Postdevelopmental State

hamper liberal and progressive political forces and requires that the latter coordinate in some manner to achieve common ends. While this ability should not distract attention away from internal problems of the pro-democratic bloc, it is important to recognize the powerful external challenges it faces, if only to appreciate how conservative actors have sought to confront progressive actors and exploit contradictions within the pro-democratic bloc for political gain.

This chapter explores this "bloc politics" in greater detail by examining the survival of the public security measures of previous developmentalist regimes, and efforts to reform the latter following the Candlelight events. To do so, it focuses on the conservative confrontation with the pro-democratic bloc that occurred during the administrations of Lee Myung-bak (2008–13) and Park Geun-hye (2013–17), and the legal reforms that occurred directly after them, as Moon sought to correct for the legal abuses of both administrations. For it was during the former period that conservative administrations used their own connections to civil society actors to target liberal and progressive political actors on both cultural and political fronts. As explored below, a tacit alliance between conservative prosecutors-cum-politicians, members of the public security apparatus, and conservative civil society organizations such as the New Right movement led to a form of confrontation known in Korea as "politics by public security." This politics targets social conflict and political dissent as threats to national security and embraces a cultural politics that seeks to revise the narrative of Korean democratization in order to obfuscate the role of the democracy movement. To do so, it criticizes specific democratic events and activists as threats to democracy while praising former dictatorships. This mode of politics is particularly salient for the role it played in provoking the renewed democratic mobilization that led to the Candlelight events and the impeachment of Park Geun-hye. But it did not end with those events. Instead, following a period of reorganization, the conservative bloc was able to exploit discontent with the liberal Moon administration's reform plans. Specifically, the Moon administration's attempt to reform the public security apparatus of the state in the form of the power of the prosecution service—which along with chaebol and labor market reform was seen as one of its three central tasks—devolved into a complex scandal that provided an opportunity for the conservative bloc to reconstitute itself.

This scandal arose around the appointment of former democracy activist and progressive legal scholar Cho Kuk to the position of minister of justice. Cho was portrayed by both Moon and by prominent politicians as a pioneering legal and democratic reformer in a manner that sought to demonstrate the administration's fidelity to the democracy movement and secure its legitimacy in a manner similar to the dynamics of inclusion already explored in previous chapters. But as discussed below, the case of Cho quickly departed from the usual legitimation-through-inclusion dynamics explored in the previous chapters and developed into something that might best be understood as a politics of personality. Specifically, the very task of prosecution reform became bound up with support for or opposition to Cho's personality itself to the degree that it appeared that the task of prosecution reform was indistinguishable from it. As such, when a scandal erupted surrounding alleged influence peddling by Cho and his family—one that involved document forgery by his wife to secure a spot for their daughter at a prestigious university, among other allegations—the administration opened itself up to the critique that its promises to eliminate vested interests and promote "fairness" had been abandoned. The creation of pro- and anti-Cho camps ultimately led to a series of protests for and against prosecution reform that allowed the conservatives to appropriate the slogan of fairness. Meanwhile, by rallying around Cho (as a charismatic reformer) the actual *content* of legal reforms proposed by the Democratic Party was obscured, or worse, the central tasks of Candlelight Democracy, such as building the "society that respects labor" or pursuing chaebol reform, became depicted as contingent on the success or failure of Cho's reforms. Such a view, I argue, distracted from the actual content of the policies pursued by the pro-democratic bloc, including its approach to legal reform, and the lack of progress explored in the preceding chapters. In this sense, the politics of personality that surrounded Cho provided both an alibi for the administration's internal problems and a tool for the conservative bloc to regain its political hegemony.

Frailty of Liberalism?

As discussed in the introductory chapter, the resilience of the repressive apparatus of the anticommunist, developmentalist dictatorships has long concerned pro-democratic intellectuals, politicians, and CSOs. The literature on overcoming the '87 regime and the problems of conservative democratization have sought to understand this issue, and authors associated with both sets of ideas have revised their work in relation to the experiences of both conservative and liberal administrations. The power of

144 | The Postdevelopmental State

what remains of this apparatus became a particularly salient topic for investigation after the election of the conservative Lee administration in late 2007. At the time, the eminent political scientist Choi Jang-jip expanded his theory of conservative democratization to better grasp the changes taking place. Lee sought to undermine institutions established by the preceding liberal administrations such as the National Human Rights Commission, the Truth and Reconciliation Commission, and the Ministry of Gender Equality and Family, which he restructured, disbanded, and subordinated, respectively (Doucette 2013a; Kim DC 2010; De Custer 2010). In response to Lee's rollback of these and other initiatives, Choi emphasized the frailty of political liberalism in South Korea. He advanced the thesis that due to ideological confrontation between the "conservatives" of the old developmentalist regimes and the "progressives" who fought for democracy in the 1980s, liberalism in South Korea was poorly established. For Choi (2009, 6), this problem was made more difficult under Lee as the former repressive apparatuses of the state, notably the judicial and police agencies, expanded their "functions and power in a manner with which the citizens were quite familiar during the authoritarian rule."

Putting this problem in perspective, Choi situates its origins in the Cold War and postliberation period. Choi notes that while the values and institutions of liberalism provided the "raison d'état" for the establishment of a separate South Korean state after emancipation from the Japanese, anticommunism came to be seen as a more urgent task than building a democratic state. The architects of the South Korean state felt that "under the circumstances, the realisation of liberal democracy was not possible without the realising of national security and internal political stability." From Choi's perspective, the two processes—"materializing liberal democracy and building an anti-Communist bulwark"—became virtually identical as state builders chose to consolidate "the political order and stability of the regime by making it a solid anti-Communist bulwark prior to building liberal democracy" (Choi 2009, 2).

> While the ultimate goal of the newly created state was the establishment of liberal democracy, the means to attain it was Cold War anticommunism. In reality, the goal and its means were displaced. Also, it accompanied an obvious discrepancy between reality and rhetoric, and between formal institutions and practices. (Choi 2009, 2)

From the perspective of Choi, this deferral and displacement of liberalism continues to shape contemporary politics. The national security issue remains an imperative that cannot be overridden by other principles and norms, "even those of democracy and liberalism," such that "the ends and the means are hardly allowed to be distinguished" (Choi 2009, 6). In other words, the frailty of liberalism leads to a lack of moral restraint on the way in which the government deals with political conflict and security pressures.

In a parallel intervention at the time, the progressive sociologist, cofounder of PSPD, and eventually Seoul Metropolitan Government education chief Cho Hee-yeon advanced a complementary argument. Cho (2012a, 7) agreed with Choi that liberal administrations have had difficulty in altering the conservative trajectory of democratization. Moreover, the appeal of Lee's pro-growth politics stemmed in part from the failure of the preceding liberal administrations to address fundamental problems in society such as income inequality, the influence of the chaebol, and the power of public security agencies. However, Cho adds, the composition of the Lee Myung-bak administration, based on an alliance of neoconservative forces and remnants of the old dictatorial regime, provided further indications of democratic rollback (Cho 2012a, 16). In Cho's (2012a) view, the Lee administration did not involve "regime reformers" or "regime challengers" as did previous liberal administrations and the conservative administration of Kim Young-sam. Instead, Lee relied on traditional pro-business and regional interests and the neoconservatives of the New Right movement who helped to undermine popular movements and state institutions designed to safeguard democratic norms and promote social equality.

Though published in 2012, Cho's analysis remained valid for describing the subsequent Park Geun-hye administration, where the alliance between older anticommunist politicians and the New Right appeared even stronger. As discussed in chapter 3, Park was elected in December 2012 by promoting a moderate vision of "economic democratization" largely borrowed from the liberal left, using it to pledge to reform the country's large business groups, the chaebol, and expand social welfare. She did so to differentiate her administration from Lee Myung-bak's pro-growth rhetoric. His 747 economic plan (according to which South Korea would achieve 7 percent annual GDP growth, US$40,000 in per capita income, and become the world's seventh largest economy) had come to be seen by the public as a failure and his Four Rivers Project a symbol of corruption and environmental destruction (see Kang HK

2011). Lee's policies had foreclosed the option of Park mounting her election with a strong emphasis on developmentalism. So, to differentiate her campaign from Lee, Park presented herself as a maternal figure who voiced concerns about inequality and welfare. This narrative was complicated, however, by events following Park's electoral victory and inauguration. Park's promise of increased welfare and economic reform went unfulfilled as she quickly backtracked on her core pledges and failed to offer key administrative posts to the moderate conservative advisors that had helped organize her election campaign.

After introducing corporate governance reforms that did little to challenge the chaebol's entrenched economic power and revising her promises to create a universal pension system, she declared that her economic democratization drive had been successfully completed and that her economic policies would now center on fostering a "creative economy"—a euphemism for economic deregulation and privatization of state-owned industries. The discourse of economic democratization vanished overnight. To the dismay of moderate conservatives such as Kim Jong-in and Lee Sang-don, as well as the liberal left, Park reshuffled her cabinet in early August 2013 to include several elderly advisors from her father's dictatorial regime and former prosecutors-turned-politicians who had held positions related to anticommunist activities and the maintenance of "public security" in past military and conservative governments. Rather than pursuing economic democratization or taking on the chaebol, Park shifted her attention toward confrontation with the country's labor unions, deregistering the Korean Teachers and Education Workers' Union on the grounds that it retained a handful of fired or dismissed workers as members. To do so, Park used an enforcement decree (which provides a way for the executive to shape how a law is enforced without revising legislation) to limit the practical recognition of labor's freedom of association on this matter.[1] Park also targeted the Korean Railway Workers' Union with obstruction of business suits for going on strike to protest plans to privatize Korea's high-speed rail system, the KTX. By February 2014, Park introduced a "Three-Year Innovation Plan" that was reminiscent of Lee Myung-bak's neoliberal 747 Plan: Park promised to "smash regulations" and introduce a "competitive system" into the public sector with the goal of achieving a 4 percent growth rate, 70 percent

---

1. Such use of executive power to limit existing rights provided a further reason for the push to ratify ILO core conventions pertaining to labor's freedom of association after the Candlelight events.

The Integral State of the Conservative Bloc | 147

employment, and per capita income of US$40,000 by 2017—in other words, hers would be a 474 plan. The old developmentalist politics associated with the conservative bloc had returned.

Politics by Public Security

The seeds of Park's authoritarian turn were planted long before her inauguration but were not fully recognized until June 2013 when it was confirmed that her allies within the state had engaged in an unlawful campaign to discredit the liberal opposition for two years prior to the election. The National Intelligence Service (NIS), South Korea's main spy organization, and other state agencies conducted a disinformation campaign by using social media sites and by supporting conservative civic groups to smear liberal-left politicians. Even before Park's election victory, hints of this campaign were detected. Liberal lawmakers had questioned the political neutrality of the NIS following an episode prior to the elections when Conservative Party lawmakers Chung Moon-hun and Kim Moo-sung used a classified transcript—illegally obtained and allegedly supplied by the NIS—to spread a false claim about the liberal Roh administration for which presidential candidate Moon Jae-in had served as the president's chief of staff. The document implied, out of context, that Roh had secretly agreed to abandon the Northern Limit Line—the de facto western maritime boundary between the two Koreas—during his summit meeting with North Korean leader Kim Jong-il in 2007, and thus cede South Korean territory to the North (Seo 2018). Then in the final days of the election campaign, dramatic evidence of further electoral interference by the NIS and other state agencies appeared. Officers from the National Election Commission were tipped off about an illegal online campaign operation and discovered an agent on the campaign at work from a small apartment in southern Seoul (Choe SH 2013).

Eventually, a special investigations team led by prosecutor (and future president) Yoon Seok-yeol revealed that the NIS's cyberwarfare unit had formed some 30 extradepartmental teams to upload and circulate posts disparaging the opposition and smearing them as pro–North Korean forces (McCurry 2017). This activity resulted in thousands of online posts and millions of tweets with political or election-related content. Subsequent parliamentary audits revealed that the Ministry of Patriots and Veterans Affairs as well as the Ministry of National Defense's Cyberwarfare Command had performed similar operations. The electoral interference

148 | The Postdevelopmental State

carried out by these agencies used popular internet forums and social networking sites to discredit key opposition figures as *chongbuk chwap'a*, a term that is commonly translated as "pro-North leftists." As mentioned in chapter 3, the term *chong* means to obey or follow, with connotations of being slavish, while *buk* means North; *chwap'a* stands for left faction or leftist. Departing from its usual Cold War anticommunist epithet for the left as "Reds" or "Commies" (*ppalgaengi*), conservatives used the term to represent the left as not only suspected sympathizers with North Korea but as actively deferential to its wishes. This use included even liberal politicians that favored Kim Dae-jung's Sunshine Policy of peaceful engagement. The overall online message was that South Korea required defending from left-wing forces who collaborate with the regime in Pyongyang to undermine the nation-state from within. Yoon's investigation eventually led to the former director of the NIS, Won Sei-hoon, being indicted for violating the Public Official Election Act, a charge that was eventually upheld following a series of trials and retrials. In Won's defence, however, the agency and its political allies presented such electoral intervention as being in the interest of public and national security. Conservative forces dismissed months of ensuing protests that decried the electoral interference, calling efforts to initiate a full investigation as destabilizing to the state and therefore unpatriotic.

Put another way, the Park administration used "politics by public security"—the labeling of dissent and activism as a threat to national security—to lend legitimacy to the actions of state agencies involved in the electoral interference and ward off questions into how the president had come to power. Moreover, the indictment and trial of NIS chief Won Sei-hoon did not discourage her administration from engaging in this form of politics. Shortly after the indictment, the Park administration brought charges of treason and National Security Law violation against a sitting lawmaker, Lee Seok-ki, a left-nationalist from the small, oppositional United Progressive Party (UPP), and his associates. Lee had allegedly held a public meeting to discuss the need to prepare to fight against American imperialism and, by extension, the South Korean government if a war broke out between the two Koreas. The transcript of the meeting leaked by the NIS implied that Lee and his colleagues had discussed strategies that included attacking transportation, energy, communication, and other key state infrastructures (*Hankook ilbo*, September 2, 2013, September 3, 2013) and had sung "revolutionary" songs from North Korea. In February 2014 Lee was convicted on most charges and sentenced to 12 years in prison. One charge was appealed at the Seoul Superior Court, where he was found not guilty of plotting a rebellion against the state. However, the court allowed the other convictions, the National Security Law violation and sedition, against Lee to stand, meaning that Lee would serve nine years of his original 12-year sentence. Given his already controversial status among the South Korean progressive left for allegedly rigging internal elections for proportional representation candidates in the UPP, and as a champion of a naïve form of anti-imperialist left-nationalism, many in South Korea expressed their belief that the NIS was pursuing the case as a distraction. Nonetheless, the case raised concerns about basic principles of freedom of association after the Constitutional Court dissolved the UPP in December 2014 on charges that its principles supported North Korean–style socialism, in violation of South Korea's basic democratic order: it was the first forced dissolution of a political party since 1958.

The Park regime's reliance on public security rationale was not confined to the case of Lee and the UPP but was used broadly to confront oppositional actors. Figures within her administration covertly blacklisted thousands of cultural and public figures critical of the administration from receiving state funding by depicting them as threats to public order (Yuk 2019). Park's administration actively used this logic in its confrontation with the labor movement discussed above. For instance, when public opinion of the KTX privatization increasingly turned negative, the police searched the homes of the Korean Railway Workers' Union leaders, who were at the forefront of the anti-privatization protests, accusing them of violating the National Security Law by forming an organization within the railway corporation that "plotted to expand *chongbuk* forces" and spread pro-North propaganda (*Yonhap News*, April 29, 2013). Even bereaved parents of the young victims of the Sewŏl ferry disaster who protested the government's poor response were targeted by supporters of the president as outside agitators and pro-North sympathizers, further adding to their trauma (Kim N 2018). To many, the labeling of almost any political criticism of the administration as pro-North seemed insane. But as Richard Hofstadter (1964, 77) pointed out long ago, this style of using such exaggerated or "paranoid" claims to justify policies is not because conservatives have profoundly disturbed minds, but rather that the fear it produces helps facilitate the leveraging of power, protection of elite interests, and aggressive confrontation with the opposition.

Anticommunist Afterlives

For the liberal-left press, the actions of conservative politicians, the NIS, and other state agencies provided a clear sign that under Park's leadership,

150 | The Postdevelopmental State

state agencies were returning to a mode of governance long described as *kongan chŏngch'i* and *kongan chŏngguk*: translated as "politics by public security" and "the political climate of public security." These phrases denote the use of public security rhetoric, often but not always framed around Cold War understandings of "national security" but certainly implying a logic of "public order," by politicians and state institutions to stifle popular dissent and criticism. Hong Yung Lee (1991, 65) notes that this phrasing dates from the Roh Tae-woo administration (1987–92) and describes the old elite's attempt to reconcile political democratization with the preservation of vested interests. Amid growing popular demands for chaebol reform, peaceful reconciliation with North Korea, and the recognition of labor rights, former prosecutors-cum-politicians in Roh's administration selectively utilized the legal system to "impose a tense political situation" (Lee 1991, 65). In other words, they characterized popular protests as a threat to both public order (by depicting student and labor protests as uncontrolled, riotous behavior) and national security (by insinuating an alliance between liberal-left political forces and North Korea). Roh's government jailed over 1,000 union and student activists engaged in political activities under the pretext that they were engaging in violent demonstrations or subversive activities that threatened public security. Observers noted at the time that the Roh regime was deliberately vague when handling student and labor activism about what constituted subversive activity and how it threatened national security (Park CG 1991).

While the phrase "politics by public security" was frequently used during the Roh Tae-woo era, the repressive tactics that fall under its umbrella have their ultimate antecedents in the anticommunist foundations of the Korean state, as Choi notes above. The Syngman Rhee regime during the First Republic (1948–60) justified similar forms of repression as being necessary in the face of a communist foe to the North. Likewise, the Park Chung-hee dictatorship used anticommunist propaganda to justify its policies. Dissidents were frequently harassed using the notion of *pan'gong*—anticommunism—and terms such as *ppalgaengi*, mentioned above, and *kanch'ŏp* or "spies" to heighten a sense of fear among the population. These terms were discursive antecedents to *chongbuk* and *chwap'a* used by his daughter's allies. As Suh Sung (2001, 98) notes, Park also revived the very laws used by the Japanese to repress political opposition: the Public Order Preservation Law, the Korea Ideological Criminal Security Surveillance Law, and the Korea Ideological Criminal Preventive Detention Law. After liberation, these laws resurfaced in the form of the National Security Law, the Anti-Communist Law, the Security Surveil-

The Integral State of the Conservative Bloc | 151

lance Law, and the Public Security Act. Park used these laws during the Third and Fourth Republics to demobilize the opposition and protect economic interests such as the chaebol by regimenting labor relations for their benefit. As Park's export drive was heavily dependent on foreign borrowing, it faced tremendous pressure to keep domestic labor costs low to facilitate loan repayment. As this economic plan became crisis-prone, he increasingly ruled by decree and used the logic of national emergency to silence not only labor but most of the political opposition. To do so he further strengthened his power under the Yushin Constitution.

Although Yushin stands for revitalization (Yushin Hŏnpŏp, or Constitution for Revitalizing Reforms), legal scholars considered it to be the death of constitutionalism, for it personalized power in the president, who was able to rule by decree, not law (Won 2001, 60). As Yi (2022) points out, Yushin's core drafter, Han T'ae Yeon, along with jurists such as Kim Kichoon and Han San Deok, imported Carl Schmitt's concept of the sovereign dictator to do so. They interpreted the decision of the president as the direct political will of the people, requiring no legitimation. In the (approving) words of contemporary pro-Park economist, Jwa Sung-hee (2017, 94), Yushin "economized" politics. It provided for an indirect election by an appointed "national conference for unification," and for the president to appoint one-third of the National Assembly, reduce the power of the legislature, and extend the power of the executive branch. In 1975 Park declared that Yushin could not be amended until the threat from the North was gone: to return to the old constitution was tantamount to endangering national security (Oh 1976, 72–73). Observers at the time discussed how the Park regime aimed to transform political democracy into what it called an "administrative democracy" (Han SJ 1974, 43). The charges against Lee Seok-ki and his associates— National Security Law violation, sedition, and plotting an armed rebellion—and the Constitutional Court's dissolution of the UPP evoked for many the experience of exaggerated national security threats during the Cold War era, when the National Security Law and Yushin Constitution were used to target social movements and the political opposition (Ryu Y 2016, 2019). The charge that the UPP's alleged support for North Korea denied the basic democratic principles of South Korea resonated with Decree No. 1 of the Yushin Constitution, which made it illegal for any person to "deny, oppose, misrepresent or defame the Constitution" as well as to "assert, introduce, propose, or petition for revision or repeal of it," including fabricating or disseminating "false rumours" (Kim YC 1990, 158).

The commonalities between the politics by public security and Korea's authoritarian era are not coincidental. Park Geun-hye's core advisors—her so-called Group of Seven Men—traced their lineage back to Yushin and were very familiar with the style of administrative democracy practiced under it. Indeed, they had helped to design it. Park Geun-hye's first chief of staff, Kim Ki-choon, who left his post after two years, was perhaps the most emblematic persona in this regard. As mentioned above, Kim helped draft the Yushin Constitution and from 1974 he oversaw the bureau responsible for anticommunist investigation in the Korea Central Intelligence Agency, the predecessor to the NIS. From 1980 until 1982, he was the head of the public security team of the Seoul District Prosecutors' Office, and as such, has been connected to high-profile political cases. Between 1988 and 1990 Kim was credited with devising a chimerical prosecutorial strategy that actively pursued major criminal cartels in the name of "public safety" (*minsaeng ch'ian*), with the knowledge that the resulting arrests would cause a sensation and obscure the state's simultaneous and vigorous prosecution of cases against opposition and labor organizations in the name of "national security" (*kukka anbo*). One key event he engineered was the indictment of 443 people including Kim Dae-jung, then leader of the Peace and Democracy Party, on charges of threatening national security.

The list of Kim's achievements does not end there. He was appointed prosecutor-general in December 1990 and minister of justice two years later. As a cabinet minister he was at the center of the notorious 1992 "Chowon Blowfish Restaurant Incident." Kim met with the mayor of Pusan, along with officials from the prosecution, police, the Agency for National Security Planning (the name of the NIS at the time), the Defense Security Command, and the municipal education office, as well as executives of the Chamber of Commerce and Industry, in a plot to drum up regional support for the ruling party candidate Kim Young-sam ahead of the presidential election later that year (Hankyoreh, 6 August 2013). Kim led the campaign to impeach liberal president Roh Moo-hyun in 2003 after Roh made remarks during a trip to Japan that "permitting the existence of a communist party will bring true democracy to Korea" (*Korea Times*, June 12, 2003, cited in Lee Y 2005, 410). Kim argued this statement undermined the principles of the Republic of Korea and used his position as chairman of the National Assembly's legislation-judiciary committee to lead the impeachment. Under the Park Geun-hye administration, Kim was later found to have orchestrated a blacklist with the help of the NIS that included over 10,000 cultural figures including artists, writers, filmmakers, and other public figures critical of the Park administration to be

The Integral State of the Conservative Bloc | 153

denied public funding, a crime for which he was later convicted along with several other officials, including the culture minister and other presidential secretaries (see Yuk 2019).

But Kim was not the only anticommunist prosecutor involved in Park's administration. The Conservative Party floor leader Hwang Woo-yea—later appointed as minister of education and deputy prime minister in 2014—was an associate judge presiding over public security cases in the Chun Doo-hwan regime (1980–87), such as in the case where workers' rights activists were tortured and charged with violation of the National Security Law in what became known as the Hangnim Incident of 1982 (Kang JK 2013). There was also Hwang Kyo-ahn, who served as the minister of justice; Park Han-cheol, the chief justice of the Constitutional Court; and Hong Kyung-shik, the senior secretary for civil affairs, among other former prosecutors in both the administration and ruling party such as Hong Joon-pyo, Kim Jin-tae, Kim Hwang-sik, and Ahn Sang-soo. The prominence of these figures within Park's administration and the broader conservative bloc raised concerns about the independence of the prosecution service. Moreover, these concerns were well justified given the power that prosecutors have within the Korean legal system, where they maintain control over the police and have a monopoly of authority over investigation (a job handled by police in most countries), indictment, and execution of a court sentence.

Old Right Meets New Right

While the staffing of Park's administration with numerous public security prosecutors and the actions of the NIS and other state agencies strongly evoked the politics of the developmentalist past, the success of the conservative bloc in the 2012 election was not simply a product of their initiative. As mentioned before, Park enlisted moderate conservatives to lead her economic democratization campaign before jettisoning its promises. Likewise, in her administration's confrontation with the pro-democratic bloc, she benefited from the support of growing conservative civil society movements. A new generation of conservative intellectuals founded these movements, known collectively as the New Right, in the wake of liberal President Roh Moo-hyun's victory in the 2004 general elections. Although many New Right thinkers once belonged to the left (Doucette 2013a), their connections with the conservative bloc demonstrate that it too has its own integral state, its own integral *nexus* between political and civil society,

154 | The Postdevelopmental State

that it mobilizes to create hegemony. In the case of the Park Geun-hye's electoral campaign and administration, the New Right sought to revise conservative discourse in order to better accommodate it to the present political climate. To do so, it revised conservative narratives of democratization.[2] Rather than staunchly defending dictatorship against democracy, the New Right affirmed Korea's democratization as a desirable outcome but only in a minimal sense. Ignoring the importance of Korea's democratic political struggle, the New Right sought to explain democratization by stressing the contribution of the Park Chung-hee regime. They credited him for laying the foundations of the market economy and building a strong middle class, which they see as the necessary precursor for democracy (Yang M 2021, 354–55). In this view, the Sixth Republic provided the telos of the Park administration, a view that is uncomfortably in line with that of many modernization theorists and admirers of Korea's "strong state" discussed in chapter 1.

While the movement had its basis in conservative civil society, like progressive reformers, members of the New Right have also held government posts or have become lawmakers, revealing the flexibility of the conservative nexus and the importance of its own integral state. New Right intellectuals who went on to become Conservative Party lawmakers in the National Assembly during the Lee and Park administrations include Shin Chi-ho, Kim Seong-hee, and Cho Cheon-hyeok, among others. The New Right were particularly known for its labeling of the Kim Dae-jung and Roh Moo-hyun years as "the lost decade," a phrase that caught on in the conservative imagination and was repeated by its allies in the media to describe these liberal administration's policy failures. Moreover, in contrast to their praise of the dictatorial foundations of Korean democracy, the New Right criticized the efforts of the Democratic Party to come to terms with the crimes of past regimes and seek reconciliation with North Korea as having impaired the identity of the Republic of Korea, damaged its national interests, and broken its national unity (Lee IH 2008). As such, they have sought to restrict the ability of state institutions to address past wrongs by, for instance, curtailing the power of the Truth and Reconciliation Commission and revising the Democratization Movement Activists' Honor-Restoration and Compensation Act. And after his election, conservative President Lee appointed a New Right–affiliated scholar, Lee Young-jo, as the commission's president, who then publicly declared that

---

2. For Sungik Yang (2021), the degree to which this revision might be considered novel, rather than simply the "old right in new bottles," is open to debate.

The Integral State of the Conservative Bloc | 155

the commission's work had been a waste of money (de Ceuster 2010, 22; Roland and Hwang 2010). The New Right also waged a campaign to disseminate history textbooks that characterize the Park Chung-hee dictatorship as strongly contributing to South Korean democratization, paint a rosier picture of Japanese colonialism,[3] and omit important events for the democracy movement, such as the Gwangju Uprising, which some conservatives continue to regard as an antistate riot supported by North Korea. As such, the cultural politics of the New Right and the public security approach of prosecutor-politicians mingle well together. For example, the deregistration of the Korean Teachers and Education Workers' Union by Park can be seen partially as retaliation for the role the teachers' union played in contesting the revision of South Korean textbooks, making it a thorn in the side of conservative forces and their efforts to create a rival, New Right–aligned teachers' union (Tikhonov 2019).

If the alliance between the old right and the New Right proved to be instrumental in shaping the politics of the Park administration, the actual policies they pursued provoked, in the end, the largest episode of civic protest since the June Democratic Uprising in 1987. The NIS electoral intervention, UPP case, schism between moderate and pro-Park conservatives with her own ruling party, Park's antilabor policies, and the administration's mismanagement of the Sewŏl Ferry sinking and hostile reaction to grieving families all prepared the kindling for the Candlelight events. But the spark was ultimately provided by revelations of influence peddling by Park's friend, spiritual advisor, and confidante Choi Soon-sil. First to be revealed were favors for Choi Soon-sil's daughter, Chung Yoo-ra, which included a literal gift horse from Samsung and a free ride at the nation's most prestigious women's university. The discovery that some of Chung's coursework was completed by the teaching assistants of the proto–New Right writer Lee In-hwa, known for his controversial pro-dictatorship praise of Park Chung-hee, added further fuel to the fire. As protests continued, revelations of Choi's personal involvement in state affairs, from cultural and development assistance policy to overseeing Park's speeches and public appearances, widened the scandal. While much of the media commentary focused on Choi as a diabolical, Rasputin-like character at the heart of the state, the activities of Park and Choi suited the interests and ambitions of other members of the elite. A number of Korea's large,

---

3. This argument evokes earlier debates surrounding historical stagnation among South Korean historians, and in which Ri Yŏng-hun—who has also coordinated the production of the New Right's history textbook—was involved (Miller 2010, 9).

156 | The Postdevelopmental State

family-led conglomerates, including Samsung, Hyundai, SK, and LG, donated millions to the foundations run by Choi. The timing of the Samsung donation came just before the National Pension Service approved a merger between Samsung affiliates that would guarantee the Samsung heir Lee Jae-young his management rights over the conglomerate (Choe and Matoko 2017). In this sense, Samsung's "donation" was not simply the result of Choi's influence peddling but stems from chaebol families' often unlawful efforts to maintain managerial control of their firms. The fact that such acts have often been followed by pardons from the state or have been left unpunished due to the failure of the prosecution service to vigorously investigate and indict the chaebol for corporate crimes further contributed to the intensity of the protests.[4]

While Park's and Choi's collusion served a variety of elite interests, the presence of Choi herself raised some important, forgotten aspects of the integral state during Korea's rapid development under authoritarian dictatorship that tend to be overlooked. Choi is the daughter of Choi Tae-min, who founded an obscure, syncretic religious cult called Yŏngsegyo, and mentored Park Geun-hye after her mother's assassination in 1974. In turn, Park helped lead his Mission for National Salvation, an organization that preached anticommunism with evangelical fervor throughout the 1970s as part of an effort to attract Christian support for her father's regime. Park Geun-hye's close friendship with Choi's daughter extends from this time. Even before the death of Park Chung-hee, Choi was alleged to be involved in influence peddling using Park's reputation. Following it, and until his own death in 1994, Choi was involved in various fundraising schemes to memorialize his legacy with other notable actors associated with Korea's rapid industrial development. A quick look at some of these actors provides an interesting contrast to the received narrative of the Park Chung-hee regime as merely a benevolent, technocratic government concerned

---

4. There was also and awkward resonance between the Choi case and the Sewŏl ferry disaster. The Sewŏl was operated by Chŏnghaejin Marine Co. Ltd., a minor chaebol controlled by Yoo Byung-eun. Yoo was the founder of another salvation cult from the Park Chung-hee era, and had alleged ties to Choi Soon-sil's ex-husband. Like other chaebol heads, Yoo controlled his company through elaborate cross-shareholding arrangements, which he used to enrich himself and his family. The staff of the overloaded ferry was predominantly made up of ill-trained employees on temporary contracts. Furthermore, regulatory failure due to self-regulation, parachute appointments, and lax enforcement in the shipping industry and naval rescue organizations further exacerbated the tragedy (You and Park 2017; You 2016) as did the government's response to grieving families and slandering of them by some conservatives as "pro-North" leftists.

The Integral State of the Conservative Bloc | 157

with economic growth (Moon 2009). Instead, these efforts reveal an extensive nexus between politics, religion, state administration, and economic planning: in other words, they reveal that even the "developmental" state needs to be regarded as an *integral* apparatus composed of both political and civil society.

To illustrate, the efforts of Choi Tae-min and others to memorialize Park and his wife ultimately resulted in the establishment of the Park Chung-hee Memorial Foundation. Park's long-serving economic planner and secretary of state Kim Chung-yum was one of the first presidents of the commission that became the foundation. His son, Kim Joon-kyung, served as president of the Korean Development Institute during the Park Geun-hye administration and promoted her father's Saemaul movement through Korea's official development assistance strategies at this time (Doucette and Muller 2016; Doucette 2020a). Former anticommunist prosecutor Kim Ki-Choon served as the Park Cung-hee Memorial Foundation's first chairman. As discussed above, during the 1970s, Kim helped to draft Park's Yushin Constitution, and served as Park Geun-hye's chief of staff. The longtime chairman of the foundation, who also served in this role during her administration, is conservative economist Jwa Sung-hee; as discussed above, Jwa is a public figure full of ardent and unapologetic praise of the former dictator. Although it was just a minor sidenote to the events, as the Candlelight protests began in fall 2016, it was discovered that a foundation set up by Choi Soon-sil—the Mir Foundation, which Choi and Park had "encouraged" many chaebol to fund—had drawn up plans to fund the renovation of the Park Chung-hee Memorial Foundation's buildings and other memorial projects. In short, these memorialization efforts show a dense and living interaction of ideology, religion, and political repression at the nexus between political and civil society rather than the conventional story of Korean development as the effect of a strong state and meritocratic economic planners.

While the figure of Choi helps to reveal this nexus, an "occulted" view of her relationship with Park can easily obscure it. In other words, focusing too intensely on her role easily distracts from the broader cult of personality built around Park Chung-hee by the old right and the New Right. In my view, it is this very "cult" that is more perverse. For it has been used to occlude political power, that is, to make it seem mysterious, as something that flowed from Park's charismatic personality, and materialized through his will and intentionality rather than through specific social relations. As discussed earlier, developmental state theorists are not immune from narratives associated with this cult that conservatives have used to

158 | The Postdevelopmental State

seek hegemony. The idea that Korea's rapid development was a virtuous technocratic affair undertaken by an insulated developmental bureaucracy, and that legitimacy merely flowed form the actions of the state itself and its leadership, are two such myths belied by the discussion of the Park Chung-hee Memorial Foundation above. The intersecting scandals that provoked Park's impeachment evoked for many the manner that the chaebol, state bureaucracies, religious elites, conservative intellectuals, the prosecution service, and prominent political figures have interacted from the developmentalist era to today. The election of liberal Moon Jae-in following the events provided an opportunity to reform the power of this nexus, particularly when it came to the power of the public security apparatus within it. But it was here, especially when it came to reform of the prosecution service, that the contradictions of Moon's policy initiatives explored in previous chapters came to be acutely felt.

The Politics of Fairness

The extent of the scandals surrounding the Park administration revealed that members of the conservative bloc and its nexus with civil society have been used to both subvert democratic norms and constrain the pro-democratic bloc. As such, it has constituted an obstacle to efforts to expand democratization and pursue social and economic justice. Furthermore, the coherence of the conservative bloc has created the need for greater cohesion and coordination among the forces that compose the pro-democratic bloc. There is a necessity for a "bloc politics" that must mediate between a range of liberal, regional, and progressive interests. But this need for coordination also limits the space available for broader representation of subaltern interests. As the experience of the minor parties has shown, it is difficult to pursue comprehensive antidiscrimination legislation or develop a political platform that suits working class interests when, strategically, the contest between the two major parties has such strong material consequences for democracy. Moreover, it is not simply the power of the minor parties that is challenged by the power of the conservative bloc and its nexus with the public security apparatus, but also the broader project of economic democracy. The ability to effectively institute regulations on monopoly power, the use of nonregular employment and exploitation of subcontractors, and the punishment of economic crimes such as collusion and bribery is directly related to the capacity of governing party to ensure the prosecution service's enforcement of the law.

The Integral State of the Conservative Bloc | 159

Hence, early in his administration, Moon announced that in addition to his pledges to pursue economic democracy and a society that respects labor, one of the central tasks for continuing the spirit of the Candlelight Revolution would be to create a country that eliminates foul play and unfairness: a task that involved reforming the Ministry of Justice, the NIS, the police, and associated organizations.

After his inauguration, Moon moved quickly on his pledges. To do so, he limited the ability of the NIS to collect intelligence on domestic trends (which are technically beyond the purview of the National Intelligence Service Act) by abolishing the offices used to collect information on domestic politics and refocusing the agency on its existing mandate toward external threats. As part of a comprehensive package of legal reforms, Moon also moved to strip the agency of its anticommunist investigation units and transfer them to the National Police Agency. Toward the end of his second year in office, Moon then moved on to the more difficult task of reforming the prosecution service. To do so, he sought to put limits on the prosecution service's powers of investigation, transfer greater investigatory power to the police, and set up a special independent body to handle investigation and indictment of high-ranking officials: the latter was a demand that originated from Korea's #MeToo movement (Choo H 2021, 265). To oversee the reforms, Moon decided to appoint his presidential secretary for civil affairs, the progressive legal scholar and former activist Cho Kuk, to the position of minister of justice. However, Cho's appointment itself became an object of controversy as the prosecution launched an investigation into possible minor fraud and influence peddling by Cho's family members. The case revolved around his wife's writing of allegedly fraudulent recommendation letters for Cho's daughter to secure her a spot in a prominent university, suspected plagiarism on her behalf, and other examples of using their influence to inflate their daughter's academic credentials. Separately, an investigation was launched into a small private equity fund invested in by Cho and his extended family, resulting in the indictment of Cho's nephew.

The corruption cases around Cho resulted in a series of rival mass protests supporting and opposing Cho's appointment. Conservative groups portrayed Cho as a diabolical figure, a corrupt "leftist" at the heart of the state. Meanwhile, liberal supporters portrayed him as an innocent victim, one forced to bear the burden of democratization through personal suffering. But the protests were not simply organized on the lines of a confrontation between political blocs. Young university students upset at the behavior of Cho's family also joined the opposition to Cho's appointment and pointed out the hypocrisy of his appointment given the discourse of fairness promoted by senior figures in the Moon administration. Ultimately, these protests created divisions within the pro-democratic bloc. On the one hand, many of Cho's supporters interpreted the actions of the prosecution service as being politically motivated in seeking to prevent reform of their agencies. For many of the 586 generation, the actions of the prosecution evoked the memory of former president Roh Moo-hyun, whose suicide in the spring of 2009 they attributed to the intensity of the prosecutor's investigation. On the other hand, the alleged crimes of Cho and his family, while minor compared to those of Park and the chaebol, evoked anger among many, and especially among the youth who had supported the Candlelight protests. Cho's family's actions seemed to be yet another case of the "gold spoons" taking advantage of their power and influence. Since access to prestigious universities is seen as a major marker of status and inequality, the fact that a professor at a prominent university would use his influence to secure special treatment for his children angered many young students who had participated in the Candlelight events. Conflicted attitudes toward Cho's appointment arose not only between generational cohorts—and even stimulated a discourse of intergenerational politics—but also among intellectuals, CSOs such as PSPD (of which Cho is a former member), and minor progressive parties. For instance, PSPD member Kim Kyung-yul resigned from his position as chair of its Center for Economic and Financial Justice after criticizing his colleagues' silence over Cho's behavior, and founded a new CSO, Economic Democracy 21, to criticize the limitations of legal, corporate, and labor reform.[5] Such conflicts animated even minor parties such as the Justice Party, which remained neutral on the matter, a move that was criticized by some of its supporters for betraying its own principles of justice and fairness.[6]

---

5. Kim would later surprise many of his former colleagues by joining the Conservative Party in late 2023.

6. The scandal around Cho eventually became so contentious in progressive circles that one's opinion on Cho became a point of tension in interpersonal relationships. One high-profile exchange between progressive media commentor Chin Jung-kwon, Roh Moo-hyun Foundation chair Rhyu Shimin, and progressive writer and novelist Gong Jiyoung was indicative of this tension. Chin's criticism of Cho received such a backlash from his colleagues that he accused his former friends of delusion and political fanaticism. Chin would eventually lend his support to the conservative candidate, Yoon Seok-yeol, in the following election. However, most critics of Cho did not see the occasion as a reason to support the Conservative Party. Nonetheless, many eventually developed conversation strategies to identify the position of their friends and colleagues before feeling that they could be open about their own opinions.

The Integral State of the Conservative Bloc | 161

What these tensions reveal is that the task of prosecution reform itself became perceived by some as a question of support for and against Cho himself. But this intense focus on Cho distracted from the actual content of legal reforms being proposed and the ability of such reforms to address the enduring problems that led to the Candlelight Revolution. For instance, CCEJ member Park Sang-in pointed out that reform of commercial law wasn't even proposed as part of his package of reforms. As such, he complained, the project of economic democratization was missing from Cho's reform plan. "The independence of the prosecution cannot be achieved without reform of the chaebol, which has become an uncontrolled economic power," argued Park (as quoted in Pan 2019). Activists from the trade union movement made similar remarks about Cho's attitude toward labor. They noted that the Moon administration had left outstanding damage claims against trade unionists on the books, took an instrumental approach in the ratification process for the ILO conventions, and failed to effectively revise TULRAA to prevent similar abuse of damage claims in the future, much less pass comprehensive antidiscrimination legislation. For labor, repression wasn't seen as simply a problem of prosecution reform but also a function of how liberal administrations had previously responded to the labor conflict. Under the liberal Kim and Roh administrations arrests of trade unionists increased along with the use of damage claims. Moreover, Cho's attitude toward labor was made clear before the scandal, when as senior secretary for civil affairs he put pressure on the KCTU to consent to Moon's agreement on working time and declared that the "government can't listen to all their [labor's] demands." Criticizing both the KCTU and PSPD, Cho argued that he felt a sense of déjà-vu that reminded him of how those organizations withdrew their support from and consequently weakened the participatory government of Roh Moo-hyun (Lee DK 2018). Ironically, Cho's comment was correct, but not in the way he intended it to be. He intended it as a criticism of what he saw as the "unreasonable demands" of the KCTU and progressive movements: demands such as ILO ratification and a 52-hour workweek that were hardly unreasonable, as others pointed out at the time (Lee TK 2018). But what Cho really pointed out, in fact, was that the Moon administration, like Roh before him, had failed to live up to its promises to pursue economic democracy and enact effective labor standards and had merely sought to discipline labor. In both cases, the result led to disillusionment with the ruling administration.

Eventually, the Moon administration's stubborn insistence on support for the figure of Cho Kuk opened itself to disillusionment from the wider

162 | The Postdevelopmental State

populace. The opportunity for it to affirm its criticism of "vested interests" by acknowledging the contradictions of Cho's alleged actions was missed. It could not separate the *policy* of prosecution reform from the *personality* of the person leading it. While eventually Cho's reforms were passed, the uncritical defense of his personality as a democratic reformer was a fatal error, an error that was repeated in several contemporaneous incidences, including several #MeToo cases involving pro-democratic politicians. It allowed the right to appropriate the discourse of fairness from the pro-democratic bloc in the lead up to the 2022 elections. To do so, the conservative bloc rallied around the figure of prosecutor Yoon Seok-yeol, the very prosecutor who led the case into Park Geun-hye, and had previously prosecuted several chaebol heads, figures involved in the 2012 interference, and opposed Cho's legal reform plans. Against the contradictions of Cho's personality, the perception of Yoon as an independent prosecutor unbeholden to the elite provided a means for the Conservative Party to rebrand itself. To do so, it promoted the idea that it was liberal administrations, and the former 586 activists who led them, who were being unfair and unlawful. Conservative politicians further weaponized this critique of the apparent hypocrisy around Cho by conjoining it with a misogynistic backlash against the #MeToo movement and claims that institutions such as the Ministry of Gender Equality promoted discrimination and "unfairness" toward men and should be abolished. In this way they connected the broader politics of resentment around Cho to rising misogyny among younger men in a time of increased economic anxiety (Kim YM 2022). Unfortunately, the Moon administration had led itself into this situation both through its support for Cho, who was for a time seen as Moon's likely successor, and through its failure to connect prosecution reform to the broader project of economic democratization in a manner that might relieve both the economic anxieties faced by many households, and not just the younger generation, and their concerns about fairness. Instead, the Cho affair came to signify for many progressive reformers the exact moment that the candlelight went out.

Conclusion

The election of Yoon reveals that despite the historic opportunity provided by the Candlelight Revolution, the conservative bloc remains a powerful actor in Korean politics. It has used its own integral state, its alliance between the old right and the New Right and recent absorption of misog-

The Integral State of the Conservative Bloc | 163

ynistic "alt-right" elements, to reconstitute itself and regain political power remarkably quickly. At the time of writing, it remains to be seen how much the politics of public security embraced by past conservative administrations will be restored under Yoon. Yoon's political capital largely rested on his reputation for independence. Nonetheless, his appointments over the first two years of his administration consisted largely of fellow prosecutors from his professional circles and a number of New Right figures associated with previous conservative administration, leading some observers to wonder if his administration will also become a "republic of prosecutors" (Shin GW 2022). By the spring of 2023, there were also signs of a return to some of the features of politics by public security in the regime's treatment of the labor movement. Yoon used back to work legislation and punitive damage claims to force striking truckers to end their strike for safe rates and employment protections, followed by similar claims against subcontracted shipbuilding workers and construction unions affiliated with the KCTU. The ESLC was scaled down to merely a discussion body and Kim Mun-su, a renegade former labor activist turned conservative politician, was appointed as its head. Meanwhile, Yoon announced plans to modify overtime regulations to permit a maximum 69-hour workweek and in his August 15 Liberation Day 2023 speech made the bizarre claim that "forces of communist totalitarianism have always disguised themselves as democracy activists, human rights advocates or progressive activists" (Yoon 2023). Finally, after the establishment of the Corruption Investigation Office for High-Ranking Officials to investigate high profile cases of collusion, prosecutors chose to target the progressive educational superintendent of Seoul, Cho Hee-yeon, for hiring irregularities as their first case. Cho had reinstated dismissed teachers from the Korean Teachers and Education Workers' Union who were targeted under the conservative administrations of Lee and Park. Cho took a principled stand that his actions were lawful and an act of social justice (Kan 2021), a stance that was later validated as he was one of the few prominent progressives to be reelected in the next local elections in early 2022. Instead of investigating many possible high-profile cases of corruption, that the investigation chose Cho as its first case provided a message to the progressive left that public security politics was alive and well.

As this chapter has shown, however, the resilience of the conservative bloc and its politics by public security is not simply a matter of confrontation between political blocs but involves dynamics internal to each bloc itself. In the case of prosecution reform discussed in this chapter, the Cho scandal revealed that the Moon administration had invested too much

164 | The Postdevelopmental State

political capital in the figures of prominent reformers at the expense of developing substantive policy that might help it fulfil its pledges to institute Candlelight Democracy. Other critics of Korean democracy have noted this trend. The political sociologist Gi-Wook Shin (2020), for instance, argued that, ironically, the Cho phenomenon, the Moon administration's campaign of fighting "vested interests," the sabotage of the mixed-member proportionate representation system, and the righteousness and arrogance of many of Cho and the president's supporters (e.g., online "fan" groups such as Moon-bba and RohSaMo) risked democratic backsliding. While Shin's assessment of democratic decay is an exaggeration, the problems he identifies are salient for the discussion of the dilemmas of economic democratization and the problem of the postdevelopmental state discussed in this book. In this regard, these tendencies are not so much an example of backsliding as much as they are an indicator that Moon lacked a hegemonic project for deepening democratization.[7] The liberal cult of personality around Cho suspended scrutiny into the very policies and imaginaries of prosecution reform embraced by the administration, which lacked substantive reform plans that might satisfy demands for alternatives to neoliberalism and developmentalism. For without addressing the rising inequality, poor labor relations, and concerns about fairness and inequality that led to the Candlelight events to begin with, the Democratic Party provided the conservative bloc an opportunity to appropriate the discourse of fairness that enabled them to regain political power.

---

7. The sabotage of the mixed-member proportionate representation system perhaps comes closest to backsliding when it comes to the party system. While dismissed as a product of the opportunism of both Conservative Party and Democratic Party bosses, this event was, at minimum, a terrible betrayal of democratic principles.

Conclusion

The Future of a Problematic?

The Cho scandal provides an appropriate end point to the book's inquiry. For it represented the exhaustion of a sequence of political economic reform that had been initiated with popular enthusiasm following the Candlelight events only to become mired in disillusionment by the time of Cho's appointment as minister of justice. In short, the Moon administration succumbed to some of the very dynamics associated with conservative democratization—a period of excitement followed by disillusionment, lack of effective labor representation, and fixation on the personalities of individual politicians—that its project of Candlelight Democracy had sought to address. This fact was noted with irony by Choi Jang-jip himself. Commenting on the Cho scandal and the discourse of good vs. evil that accompanied it, Choi argued that it represented a form of populist politics encouraged by the campaign against "deep-rooted evils" (Park SH and Ko JA 2020). For Choi, this kind of rhetoric led to greater polarization between the parties, when, in fact, what he felt was needed following Park's impeachment was greater consensus between the parties on what a better system of checks and balances on the power of the president and the broader institutions of government might be. Commenting on the phenomenon of "plaza democracy" as seen in the protests for and against Cho Kuk, Choi argues that instead of "relying on political parties or the National Assembly to represent societal opinions," this form of populist politics "allows a president and his administration to lead domestic politics" (Choi as quoted in Park and Ko, 2020). Political authority, and ultimately legitimacy, comes to focus on the president, facilitating such cycles of popular enthusiasm and disillusionment.

While I agree with Choi's identification of the cyclical nature of this phenomenon, and his description of the problematic politics of personality it involves, the problem as I see it is not one that can be resolved simply through the party system and institutions of representative democracy. There is a wider political and material basis to it that involves both the structure of historical blocs that shape Korean politics—and that make such a consensus unlikely—and the legacy of inequality that has accompanied rapid development and its neoliberal restructuring. A focus merely on the formal institutions of representative politics risks neglecting the structural conditions that helped to generate the Candlelight events, and the integral relations between political and civil society that have shaped the response to them. In this sense, the Cho scandal did not so much represent the failure of a populist politics as it spoke to the lack of an effective hegemonic project within the pro-democratic bloc that might resolve the political economic problem represented by the postdevelopmental state. In other words, what Choi sees as populism here—the fact that the administration has come to embrace a script of the good (people) versus the bad (elite) that centers itself on the integrity of specific personalities for its authority—is a symptom of its failure to create a substantive alternative to the status quo and to effectively utilize the nexus between political and civil society in order to achieve it. Without such a project that might address issues from inequality to irregular work, the Cho scandal came to concentrate the dilemmas outlined in this book into a single conjunctural event.

Cho's appointment by Moon as a progressive, pro-democracy activist and charismatic public intellectual, one who could address the power of the prosecution and public security apparatus, speaks directly to the *legitimation* dynamics explored in this book. For it highlights how the nexus between political and civil society has been drawn on as a source of ideas and to display the democratic credentials of liberal administrations. However, as chapters 3–5 described, this *inclusion* of prominent figures from civil society does not necessarily ensure that their *imaginaries* of reform were progressive or substantive enough to fulfill broad demands for equality and fairness. In this manner, the Cho scandal demonstrated the lack of a broader progressive plan for coordinating political and economic reform within the integral state. Without such a plan, and a means to implement it, politics came to hinge on the respectability of specific reformers per se. This fact allowed the conservative bloc—with its resilient nexus between former prosecutors and the New Right—to exploit contradictions in the personal lives of individual figures to regain public support. To do so, it appropriated the discourse of fairness—using it to articulate economic anxieties, misogynistic resentment, and intergenerational grievances—

Conclusion | 167

and combined it with the bloc's usual public security rhetoric to portray the behavior of Cho and other reformers of his generation as threats to democracy.[1]

Ultimately, the Cho scandal signified the exhaustion of the energy of the Candlelight Revolution and the various initiatives tasked with solving the problems that had led to it. This result was unfortunate, for the conservative bloc's victory in the 2022 elections demonstrates the need for a cohesive pro-democratic bloc that might advance an alternative to the status quo. This necessity, however, raises the question what new progressive imaginary might mobilize the pro-democratic bloc in a coherent fashion given the exhaustion of imaginaries such as economic democracy and its associated projects such as the society that respects labor and a people-centered economy? The answer to this question is obviously beyond the scope of the present work. Nonetheless, whatever project is embraced by the pro-democratic bloc will need to critically understand why the project of economic democracy failed. In this regard, this concluding chapter reviews some of the book's arguments as to why this has been the case. It then discusses how the book's broader problematic of the postdevelopmental state and focus on the integral state remains relevant in other areas of political and economic reform in contemporary Korea. Finally, this chapter discusses why this book's conceptual and empirical reframing of the priorities of developmental state research resonates beyond the case of Korea and East Asia. For the renewed interest in the role of the state in development—especially in a climate of geopolitical turbulence—has led to a resurgence of the idea of the developmental state as a model for policy. Without correcting the democratic deficit outlined in this book, such studies risk replicating celebratory praise for authoritarian, growth-

---

1. While the Cho scandal was the most pronounced episode of this kind, the wealth and behavior of other reformers received similar public attention. These figures include politicians and officials such as Choo Mi-ae, who replaced Cho to lead prosecution reform, who was accused of seeking preferential treatment for her son during his military service; Kim Sang-jo, for his behavior as a landlord; and Jang Ha-sung, for alleged misuse of a corporate credit card. These scandals did not "stick," however, in the ways that the Cho scandal did. Nonetheless, the behavior of these reformers, along with that of other prominent members of the 586 generation identified during Korea's #MeToo movements, such as Mayor Park Won-soon and South Chungcheong governor Ahn Hee-jung, among others, combined to create a discourse of generational politics. In short, the idea that Korea's political economic problems was the problem of a particular generation exploiting another (rather than, say, the lack of a substantive political project) came to gather currency. For a critique of the discourse of generational politics in Korea, see Shin JW 2022.

168 | The Postdevelopmental State

oriented politics and provide little in the way of an alternative to the Scylla and Charybdis of developmentalism and neoliberalism.

Pursuing Economic without Social Democracy

When writing this book, I toyed with an alternative subtitle, *Pursuing Economic and Social Democracy in South Korea*. The question of why this subtitle wasn't ultimately used provides something of the answer to the broader problem the book seeks to tackle. That is, why did the project of economic democracy lead to such minimal results? Why didn't it reorient, in a substantive sense, the broader structures of Korean political economy and the various inequalities upon which it rests? In short, the answer is that it failed largely because economic democracy was not pursued *with* or *as* social democracy. Despite its origins in the radical democracy movements of the 1980s and 1990s, its dominant pro- and antichaebol proponents gradually came to imagine the project as one largely concerned with corporate governance. Consequently, as its critics pointed out, the administration neglected the "material substance of economic and social democracy" (Rhyu SY 2018, 27). As discussed in chapter 3, this was a disappointing result given that both major camps explicitly argue that a system approximating the ideal of a Scandinavian welfare state was their goal. Unfortunately, however, the relational and class context of social democratic struggle received little consideration in their strategies.

Progressive critics involved in the Intellectuals Declaration Network made cognate remarks. They argued that the real failure of the Moon administration was its inability to create an effective *reform bloc*. As Cho Don-mun (as quoted in Park SY and Cho SE 2021a) argues, there was an absence of a policy alliance to bring potential beneficiaries of economic democratization and its associated initiatives such as income-led growth and the society that respects labor into the ruling alliance. Without such a plan, Cho argues, the administration became strongly influenced by the Ministry of Finance and returned to a profit-led growth strategy (Park SY and Cho SE 2021a). As Lee Byeong-cheon (as quoted by Park and Cho 2021b) puts it, using Gramscian terminology, the government failed to form a reform coalition for securing hegemony. Consequently, it lacked a "control tower" to oversee reform, which allowed the bureaucracy to set the course of policy once Moon's initial reforms met with criticism or negative public opinion polls. Rhyu (2018, 29) makes a similar criticism, and argues that the administration's "policies should have been premised on a

Conclusion | 169

careful roadmap and a detailed action plan to overcome these unintended consequences." Labor critics of the Moon administration made cognate criticisms. As Lee Jeong-hee (2019, 767, 777) points out, the labor movement welcomed the idea of creating an alternative labor regime to overcome the structure of the '87 regime in the sense of the resilient power of the conglomerates and the subordinate role accorded to labor. However, she argues, the government did not seem to want to use social dialogue to do so but used it instead to present policy directions whose parameters were mostly decided in advance.

The Intellectuals Declaration Network led by Lee and Cho contrast this failure to create such a coalition to the historical experience of Scandinavian social democracy and New Deal America, which, they argued, incorporated workers and low-income earners into a political alliance. In making this claim, these authors are not seeking to validate an Occidentalist ideal type of social democracy. Rather, in this instance, they provide an immanent criticism of the liberal administration's own attempts to promote the *form* of institutions associated with social democracy without the relational *content*. They do so by emphasizing the *relational* lessons of social democratic and democratic socialist struggle along the lines of what I would call a spirit of democratic experimentalism akin to that embraced by radical thinkers such as Gramsci and John Dewey (West 1988; Liguori 2015, 192–199). Unfortunately, such an experiment is difficult to achieve using the pro-capital "models" that were used to pursue economic democracy. In this case the democratic deficit seen in neoliberal and developmentalist perspectives—that posit state and market as cohesive, coherent actors—was replicated in political strategies that did little to substantively incorporate the labor movement or address interclass disparities much less the demands of other subaltern actors. This critique raises the broader issue of comparison: that is, the way different "models" are understood and incorporated into practice. While Scandinavian and New Deal imaginaries have been particularly prevalent among post-Keynesian and institutionalist thinkers within the progressive bloc, they have often been understood in a manner that sees them nationally delimited, pregiven policy options rather than as geographically interconnected sites with the global political economy.[2] In contrast, the critique of such imaginaries by

---

2. These imaginaries are somewhat fluid. For instance, reformers have highlighted features of Pink Tide governments in Latin American, neo-Bolivarian models: the work of Saesayŏn (New Society Institute) among others was popular in the early 2000s in this regard, for instance.

170 | The Postdevelopmental State

more progressive or radical thinkers often highlights the *relational* aspects of such models rather than their strictly institutional or ideal type features, so as to correct for the fetishization of abstract models over inclusive political struggles.

Chang Seok-jun (2019a, 2019b) makes cognate remarks in his criticism that reformers in the Moon administration failed to exercise intellectual and moral leadership by neglecting the principles of freedom, equality, and solidarity in their proposals for social democratic reform, fetishizing institutional form instead. To emphasize these principles, he argues, does not mean that "Swedish social democracy is an alternative to Korean society." Acknowledging Korea's more difficult geopolitical conditions, Chang argues that adherence to these principles might lead to its own distinct egalitarian model. For progressive critics of the Moon administration such as Chang and others, it was obvious that economic democracy was not theorized as a mixed economy model, an episode of historical and social justice, nor as industrial democracy, but rather as an elite, or technocratic, arrangement between the state and the chaebol. Unfortunately, this vision of reform did little to depart from the traditional positions of supporting the chaebol as national champions and seeking to reform them in line with market-based principles. In this manner, the Moon administration failed to depart from the policies of previous administrations that have vacillated between these positions, often beginning with promises of chaebol reform but ending on a pro-chaebol stance. Moon's pardoning of Samsung heir Lee Jae-young and his pro-business New Southern Policy (targeting aid and investment into Southeast Asia, a key production platform for Korean firms) are indicative of this trend. As such, the development of a transformative platform for chaebol reform that might include the participation of labor and other subaltern actors remains an important concern for future reform efforts.

The problem of developing an inclusive and transformative policy framework has been even more pronounced, unfortunately, when it has come to labor market reforms that might address the problems of inequality and irregular work. As discussed in chapter 4, despite the inclusion of veteran labor activists and reformers from pro-labor CSOs, Moon's attempt to create a "society that respects labor" resulted in a similar dilemma. In this case, the problem could be rephrased as one of pursuing social democracy without labor, or social democracy without content. For despite endorsing policies and institutions associated with social democracy—such as social dialogue, an employee representative system, and other forms of social partnership—the way Moon's labor reforms

Conclusion | 171

were implemented left much to be desired. Ultimately, the administration sought to use the presence of labor and CSO activists to accord legitimacy to its labor policies, rather than to develop substantive policy through interaction with labor as a difficult but worthy partner. As such, the Moon administration could not effectively defend its regularization and minimum wage policies when they faced backlash, and its use of the dialogue body to push through an agreement on flexible working time further alienated the labor movement and innovative public interests that participated within it. This episode reveals how the nexus between movements and the state is used to pursue legitimation, but, more so, how such legitimation efforts have failed largely because they lack a stronger, comprehensive vision of economic reform and political coordination.

On the surface, the remedy to this problem might involve cultivating a stronger relationship between the trade union movement and the Democratic Party. The natural place to begin here would be before the election cycle and might involve cultivating a strong set of policy prescriptions in advance in full recognition that this might be a contentious and difficult process. As the Democratic Party has formed alliances with the relatively conservative FKTU in the past, such an exercise should not be impossible to concieve. This proposal may seem naïve given the diversity of voices within the Democratic Party and the fact some may intentionally work against labor inclusion. And yet since leaders within the party have embraced ideas associated with social democracy and a philosophy of progressive liberalism, if they are to express some fidelity to these goals, such a strategy should not be ruled out. Beyond this strategy, support for comprehensive labor and civil rights legislation, including the "yellow envelope bill" revising TULRAA to extend the rights of irregular workers and the long promised antidiscrimination law, would be a good starting point. It is one that might signal an effort to make an egalitarian vision of economic and social democracy hegemonic, and to address forms of discrimination that intersect with and inform labor issues such as gender, sexuality, ability, and migrant status. Indeed, it might be more effective than the current pattern of veteran trade unionists, labor, and democracy activists joining the party as officials, advisors, and elected members of the National Assembly. As Lee Yoonkyung (2022) notes, once in power, many progressives have difficultly coordinating policy when in office, and, unfortunately, the result is often that their reputations come to obscure the lack of progressive policy.

These intersecting problems of legitimation-through-inclusion and lack of substantive reform imaginaries proved to be particularly problematic in the case of prosecution reform and the wider bloc politics explored in chapter 5. In many ways, the problems evoke the necessity of having a pro-democratic bloc to begin with, for the power of the conservative bloc means that the various liberal and progressive actors that compose the pro-democratic bloc must find ways to mobilize and coordinate together. This reality, however, does not mean that the failures of the democratic bloc can simply be explained by the strength of the conservative one, and, indeed, there is some fluidity and connection between blocs. Their ability to address the rival bloc's power hinges not only on external constraints but also on the internal dynamics of the bloc itself. As the case of prosecution reform examined in chapter 5 shows, the fixation on the virtues and vices of Cho Kuk obstructed the task of pursuing legal reform that might resolve economic and social polarization. Ironically, the subsequent Yoon administration has not been as sensitive to this problem despite his appropriation of the mantle of fairness. While his appointments have faced similar probes into their efforts to provide educational privileges to their children, the same charges of hypocrisy did not generate mass protest during his first months in office. This is most likely because the stakes of such appointments in terms of prosecution reform is much less (for the conservative bloc represents the status quo rather than a departure from it) and the expectation around the virtues of conservative figures less intense. Indeed, for some young, alt-right voters, as in the case of the United States and elsewhere, it is the appeal of a might-equals-right politics that has drawn them to the Conservative Party to begin with.

A Broader Dilemma

As discussed in the introduction, this book uses the term "postdevelopmental state" to connote the dilemmas explored above. The term does not describe an ideal type of state, but rather an unresolved set of strategic and relational challenges involved in seeking to overcome the intersecting legacies of developmentalism and neoliberalism in a time of expanding inequality. The challenges, I argue, are best viewed from a perspective sensitive to the *integral* nature of political and civil society and the manner that the nexus between them has been mobilized to pursue political and economic reform. While this book explores these challenges in the three key policy areas—chaebol, labor, and prosecution reform—they do not exhaust the possibilities of this terminology. Rather, it remains relevant to other areas of reform and restructuring that, for reasons of space, are not

Conclusion | 173

analyzed in this book. For instance, the task of creating alternatives to both developmentalist and neoliberal policies toward the environment has witnessed similar dynamics. Liberal administrations, as much as their developmentalist predecessors and conservative rivals, have depended on massive construction and infrastructure plans that raise difficult questions about environmental justice. Likewise, intellectuals and environmental activists have been incorporated into state policy-making under liberal administrations, many of whom have been criticized by their colleagues for backtracking on their green pledges and for treating environmental problems with a neoliberal logic of profitability and efficiency (Choi YR 2014, 2019).

A similar dilemma can also be seen in broader issues concerning urban development. As discussed in chapter 2, the historic rise in household debt following the Asian financial crisis has contributed to speculative bubbles in credit, stocks, and real estate. This investment has helped to drive inequality directly in terms of wealth inequality but also indirectly in the sense that the appropriation of workers' income through debt affects the compulsion to engage in irregular work, shaping income inequality, and raises broader questions about fairness and justice within the economy. The increased cost of living due to rising house prices and rent also contributed to disillusionment in the Moon administration and his largely property-led urban development strategies. Moreover, as interest rates rose to combat inflation during 2022 and 2023, observers worried that Korea might face its own version of a Japanese bubble crash of the late 1990s due to its highly leveraged households. Despite the appointments of critical urban scholars—themselves experts on gentrification, displacement, and redevelopment in Korea—to prominent positions in his administration, Moon's policies failed to quell the speculative rise in house prices. Despite some expansion of social housing and taxation of additional properties, Moon's discussion of developing Seoul's greenbelt and plan to build a Great Train Express line to facilitate apartment construction were seen by critics as an attempt to prop up developers, a criticism other urban-level governments have also witnessed despite the inclusion of progressive policy "experts" (Doucette and Hae 2022).

Similar problems of overcoming developmentalist and neoliberal structures can be seen in the efforts of a variety of struggles for social justice. For instance, despite calling himself a "feminist president" and including veteran feminist CSO activists in prominent positions in his administration, the demands of various sexual and social minorities who participated in the Candlelight events were neglected after Moon's election. As Ju Hui Judy Han (2022) has described, the recognition of same-sex marriage and creation of comprehensive antidiscrimination legislation requested by a variety of social movements came to be seen by the Democratic Party as being "too early" (*shigisangjo*) and met with a logic of deferral (*najunge*). As Han argues, this hetero-patriarchal ranking of priorities evokes a developmentalist temporality of postponement (not now but later) and is in contrast to the actual participation of minorities in the Candlelight events. "Alongside feminist and youth activists, gender and sexual minorities advocated for conscientious speech and a public culture of mutual respect and accountability, seeking to build inclusive spaces that did not condescend toward youth or stigmatize mental illness or disability" (Han 2022, 127). To have participated in the democratic event of the Candlelight Revolution only to have one's demands excluded was seen as betrayal and points to the limits of Moon's envisaging of Candlelight Democracy. Unfortunately, only the minority Justice Party has consistently worked to develop comprehensive antidiscrimination legislation, but despite a parliamentary majority the Democratic Party refused to pass it, bowing to pressure from conservative Christian groups. This situation has evoked significant commentary on who and what the Candlelight Revolution was for. If its various visions of economic democracy and a society that respects labor did not consider the rights of various forms of social difference, then what kind of vision was it?

In light of the exhaustion of Moon's reform agenda and that of previous liberal administrations, the frustrations of social movements have generated calls for a more comprehensive and egalitarian approach to solving the dilemmas of the postdevelopmental state. Some progressive intellectuals, such as Cho Hee Yeon (2016), have argued for more comprehensive "two-track" approaches that simultaneously work toward the democratization of state and society. But, as mentioned above, the shape of such a project is currently difficult to discern. Following Yoon's election, the pro-democratic bloc found itself in disarray. Some, such as the Democratic Party's emergency steering committee cochair Park Ji-hyun, represented the problem as one of the 586 generation itself, but such an approach largely fails to consider the structural challenges that any counterhegemonic project must address, and instead represents the failures of the Moon administration as a generational issue. Meanwhile, the roots of a more substantive alternative might be found in the feminist, antidiscrimination, and urban social movements that have grown during the Moon administration, but at present it remains to be seen how their ideas will filter up into the integral state as part of a broader pro-democratic project.

Conclusion | 175

Moreover, the incorporation of such movements into the policy-making apparatus of Democratic Party administrations may itself be undesirable. As Lee Yoonkyung (2022) argues, despite the incorporation of progressive activists into the Democratic Party, the attempt to create progressive policy has often faced disappointing results. She contrasts the lack of coordination between progressive actors in the party to stronger integration between social movements and CSOs that, she argues, has been far more successful at coordinating for political change at the national level.

Lee's argument here is a salient one that she also uses to broaden political analysis of democratization beyond the party system in order to show how the politics of the "street" (or, plaza, in Choi Jang-jip's terminology) has often been more effective than that of the Democratic Party (or "assembly" as she puts it). A note of caution is needed here, however, as progressive civil society itself does not have a limitless capacity to organize and propose alternatives. It has often been dependent on government funding during liberal administrations, and itself has witnessed a reproduction problem, as many progressive CSOs tend to have their own internal tensions between older 586 activists in leadership positions and younger staffers who find it difficult to gain opportunities to move into leadership roles or to make a secure livelihood in the CSO sector.[3] Rather than seeing the modes of activism she describes—the street, the ruling party, and small progressive party—as separate spheres or "types" of political action, it is important to see them as recursive aspects of the broader politics of the pro-democratic bloc.[4] In this sense, it is the disappointment with the Democratic Party's fidelity to the aspirations of the pro-democratic bloc, as well as the resilient strength of the conservative bloc, that contributes to the politics of the street. Likewise, Lee makes the excellent point that rather than seeing the Democratic Party itself as a relatively inert structure that limits progressive initiatives, what should instead be analyzed is the failure of progressive actors who have been incorporated into it to develop mechanisms of policy coordination among themselves and with other social actors. In Gramscian terms, the problem that Lee describes is one of turning a war of position (the inclu-

---

3. In many ways, the sociologist Kim Dong-choon noticed this trajectory developing in the mid-2000s as he argued that the citizens' movement was failing to effectively reproduce itself. See Kim DC (2006).

4. Lee CS and Yoo HC (2023) make a similar argument through a stylized typology of irregular worker initiatives. Again, rather than seeing these as "types" it is perhaps better to see them as recursive strategies within a situation conditioned by the dynamics of historical blocs.

sion of progressive figures and CSOs in the party and liberal administrations) into a war of maneuver (the creation of a comprehensive plan for political economic reform).

The need for such a plan, one that goes beyond the mere inclusion of progressive personalities, was highlighted late in the Moon administration by the scholar of progressive parties Chang Sok-joon. Chang revisited a proposal made by the late Justice Party politician Roh Hae Chan for the creation of a seventh republic as a potential basis for a strategy. Roh had argued that neoliberalism had only strengthened the dominant actors of the Sixth Republic (party bosses, bureaucrats, and chaebol), so a constitutional revision to limit their powers was necessary (see Chang SJ 2019a, 2019b; Roh HC 2007). The revision would prioritize a variety of pro-democratic demands, including equality and engagement, economy and welfare, ecology, minority human rights, labor and agriculture, peace and unification, and people's sovereignty. Roh's economic proposals included the legislation of an Equal Economic Committee consisting of business, government, labor, farmers, and common people to secure the integrity of the public sector (especially in relation to education, medical care, jobs, and housing) and to develop a comprehensive economic plan. In essence, the idea was to use constitutional revision to legislate more participatory and representative forms of planning instead of relying on the inclusion of elite reformers and incomplete social dialogue to legitimize policy. While the experience of the social dialogue initiatives explored in this book raises doubts about the feasibility of such a proposal, Roh's proposal that a committee of popular forces be used to articulate a broad set of progressive demands, to legislate a participatory framework for doing so, and to institutionalize it through constitutional reform, is a novel starting point.

The Future of a Problematic

While the findings of this book are relevant for a range of political and economic struggles in contemporary Korea, its conceptual intervention is farther reaching. It seeks to address the democratic deficit in developmental state research by reframing its focus away from a fixation on economic growth and ideal type depictions of bureaucratic autonomy and toward the concerns of progressive pro-democratic actors. To do so, it employs a Gramscian focus on the integral state and highlights the importance of the nexus between political and civil society as a site from which to examine the challenges of addressing inequality and injustice. As chapter 1 argues, this is not simply an empirical intervention but also a conceptual one that seeks to reframe the standpoint from which research on development and democratization is undertaken in order to prioritize the experience of pro-democratic actors and to situate ideas within their political context. Hence, the way that the experience of developmentalist dictatorships and neoliberal political economic restructuring have shaped the project of economic democracy is highlighted in this book. The same can be said for the idea of the developmental state. Rather than seeing this idea as an abstract ideal type, its role in both the politics of its neo-Weberian theorists—including the awkward political affinities that result from their critique of neoliberalism and praise of state-led development strategies—and a variety of Korean economic reformers is considered. This intervention posits that the standpoint of the researcher does not exist in a contemplative relationship outside of the context under study but rather in a relation of interested interaction with the normative ideas, evaluative concerns, and political imaginaries of actors within that context, a fact that is much better to recognize rather than to deny.

In this sense, the current book explicitly shares the pro-democratic bloc's critique of the relations that have shaped Korea's rapid economic development and its desires for a more egalitarian political economic system. And, at the same time, it uses this concern to advance a broader critique of knowledge about the role of the state in development that neglects such viewpoints. In this regard, the problematic of the postdevelopmental state offered here represents an attempt to realign research in the broad field of the political economy of development with the experience of progressive actors involved in social change by foregrounding the dilemmas and challenges they have encountered. This has meant sacrificing the shibboleth of the state vs. market approach, which ignored the complex interpenetration of both the state and the market, tracing instead the contours of specific reform imaginaries and the dynamics they have experienced within the integral state. The result is an approach that reveals the contested meaning of development, the agency of pro-democratic forces, and the politics of hegemony and legitimacy much more than standard accounts of rapid development. What is gained is knowledge of the various social forces pursuing social change and a deeper sense of their historical and geographical context, whereas what is lost is a set of parsimonious policy prescriptions based on an idealized sense of what is unique about specific models of development. In my opinion, the gains far outweigh the losses here for they can provide a much more evaluative reading of development. In perhaps a postcolonial manner, it offers researchers a chance to align themselves with actors at sites of political struggle and, consequently, support solidaristic practices of knowledge production oriented toward more egalitarian imaginings of development and democracy.

This reframing of the developmental state research program remains relevant for contemporary research on states and development well beyond Korea for several reasons. The first is that despite the decline of its program, the idea of the developmental state has recently returned as a policy model. Among the reasons for this return are the declining popularity of neoliberal visions of economic growth, resurgent forms of nationalism, and rising geopolitical tensions that highlight the need for a more active role for the state in shaping economic growth. This renewed popularity has particularly been the case in the growing literature on "democratic" developmental states in Africa, in which Korea's experience has figured prominently (Edigheji 2010; Mkandawire 2001; Yi and Mkandawire 2014). But the idea of the developmental state has also been embraced elsewhere, and by governments of both authoritarian and left-nationalist persuasions. For example, Vietnam has sought to model institutions described by developmental state theorists such as Korea's Economic Planning Board in its practices of long-range planning (Kim PH and Jung W 2018). At the same time, Korea has also provided inspiration for Ecuador's attempts to create something of a democratic and de-colonial developmental state that advances a green agenda of a "bio-socialism" that includes respect for indigenous knowledges and identity (Childs and Hearn 2017). Correspondingly, Korea's foreign ministries and other emerging donors have been attuned to this interest. For example, through its Knowledge Sharing Program and cognate initiatives, the Korean government has also been happy to supply celebratory narratives of its development experience that seek to satisfy demand for knowledge of its history as a "development alternative" to mainstream development advice (Doucette and Muller 2016).

But this turn of events also risks replicating the same assumptions about state autonomy and bureaucratic rationality that figured in classic studies of the developmental state. What a lot of these policy models share is an overidealization of the cohesion of the state, the coherence of development plans, and the "rationality" of its practitioners (Doucette 2020a). But as this book has shown, state policy cannot be understood without examining the broader social relations that political and civil society are enmeshed in. This isn't to say that the state isn't a powerful actor within the economy, but that the agency of its various parts are

Conclusion | 179

conditioned by a variety of ideas, alliances, and experiences that are densely connected to civil society. Moreover, in many contexts, the embrace of the idea of the developmental state is a way of depoliticizing social conflict and demobilizing other egalitarian options by treating development as largely a technical problem for elite actors. It speaks to a limiting of democratic imaginaries rather than an expansion of them. Hence, a better understanding of both the social context of Korea's developmentalist policies and their neoliberal restructuring, as well as the challenges faced by progressive forces in promoting egalitarian and democratic reform, can help to better situate the lessons the experience of Korean development might provide when made to travel to different places (see Park SH et al. 2020 for a discussion).

The second reason is slightly more prosaic and that is that the relational and processual approach to the state embraced here is also germane for contemporary geographical scholarship, particularly the wider literatures on state rescaling and "variegated capitalism" (Brenner 2004; Jessop 2016; Peck and Theodore 2007; Peck 2023). This literature shares a cognate agenda with research into East Asian developmentalism but often lacks a granular focus on grassroots and pro-democratic actors. In part, this is a consequence of the decline of the area studies tradition in geography for reasons both for the better and for the worse (cf. Ashutosh 2017; Sidaway 2013; Harootunian 2002). For the better in that the Cold War context of area studies was deeply problematic, but for the worse in that idle conceptual speculation based on limited area knowledge or, worse, orientalist stereotypes often replaced it. Hence, the focus in this book on how pro-democratic actors have actively sought to *upscale* social partnership from the urban to the national level and have *jumped scale* to the global level to ratify international labor standards and modify national laws provides a chance to deepen this literature's insight into the "strategic selectivity" of the state and the sources of institutional variegation at the global level. It does so by examining social movements as scale-making agents in their own right and the integral state as an important site of transformation. Moreover, as the book explores the practical dilemmas involved when social movements work to "import" and modify national institutions associated with divergent economic imaginaries such as Nordic institutions of social partnership and Anglo-American corporate governance practices, its focus is also novel for the state rescaling literature on East Asia. To date, much of the latter has focused largely on *sub*national rescaling such as special economic zones, regional clusters, and site-specific places of policy experimentation rather than national policy per se (Lim

2019; Kleibert 2018; Zhang and Peck 2016), hence there is room here for connecting democratic mobilization to new modes of national change and transformation.

The third reason is similar dynamics within the integral state have been witnessed by social movements and democratic struggles elsewhere in East and Southeast Asia. Democratic events such as Korea's Candlelight Revolution are not isolated but have been complemented by cognate events in the region such as Taiwan's Sunflower Revolution, Hong Kong's Umbrella Revolution, Thailand's Red Shirt Movement, and more. There is ample room for relational comparison and an "eventful geography" (cf. Lee CK 2019; Ho MS 2019) here both in terms of the processes that led up to such events and the different ways in which such events have been shaped by or led to new connections within the integral state. Learning from such democratic struggles, their successes, failures, and interconnections, seems to be an excellent way to see not only how the politics of East Asian development have been contested but also to find lessons that might be drawn for similar conjunctures elsewhere. For the problems described in this book do not apply to Korea or East Asia alone as much as they may share interconnections and correspondences with other places. The right-wing politics of personality they have combated is now a persistent political problem in America and Europe. Moreover, the lack of a progressive social democratic imaginary of the future animates a range of Anglo-American and Nordic democracies. As it has often been a lack of political literacy of struggles elsewhere that has bound the progressive left in certain contexts to Eurocentrism and nationalism, my hope is that the present work can contribute to better global knowledge of pro-democratic struggles and, ultimately, the egalitarian lessons that can be drawn from them.

Conclusion

Ultimately, however, the future of the problematic of the postdevelopmental state advanced in this book depends on the efforts of social movement and progressive political forces to tackle the challenges outlined in its chapters. The utility of the idea in the Korean context will perhaps be tested by the degree to which these actors are able to devise an alternative to structures inherited from the developmentalist era and their neoliberal transformation. What the content of this project might be is up for grabs, but it must address several challenges. These include the power of the

Conclusion | 181

chaebol (and with it other forms of "international" capital), the resilience of the conservative bloc, and the problem of irregular work and with it the interconnected problems of welfare, social protection, and the cost of living. Some might argue that the question of the environment and the division system are also essential here, as, indeed, in the long run they are. For there is no future economy without the environment, and the existence of the division system has long emboldened conservative forces to subvert democratic institutions. But the immediate problem as I see it places the most emphasis on addressing the factors behind contemporary inequality that provoked the Candlelight Revolution. As this book has shown, overcoming that dilemma needs to involve as many actors within political and civil society as possible in new forms of democratic organization, and thus the willingness of the pro-democratic bloc to hold together demands for liberty and equality, along with environmental justice and peaceful engagement, may well determine its ability to create a substantial alternative. The Gramscian approach in this book provides a way to track such a project and is indeed no stranger to many of the intellectuals and political actors discussed within its pages. In the spirit of Gramsci's contrast of the pessimism of the intellect to the optimism of the will, then, I offer a final closing note. While it certainly seems that the problems described in this book can be overcome, whether the pro-democratic bloc ultimately finds a way to do so will have to be the topic of further scholarship.

Methodological Appendix

As discussed in the introduction, this book uses an extended case study method to examine the challenges of progressive political economic reform in South Korea. This reflexive approach to case study construction is influenced by a "political gnoseological" strategy of "interested interaction" (as explained in chapter 1) with the standpoints of the actors it studies and builds upon the researcher's own modest engagement with progressive movements in South Korea. Consequently, this situatedness raises the challenge of delineating between the formal and informal "fields" in which the research takes place: between formal research interviews recorded and analyzed to aid with case construction, process tracing, and interpretation, and more informal observation, conversation, and experience accumulated over time. As this book is the result of both strategies, this methodological appendix provides further context in relation to its individual chapters.

The discussion of the economic democracy debate in chapter 3 began with fieldwork for my doctoral dissertation, which involved interviews with intellectuals from a variety of reform factions. I was interested in the passion that the debates over chaebol reform provoked at the time, and was fortunate enough that Sungkonghoe University, where I was a visiting researcher, hosted a semester of talks by prominent reformers who had been involved in advising the liberal administration of Roh Moo-hyun. Some of my informants at the time held formal roles in Roh's administration and others in civil society. Many went on to serve in the subsequent liberal administration of Moon Jae-in. I followed the careers of my informants since this time to better understand both the practical aspects and political stakes of their debates. As the 2012 elections provided a crystallization of the main two poles of the debate, the chapters make use of published exchanges between these camps during the campaign. I also carried out interviews with some of the participants following it and have

184 | Methodological Appendix

interacted with a number of its participants and critics over the last 15 years. The analysis in this chapter has also benefitted from discussion among my peers and collaborators in various small economic reform CSOs over the years. The tension between these camps and exchanges between post-Keynesian, institutionalist, heterodox, and post-Marxist economists within them has been a frequent point of conversation with these peers as have the careers of those who have gone into the Blue House, so to speak. But, of course, all errors of interpretation are my own.

In some ways, my situated experience with progressive actors blurs the conventional borderline between formal and informal research in that my own knowledge of tensions within the pro-democratic bloc has been produced through broader observation and social interactions that involve both chance and circumstance. In some cases, the "site" from which my general understanding of these debates has emerged includes formal interviews, secondary literature, and statistical interpretation. At the same time, my general understanding of reform politics in Korea has benefited from long dinners, weekend hikes, chance meetings at protests and conferences, Facebook and social media posts, personal communication, and occasional collaboration on solidarity campaigns. I refrain from citing these informal moments here as such interactions were not formally part of the research process; nonetheless, in many cases they contributed more than formal interviews to my understanding of the emotional valences and political stakes of what can often seem to be largely technical debates. This dynamic shapes my citational strategy in this book. As such contextual knowledge has been gained through observation and experience, and because I offered my research informants confidentiality (though most were happy to be identified with few qualifications, e.g., "after the election"), I have found it much easier and more precise to cite the published outputs that shaped this debate rather than interview transcripts per se. It is also a better strategy, I feel, for crediting the perspectives of actors involved in the debate on areas explored across chapters. Hence, I found interviews to be more useful for identifying the key ideas, camps, actors, viewpoints, and policies: these then shaped further case construction through secondary literature, policy reports, and statistical interpretation. Regarding the latter, while the approach in chapter 2 is mostly quantitative, it was in many ways provoked by the research for chapter 3 along with other interviews in the early 2010s with various financial organizations and think tanks about Korea's financial transformation and its urban effects.

A similar context influenced the other chapters of this book. For chapter 4, on the question of labor reform, my initial interest in the struggles of irregular workers and the politics of social dialogue was catalyzed by minor solidarity activism and journalism I carried out in the early 2000s with the Equality Trade Union–Migrants Branch (ETU-MB, the predecessor to the Migrant Trade Union) and its successor, the Migrant Trade Union (MTU). At the time, I was shocked by several protest-suicides by irregular worker activists who were solidarity partners of these unions following the application of damage claims against them for taking part in industrial action. These events, which occurred under liberal administrations, spurred my interest in the question of changing modes of labor control and labor's role in the integral state. The understanding of the legal application of damage claims and the politics of social dialogue explored in this chapter stem from conversations with labor lawyers, legal activists, members of the nonregular workers policy team of the Ministry of Labor, members of labor-oriented CSOs such as the Korea Labour and Society Institute (KLSI), among others, and officials with the Korean Labor Institute (KLI) and social dialogue body ESLC from the late 2000s to 2022. Here again, I am indebted not only to formal interviews for my understanding of these issues but also to many personal conversations, email queries, more hikes, and other interactions among peers and colleagues. Once again, all errors are my own. Many thanks also to Susan Kang with whom I cowrote an earlier version of an article that shapes part of this chapter for alerting me to the ILO's Committee on Freedom of Association database of complaints, which proved to be an excellent resource for tracking the use of damage claims. Other informal interactions and participation also influenced some of the arguments in this chapter. For instance, I was invited to speak at a high-profile event discussing Candlelight Democracy in the autumn of 2018 that provided an opportunity to meet some members of Moon's former transition team and future high-ranking officials. It was clear from that event that the ILO ratification would not be straightforward and that some within the administration saw the conventions as something to be bargained over. Likewise, a dinner associated with that event also witnessed some gold spoon behavior that planted some doubts about the likelihood of Moon's Candlelight plans bearing substantive fruit. In addition, the analysis also benefited from observation of various forums on labor, inequality, and social dialogue in Korea, and much personal communication on the finer points of Korean labor relations with old friends and colleagues. I am grateful to Hanee Choi for attending and taking notes at one of these events in my absence, though, again, I bear responsibility for any errors.

Finally, chapter 5 initially began as a more long-distance project based

186 | Methodological Appendix

on observation and concern over the events that followed the 2012 elections as details of the NIS intervention came to light. The first part of this chapter is based on an earlier article with my colleague Se-woong Koo that began as an attempt to provide context for a broader effort by a group of concerned Korean studies scholars, and local groups such as the National Association of Professors for Democracy (Mingyohyup), to generate awareness of the issue. The approach to case construction in the first half of this chapter, then, relies more on secondary literature than the others. The second half, which includes discussion of the Cho Kuk scandal, is indebted to broader observation of the role that the scandal played among civil society organizations and many of my progressive peers. While the argument is my own, it is informed by conversations about the politics implied by that event. The scandal became such a divisive topic of conversation across progressive CSOs and among intellectuals and reformers that by the summer of 2022 many of my close friends expressed that they were experiencing fatigue with the longevity of the topic. While I did not carry out formal interviews surrounding the Cho scandal, but instead rely on published commentaries and other literature, the fact that it kept surfacing in news and conversations highlighted, for me, its significance as a turning point in Moon's project of Candlelight Democracy. It was the moment the tide began to ebb, so to speak.

While in the introduction I use the phrase "fellow traveling as method" to describe the situatedness of the research for this book discussed above, I must admit feeling reticent about discussing such connections here. For I regard my own political experience as fairly prosaic compared to the efforts of my peers and colleagues in South Korea. If I had to deepen the metaphor, my mode of travel feels more like hitching a ride than driving a car. The metaphor can be taken quite literally sometimes as I have attended several events, protests, workshops, and meetings with such peers over the years. Nonetheless, to provide a brief sketch of how data for this study emerged from this broader set of relations and connections, table A1 provides a rough list of the types of research informants interviewed and consulted for the chapters that make up this study with the caveat that this only scratches the surface of broader informal context. The time span of these encounters runs roughly from 2006 to 2022, with extended research trips in 2006–7, 2012, 2016, and 2018 and almost yearly (and sometimes more) revisits since then. In the interest of maintaining confidentiality, the table does not list informants by name. Instead, it provides a general sense of the types of roles they have occupied and organizations they have belonged to.

TABLE A1. Research Informants ($N > 50$)

Description	Organizations
Interviews and communication with various economic and pro-democracy reform CSOs: staff, founders, and personnel	Members and formers members of PSPD, CCEJ, SER, ODA Watch, Speculative Capital Watch Korea, Welfare State Society, Alternatives Network, Karl Polanyi Social Economy Institute, Global Political Economy Institute, Intellectuals Declaration Network, NAPD, KWWA, various progressive and post-Keynesian economists
Interviews and communication with trade union activists, staff, and officials, and with labor-oriented CSOs	Members and former members of the KCTU from various national, regional, and local branches. FKTU officials. Members of KLSI, Korea Society for the Abolition of Irregular Work, Songjapgo (anti-damage claims CSO), PSSP, Korean House for International Solidarity, International Strategy Center, GongGam (public interest law organization).
Interviews and communication with government officials involved in labor and development policy and research	ESLC, Ministry of Labor, KOILAF, KLI, STEPI, KDI, KOICA, EDCF, SMG, National Assembly researchers.
Interviews and communication with intellectuals and politicians with prominent roles in liberal and conservative administrations	Several former Blue House secretaries, including former chief secretaries of policy planning; members of the State Affairs Planning Advisory Committee (Moon's transition team), prominent intellectuals, and senior national assembly members who went on to occupy prominent positions in the administration, former KDI president, former KDLP officials, among others.
Interviews with researchers from various private sector organizations and economic think tanks	IMF Office Korea, SERI, FKI, Finance and Economy Institute, various bank officials involved in urban development, among others.

Note: The acronyms in the table are as follows: Citizen's Coalition for Economic Justice (CCEJ), Economic Development and Cooperation Fund (EDCF), Federation of Korean Industries (FKI), Federation of Korean Trade Unions (FKTU), International Monetary Fund (IMF), Korean Confederation of Trade Unions (KCTU), Korea Development Institute (KDI), Korea Labor Institute (KLI), Korea Labor and Society Institute (KLSI), Korea International Labor Foundation (KOILAF), Korean Women Workers Association (KWWA), National Association of Professors for Democracy (NAPD), People's Solidarity for Participatory Democracy (PSPD), People's Solidarity for Social Progress (PSSP), Solidarity for Economic Reform (SER), Samsung Economic Research Institute (SERI), Seoul Metropolitan Government (SMG), Science and Technology Policy Institute (STEPI).

References

Agnew J. 1994. "The Territorial Trap: The Geographical Assumptions of International Relations Theory." *Review of International Political Economy* 1: 53–80.

Agnew J and Corbridge S. 1995. *Mastering Space: Hegemony, Territory and International Political Economy*. New York: Routledge.

Alami I, Alves C, Bonizzi B, Kaltenbrunner A, Koddenbrock K, Kvangraven I, and Powell J. 2023. "International Financial Subordination: A Critical Research Agenda." *Review of International Political Economy* 30 (4): 1360–86.

Amnesty International. 1999. *Republic of Korea (South Korea): Summary of Concerns for 1999 AI Index: ASA 25/01/99*. https://www.amnesty.org/download/Documents/1440 00/asa250011999en.pdf

Amsden A. 1989. *Asia's Next Giant: South Korea and Late Industrialization*. Oxford: Oxford University Press.

Amsden A. 1995. "Like the Rest: Southeast Asia's Late Industrialization." *Journal of International Development* 7 (5): 791–99.

Ashutosh I. 2017. "The Geography and Area Studies Interface from the Second World War to the Cold War." *Geographical Review* 107 (4): 705–21.

Arato A. 1974. "The Neo-Idealist Defense of Subjectivity." *Telos* 21:108–61.

Back A. 2014. "Samsung Restructuring Could Offer Opportunities: Hospitalization of Patriarch Lee Kun-hee Raises Expectations for Changes to Chaebol." *Wall Street Journal*, June 17. https://www.wsj.com/articles/samsung-restructuring-could-offer -opportunities-1402849806

Bae J. 2010. "The South Korean Left's 'Northern Question.'" In *Korea Yearbook 2009*, edited by Frank R, Hoare J, Kollner P, and Pares S, 87–116. Leiden: Brill.

Baek SH and Ahn SH. 2012. "A Comparative Social Policy Study on the Structure and Characteristics of the Korean Welfare State: Focusing on the Analysis of Public Social Expenditures." *Korean Social Sciences Review* 2 (2): 63–92.

Bhagwati J and Krueger A. 1973. "Exchange Control, Liberalization, and Economic Development." *American Economic Review* 63 (2): 419–27.

Bloch B. 2019. "The Origins of Adorno's Psycho-Social Dialectic: Psychoanalysis and Neo-Kantianism in the Young Adorno." *Modern Intellectual History* 16 (2): 501–29.

Bortz P and Kaltenbrunner A. 2018. "The International Dimension of Financialization in Developing and Emerging Economies." *Development and Change* 49 (2): 375–93.

Bourdieu P. 1998. *Practical Reason: On the Theory of Action*. Stanford: Stanford University Press.

190 | References

Boyer R. 2000. "Is a Finance-Led Growth Regime a Viable Alternative to Fordism? A Preliminary Analysis." *Economy and Society* 29 (1): 111–45.

Brenner N. 2004. *New State Spaces: Urban Governance and the Rescaling of Statehood*. Oxford: Oxford University Press.

Brown W. 2023. *Nihilistic Times: Thinking with Max Weber*. Cambridge: Harvard University Press.

Burawoy M. 2009. *The Extended Case Method: Four Countries, Four Decades, Four Great Transformations, and One Theoretical Tradition*. Berkeley: University of California Press.

Burawoy M, Blum J, George S, Gille Z, and Thayer M. 2000. *Global Ethnography: Forces, Connections, and Imaginations in a Postmodern World*. Berkeley: University of California Press.

Burkett P and Hart-Landsberg M. 2000. *Development, Crisis, and Class Struggle: Learning from Japan and East Asia*. New York: St. Martin's Press.

Castells M. 1992. "Four Asian Tigers with a Dragon Head: A Comparative Analysis of the State, Economy, and Society in the Asian Pacific Rim." In *States and Development in the Asian Pacific Rim*, edited by Appelbaum R and Henderson J, 33–70. Newbury Park, CA: Sage.

Chang DO. 2002. "Korean Labour Relations in Transition: Authoritarian Flexibility?" *Labour, Capital and Society* 35: 10–40.

Chang DO. 2009. *Capitalist Development in Korea: Labour, Capital and the Myth of the Developmental State*. New York: Routledge.

Chang HJ. 1998. "Korea: The Misunderstood Crisis." *World Development* 26 (8): 1555–61.

Chang HJ. 2002. *Kicking Away the Ladder: Development Strategy in Historical Perspective*. London: Anthem Press.

Chang HJ, Jeong SI, and Lee JT. 2012a. *Muŏsŭl sŏnt'aek'al kŏshin'ga?* [The choices we have to make]. Seoul: Boo-Kie.

Chang HJ, Jeong SI, and Lee JT. 2012b. *Igŏnhŭiwa samsŏnggŭrupto kubyŏl mot'ana* [You cannot even tell Lee Kun-Hee from Samsung?]. *Pressian*, April 28. http://www.press ian.com/article/article.asp?article_num=60120528133703&section=02

Chang HJ, Jeong SI, and Lee JT. 2012c. *Chaebŏlgaehyŏk mannŭngnonŭn panminjujŏk haengwi* [The almighty *chaebol* reform theory is an antidemocratic deed]. *Pressian*, April 30. http://www.pressian.com/article/article.asp?article_num=6012053011011 5&Section=02

Chang HJ, Jeong SI, and Lee JT. 2012d. *Pakchŏnghŭi ch'eje=chŏltaeak? ŏrisŏkŭn kyujŏng* [Park Chung-hee System = Evil? A Ridiculous Notion]. *Pressian*, June 8. http://www .pressian.com/news/article.html?no=106485

Chang HJ and Park HJ. 2004. "An Alternative Perspective on Government Policy towards the *Chaebol* in Korea: Industrial Policy, Financial Regulations, and Political Democracy." In *Competition and Corporate Governance in Korea: Reforming and Restructuring the Chaebol*, edited by Jwa SH and Lee IK, 24–63. Cheltenham, UK: Edward Elgar.

Chang HJ, Park HJ, and Yoo CG. 1998. "Interpreting the Korean Crisis: Financial Liberalization, Industrial Policy and Corporate Governance." *Cambridge Journal of Economics* (22): 735–46.

Chang KS. 2019. *Developmental Liberalism in South Korea: Formation, Degeneration, and Transnationalization*. Cham, Switzerland: Palgrave Macmillan.

Chang SJ. 2019a. *Nohoech'ani namgin kkum, che7konghwaguk* [Roh Hae-chan's dream of the 7th republic]. *Hankyoreh*, July 18. https://www.hani.co.kr/arti/opinion/column /902404.html

Chang SJ. 2019b. *Nohoech'anŭi che7konghwagung kusangŭl torik'yŏbonda* [A look back at Roh Hae-chan's 7th republic initiative]. *Pressian*, August 12 https://www.pressian.com/pages /articles/252892

Chen KH. 2010. *Asia as Method: Toward Deimperialization*. Durham: Duke University Press.

Chibber V. 2003. *Locked in Place: State-Building and Late Industrialization in India*. Princeton: Princeton University Press.

Childs J and Hearn J. 2017. "'New' Nations: Resource-Based Development Imaginaries in Ghana and Ecuador." *Third World Quarterly* 38 (4): 844–61.

Cho DM. 2021a. *Munjaein chŏngbu, chipkwŏn ch'owa talli nodongjŏngch'aeng yut'ŏnhaetta*. [The Moon Jae-in administration made a U-turn in the labor policy unlike the beginning of the administration]. *Pressian*, July 13. https://www.pressian.com/pages /articles/2021071209265322313#0DKU

Cho DM. 2021b. *Pijŏnggyujigŭi chŏnggyujik'waoka 'kyŏngjeŭi todŏk'waoranŭn kangjun-mane panbak'anda* [The 'regularization' of non-regular workers' refutes Kang Jun-man's 'economic moralization']. *Pressian*, July 13. https://www.pressian.com/pages/art icles/2021071209564858019#0DKU

Cho DM. 2021c. *Munjaein chŏngbu, namŭn imgi tongan 'taesŏn kongyak' tashi torabogil* [The Moon Jae-in administration wants to revisit the 'election promises' for the rest of his term]. *Pressian*, July 14. https://www.pressian.com/pages/articles/2021071210 503921516#0DKU

Cho HY. 2000. "The Structure of the South Korean Developmental Regime and Its Transformation—Statist Mobilization and Authoritarian Integration in the Anti-communist Regimentation." *Inter-Asia Cultural Studies* 1 (3): 408–26.

Cho HY. 2008. "Re-Analysis of Contemporary Political Change in Korea from the Per-spective of the 'Fissure of Hegemony'—Based on the Re-Interpretation of A. Grams-ci's Theory of Hegemony." *Korean Marxism* 21 (9) (Spring): 90–133.

Cho, HY. 2009. "Confronting Dictatorship, Democratization, and Post-Democratization: Personal Reflections on Intellectual and Social Practices in the Context of Dictator-ship, Democratization and Post-Democratization." *Inter-Asia Cultural Studies* 10 (1): 119–37.

Cho HY. 2010. *Tongwŏndoen kŭndaehwa* [Mobilized modernization]. Seoul: Humani-tas.

Cho HY. 2012a. "Changes in Social Movements as Counter-Hegemonic Practices and Their Reconstruction in Asian Democratization: From Convergence to Competitive Differentiation." In *From Unity to Multiplicity: Social Movement Transformation and Democratization in Asia*, edited by Cho HY, Aeria A, and Hur SW, 3–44. Selangor, Malaysia: SIRD.

Cho HY. 2012b. "Democratization as De-Monopolization and Its Different Trajectories: No Democratic Consolidation without De-Monopolization." *Asian Democracy Review* 1 (1): 4–36.

Cho HY. 2016. *T'u t'ŭraeng minjujuŭir chedo chŏngch'i wa undong chŏngch'i ŭi pyŏnghaeng chŏpkŭn* [Two-track democracy: A parallel approach to institutional politics and movement politics]. Seoul: Sogang University Press.

192 | References

Cho SJ. 2016. "The Struggle with Labor Issues in South Korea." *East Asia Foundation Policy Debates* No. 57, August.

Cho YC. 2006. "The *Chaebol* Regime and the Developmental Coalition of Domination." In *Developmental Dictatorship and the Park Chung Hee Era: The Shaping of Modernity in the Republic of Korea*, edited by Lee BC, 108–33. Paramus, NJ: Homa and Sekey.

Choe SH. 2013. "South Korean Intelligence Officers Are Accused of Political Meddling." *New York Times*, April 18.

Choe SH and Motoko R. 2017. "As Scandal Roils South Korea, Fingers Point to Mixing of Politics and Business." *New York Times*, January 2. https://www.nytimes.com/2017/01/02/world/asia/south-korea-park-geun-hye-samsung.html

Choi BC. 2012. '*Chaebŏlonghoowa 'chujujabonjuŭi' chunge mwŏga tŏ chonnyago?* [You are asking which is better: 'Defending the Chaebol' or 'Shareholder Capitalism'?) *Pressian*, May 22. http://www.pressian.com/news/article.html?no=38841

Choi CL. 2020. "Subordinate Financialization and Financial Subsumption in South Korea." *Regional Studies* 54 (2): 209–18.

Choi HS. 2013. "Ahn Sparks Battle over Liberalism." *Korea Herald*, June 19. http://www.koreaherald.com/view.php?ud=20130619000817&mod=skb

Choi JJ. 1989. *Labor and the Authoritarian State: Labor Unions in South Korean Manufacturing Industries, 1961–1980*. Seoul: Korea University Press.

Choi JJ. 2009. "The Frailty of Liberalism and Its Political Consequences in Democratized Korea." Transcript of a paper delivered at Stanford University, May 15. Published in Korean in *Asia Yŏngu* (Asian Studies) 52 (3): 252–84.

Choi JJ. 2012a. *Democracy after Democratization: The Korean Experience*. Palo Alto: Walter H. Shorenstein Asia-Pacific Research Center, Stanford University.

Choi JJ. 2012b. "Democracy in Contemporary Korea: The Politics of Extreme Uncertainty." Transcript of lecture delivered at Shorenstein Asia-Pacific Research Center, Stanford University. October. http://aparc.fsi.stanford.edu/events/democracy_in_korea_the_politics_of_extreme_uncertainty/

Choi JJ. 2018. *Mun taet'ongnyŏng chewangjŏng anijiman, kujojŏkŭro chewang toel wihŏmt'e* [Moon is not an imperial president, but at risk of becoming one]. Interview. *Joongang Ilbo*, March 9. https://www.joongang.co.kr/article/print/22426148#home

Choi JJ. 2020. "Moon Blew His Chance, Says Scholar." *Joongang Daily*, January 6. https://koreajoongangdaily.joins.com/2020/01/06/people/Moon-blew-his-big-chance-says-scholar/3072297.html

Choi SW. 2022. "Democracy and South Korea's Lemon Presidency." *Asian Perspective* 46 (2): 311–41.

Choi YJ and Glassman J. 2018. "A Geopolitical Economy of Heavy Industrialization and Second Tier City Growth in South Korea: Evidence from the 'Four Core Plants Plan'." *Critical Sociology* 44 (3): 405–20.

Choi YR. 2014. "Modernization, Development and Underdevelopment: Reclamation of Korean Tidal Flats, 1950s–2000s." *Ocean & Coastal Management* 102: 426–36.

Choi YR. 2019. "Profitable Tidal Flats, Governable Fishing Communities: Assembling Tidal Flat Fisheries in Post-Crisis South Korea." *Political Geography* 72: 20–30.

Choo HY. 2021. "From Madwomen to Whistleblowers: MeToo in South Korea as an Institutional Critique." *Feminist Formations* 33 (3): 256–70.

References | 193

Chu YH. 2002. "Re-engineering the Developmental State in an Age of Globalization: Taiwan in Defiance of Neo-liberalism." *China Review* 2 (1): 29–59.

Chun HW. 2019. *Yŏsŏng chŏngnyŏn pijŏnggyujik taep'yonŭn wae kyŏngsanowie pulch'amhaenna* [Why the representatives of youth, women, and irregular workers did not participate in the ESLC's decision]. *Sisain*, March 27. https://www.sisain.co.kr /news/articleView.html?idxno=34178

Chun JJ. 2009. "Legal Liminality: The Gender and Labour Politics of Organising South Korea's Irregular Workforce." *Third World Quarterly* 30: 535–50.

Chun JJ. 2011. *Organizing at the Margins: The Symbolic Politics of Labor in South Korea and the United States*. Ithaca: Cornell University Press.

Chun S. 2003. *They Are Not Machines: Korean Women Workers and Their Fight for Democratic Trade Unions in the Seventies*. Aldershot: Ashgate.

Chung TI .2012. *Samsŏng mokchul t'ŭrŏjwiji anŭmyŏn pokchigukkado ŏpta* [If we do not hold Samsung accountable, we cannot have a welfare state]. *Pressian*, April 2. http:// www.pressian.com/news/article.html?no=67624

Chung UC. 1997. "A Critical Look at the Korean Economy." *Korea Journal* 37 (4): 15–24.

Chung UC. 1999. "East Asian Economic Crisis: What Is and What Ought to Be Done? The Case of Korea." *Institut für Europäische Wirtschaft Discussion Paper* 26. Bochum, Germany: Ruhr University.

Citizens Committee for Economic Justice. N.d. "Who We Are." http://ccej.or.kr/eng /who-we-are/about-us/ (accessed 12 May 2020).

Clarke S. 1991. *The State Debate*. London: Macmillan.

Clifford J. 1996. "Anthropology and/as Travel." *Etnofoor* (2): 5–15.

Constitution of the Republic of Korea. 1987. Available at http://korea.assembly.go.kr (accessed July 2022).

Crotty J and Lee K. 2009. "Was IMF-Imposed Economic Regime Change in Korea Justified? The Political Economy of IMF Intervention." *Review of Radical Political Economics* (41): 149–70.

Cumings B. 1999. "Webs with No Spiders, Spiders with No Webs: The Genealogy of the Developmental State." In *The Developmental State*, edited by Woo-Cumings M, 61–92. Ithaca: Cornell University Press.

De Ceuster K. 2010. "When History Is Made: History, Memory and the Politics of Remembrance in Contemporary Korea." *Korean Histories* 2 (1): 13–33.

Dong-a Ilbo. 2006. "Uri Economic Reforms Draw Skepticism." August 12. http://english .donga.com/srv/service.php3?biid=2006081227978&path_dir=20060812

Doucette J. 2013a. "The Korean Thermidor: On Political Space and Conservative Reactions." *Transactions of the Institute of British Geographers* 38 (2): 299–310.

Doucette J. 2013b. "Minjung Tactics in a Post-Minjung Era? The Survival of Self-Immolation and Traumatic Forms of Labour Protest in South Korea." In *New Forms and Expressions of Conflict in the Workplace*, edited by Gall G, 212–32. London: Palgrave Macmillan.

Doucette J. 2015. "Debating Economic Democracy in South Korea: The Costs of Commensurability." *Critical Asian Studies* 47 (3): 388–413.

Doucette J. 2016. "The Postdevelopmental State: Economic and Social Change since 1997." In *Routledge Handbook of Modern Korean History*, edited by Seth M, 343–56. New York: Routledge.

References

Doucette J. 2017. "The Occult of Personality: Korea's Candlelight Protests and the Impeachment of Park Geun-hye." *Journal of Asian Studies* 76 (4): 851–60.

Doucette J. 2018. "Flexible Exportism: Situating Financialization within the Korean Political Economy." *Marxism 21* 15: 248–82.

Doucette J. 2020a. "Anxieties of an Emerging Donor: The Korean Development Experience and the Politics of International Development Cooperation." *Environment and Planning C: Politics and Space* 38 (4): 656–73.

Doucette J. 2020b. "Political Will and Human Geography: Non-Representational, Post-Political, and Gramscian Geographies." *Progress in Human Geography* 44 (2): 315–32.

Doucette J and Hae L. 2022. "The Politics of Post-Developmentalist Expertise: Progressive Movements, Strategic Localism, and Urban Governance in Seoul." *Urban Geography* 43 (1): 134–52.

Doucette J and Kang S. 2018. "Legal Geographies of Labour and Postdemocracy: Reinforcing Non-Standard Work in South Korea." *Transactions of the Institute of British Geographers* 43 (2): 200–214.

Doucette J and Koo SW. 2016. "Pursuing Post-Democratization: The Resilience of Politics by Public Security in Contemporary South Korea." *Journal of Contemporary Asia* 46 (2): 198–221.

Doucette J and Lee SO. 2015. "Experimental Territoriality: Assembling the Kaesong Industrial Complex in North Korea." *Political Geography* 47: 53–63.

Doucette J and Muller AR. 2016. "Exporting the *Saemaul* Spirit: South Korea's Knowledge Sharing Program and the 'Rendering Technical' of Korean Development." *Geoforum* 75: 29–39.

Doucette J and Park BG. 2019. *Developmentalist Cities? Interrogating Urban Developmentalism in East Asia.* Leiden: Brill

Doucette J and Seo B. 2011. "Limits to Financialization? Locating Financialization within East Asian Exportist Economies." *Hitotsubashi University Invited Fellows Program (21) (Discussion Paper).* Tokyo: Hitotsubashi University.

Edigheji O, ed. 2010. *Constructing a Democratic Developmental State in South Africa: Potentials and Challenges.* Cape Town: HSRC Press.

Ekers M, Kipfer S, and Loftus A. 2020. "On Articulation, Translation, and Populism: Gillian Hart's Postcolonial Marxism." *Annals of the American Association of Geographers* 110 (5): 1577–93.

Ekers M and Loftus A. 2020. "On 'the Concrete': Labour, Difference and Method. *Antipode* 52 (1): 78–100.

Escobar A. 1995. *Encountering Development: The Making and Unmaking of the Third World.* Princeton: Princeton University Press.

Eun SM. 2010. "Non-Regular Workers in Korea: Labor Market and Industrial Relations." In *Non-Regular Workers and Changes in Industrial Relations in Korea (I)I: With a Focus on Korea, the U.S. and Japan,* edited by Eun SM, Oh HS, and Yoon JD. Seoul: Korea Labor Institute.

Evans P. 1995. *Embedded Autonomy: States and Industrial Transformation.* Princeton: Princeton University Press.

Evans P. 2014. "The Capability Enhancing Developmental State: Concepts and National Trajectories." In *The South Korean Development Experience: Beyond Aid,* edited by Kim EM and Kim HP, 83–110. London: Palgrave Macmillan.

Evans P and Rauch J. 1999. "Bureaucracy and Growth: A Cross-National Analysis of the

Effects of 'Weberian' State Structures on Economic Growth." *American Sociological Review* 64 (5): 748–65.

Evans P, Rueschemeyer D, and Skocpol T, eds. 1985. *Bringing the State Back In*. Cambridge: Cambridge University Press.

Farris S. 2013. *Max Weber's Theory of Personality: Individuation, Politics and Orientalism in the Sociology of Religion*. Leiden: Brill.

FKTU. 2020a. "FKTU Strongly Condemns Retrogressive Revision of Trade Union Law and Labor Standards Law." FKTU. http://fktu.or.kr/index.php?mid=activities&document_srl=35509&ckattempt=2

FKTU. 2020b. "We Are Strongly Opposed to the Government's Anti-Labour Bill." FKTU. http://fktu.or.kr/index.php?mid=activities&document_srl=35277&ckattempt=1

Friedman T. 2005. *The World Is Flat: A Brief History of the Twenty-First Century*. London: Macmillan.

Gallas A. 2016. *The Thatcherite Offensive: A Neo-Poulantzasian Analysis*. Leiden: Brill.

Gilman N. 2007. *Mandarins of the Future: Modernization Theory in Cold War America*. Baltimore: Johns Hopkins University Press.

Gilman N. 2018. "Modernization Theory Never Dies." *History of Political Economy* 50 (S1): 133–51.

Glassman J. 2018. *Drums of War, Drums of Development: The Formation of a Pacific Ruling Class and Industrial Transformation in East and Southeast Asia, 1945–1980*. Leiden: Brill.

Goswami M. 2020. "The Political Economy of the Nation Form." *Geografiska Annaler: Series B, Human Geography* 102 (3): 267–72.

Gottfried H. 2015. *The Reproductive Bargain: Deciphering the Enigma of Japanese Capitalism*. Leiden: Brill.

Gramsci A. 1971. *Selections from the Prison Notebooks*. Edited and translated by Hoare Q and Smith G. New York: International Publishers.

Gray K. 2009. *Korean Workers and Neoliberal Globalization*. London: Routledge.

Gray K. 2013. "The Political Cultures of South Korea." *New Left Review* (79): 85–101.

Gray K. 2014. *Labour and Development in East Asia: Social Forces and Passive Revolution*. London: Routledge.

Grubb D, Lee JK, and Tergeist P. 2007. "Addressing Labour Market Duality in Korea." *OECD Social, Employment and Migration Working Papers* 61. Paris: OECD.

Ha B and Lee S. 2013. "Dual Dimensions of Non-Regular Work and SMES in the Republic of Korea: Country Case Study on Labour Market Segmentation." *International Labour Office, Employment Sector Employment Working Paper No. 148*. Geneva: ILO.

Haggard S. 1990. *Pathways from the Periphery: The Politics of Growth in the Newly Industrializing Countries*. Ithaca: Cornell University Press.

Hall S. 1985. "Authoritarian Populism: A Reply to Jessop et al." *New Left Review* 151 (1): 115–23.

Hallett N. 2015. "From the Picket Line to the Courtroom: A Labor Organizing Privilege to Protect Workers." *NYU Review of Law & Social Change* 39: 475–524.

Hamlin K. 2001. "Scourge of the *Chaebol*." *Institutional Investor Magazine*, April 1. https://www.institutionalinvestor.com/article/2btfm6ll7mr13f68vzh1c/home/scourge-of-the-chaebol (accessed July 2022).

Han JJH. 2022. "Out of Place in Time: Queer Discontents and Sigisangjo." *Journal of Asian Studies* 81 (1): 119–29.

196 | References

Han SJ. 1974. "The Political Economy of Dependency." *Asian Survey* 14 (1): 43–51.

Hankook Ilbo. 2013a. *UPP RO chŏnch'e hoeŭi kirok, 1pu* [UPP RO meeting transcript in full, part 1.] September 2, A10–11.

Hankook Ilbo. 2013b. *UPP RO chŏnch'e hoeŭi kirok, 2pu* [UPP RO meeting transcript in full, part 2.] September 3, A10–11.

Hankyoreh. 2013. "Pres. Park Turns Back the Clock with Personnel Reshuffle." 6 August. https://english.hani.co.kr/arti/english_edition/english_editorials/598515.html

Harding S, ed. 2004. *The Feminist Standpoint Theory Reader: Intellectual and Political Controversies*. London: Routledge.

Harootunian H. 2002. *History's Disquiet: Modernity, Cultural Practice, and the Question of Everyday Life*. New York: Columbia University Press.

Hart G. 2018. "Relational Comparison Revisited: Marxist Postcolonial Geographies in Practice." *Progress in Human Geography* 42 (3): 371–94.

Hart G. 2020a. "Resurgent Nationalisms and Populist Politics in the Neoliberal Age." *Geografiska Annaler: Series B, Human Geography* 102 (3) 233–38.

Hart G. 2020b. "Why Did It Take So Long? Trump-Bannonism in a Global Conjunctural Frame." *Geografiska Annaler: Series B, Human Geography* 102 (3): 239–66.

Hart G. 2023. "Modalities of Conjunctural Analysis: 'Seeing the Present Differently' through Global Lenses." *Antipode*. https://doi.org/10.1111/anti.12975

Hart-Landsberg M. 1993. *The Rush to Development: Economic Change and Political Struggle in South Korea*. New York: Monthly Review Press.

Hart-Landsberg M. 2001. "Economic Crisis and Restructuring in South Korea: Beyond the Free Market-Statist Debate." *Critical Asian Studies* 33 (3): 403–30.

Henderson J, Hulme D, Jalilian H, and Phillips R. 2007. "Bureaucratic Effects: Weberian State Agencies and Poverty Reduction." *Sociology* 41 (3): 515–32.

Hinkle RC. 1994. *Developments in American Sociological Theory, 1915–1950*. Binghampton: SUNY Press.

Ho MS 2019. *Challenging Beijing's Mandate of Heaven: Taiwan's Sunflower Movement and Hong Kong's Umbrella Movement*. Philadelphia: Temple University Press.

Hofstadler R. 1964. "The Paranoid Style in American Politics." *Harper's Magazine*, November, 77–86.

Hong GB. 2011. *Bigŭp'orŭsŭ, pokchi kukkawa chamjŏngjŏk yut'op'ia* [Wigforss: Provisional Utopia and Welfare State]. Seoul: Chaeksesang.

Hur SW. 2013. "Expanding the Feminist Politics of Reproduction in the Context of the Developmental Hegemony of South Korea." *Asian Journal of Women's Studies* 19 (3): 116–48.

Hwang JT. 2016. "Escaping the Territorially Trapped East Asian Developmental State Thesis." *Professional Geographer* 68 (4): 554–60.

Hwang JT and Park BG. 2014. "A Study on the Multi-Scalar Processes of Gumi Industrial Complex Development, 1969–1973." *Journal of the Economic Geographical Society of Korea* 17:1–27.

Im HB. 2018. "Korea Tripartism in Retrospect." In *Korea's Quest for Economic Democratization: Globalization, Polarization and Contention*, edited by Kim YM, 89–118. London: Palgrave Macmillan.

International Labour Organization. 2000. "Report of the Committee of Freedom of Association (320th Report)." *ILO Official Bulletin* 83, ser. B, no. 1.

References | 197

International Labour Organization. 2004. "Report of the Committee on Freedom of Association (334th Report)." *ILO Official Bulletin* 88, ser. B, no. 1.

International Labour Organization. 2007. "Report of the Committee on Freedom of Association (346th Report)." *ILO Official Bulletin* 90, ser. B, no. 2.

Jang HS. 2001. "Corporate Governance and Economic Development: The Korean Experience." In *Democracy, Market Economics, and Development: An Asian Perspective*, edited by Iqbal F and You JI, 73–94. Washington, DC: World Bank.

Jang JH, Kim SH, and Han CH. 2010. "Advocacy Coalitions in Regulating Big Business in South Korea: Change of Chaebol's Holding Company Policy." *Korea Observer* 41 (2): 161–88.

Jang S. 2007. "The Unification of the Social Insurance Contribution Collection System in Korea." OECD Social, Employment and Migration Working Papers No. 55. Paris: OECD.

Jang SW. 2004. "Continuing Suicide among Laborers in Korea." *Labor History* 45: 271–97.

Jayasuriya K. 2005. "Beyond Institutional Fetishism: From the Developmental to the Regulatory State." *New Political Economy* 10 (3): 381–87.

Jayasuriya K. 2018. "Authoritarian Statism and the New Right in Asia's Conservative Democracies." *Journal of Contemporary Asia* 48 (4): 584–604.

Jeon JJH. 2019. *Vicious Circuits: Korea's IMF Cinema and the End of the American Century*. Stanford: Stanford University Press.

Jeong GH and Jeong SJ. 2020. "Trends of Marxian Ratios in South Korea, 1980–2014." *Journal of Contemporary Asia* 50 (2): 260–83.

Jeong SI. 2004. *Crisis and Restructuring in East Asia: The Case of the Korean Chaebol and the Automotive Industry*. New York: Palgrave Macmillan.

Jeong SI. 2006. "Leading Social Contribution by Forming Public Foundations." *Hankyoreh*, May 19. http://english.hani.co.kr/arti/english_edition/e_national/124864.html

Jeong SJ. 2007. "Trend of Marxian Ratios in Korea: 1970–2003." In *Marxist Perspectives on South Korea in the Global Economy*, edited by Hart-Landsberg M, Jeong SJ, and Westra R. Burlington, VT: Ashgate.

Jeong SJ. 2010. "Korean Left Debates on Alternatives to Neoliberalism." In *Economic Transitions to Neoliberalism in Middle-Income Countries: Policy Dilemmas, Economic Crises, Forms of Resistance*, edited by Saad-Filho A and Yalman G, 154–65. London: Routledge.

Jeong SJ. 2013. "Marx in South Korea." In *Marx for Today*, edited by Musto M, 221–27. New York: Routledge.

Jeong SJ and Shin JY. 1999. "Debates on the Economic Crisis within the Korean Left." *Rethinking Marxism* 11 (2): 85–97.

Jessop B. 2005. "Gramsci as a Spatial Theorist." *Critical Review of International Social and Political Philosophy* 8 (4): 421–37.

Jessop B. 2016. *The State: Past, Present, Future*. Cambridge: Polity.

Johnson C. 1982. *MITI and the Japanese Miracle: The Growth of Industrial Policy: 1925–1975*. Stanford: Stanford University Press.

Johnson C. 1999. "The Developmental State: Odyssey of a Concept." In *The Developmental State*, edited by Woo-Cumings M. Ithaca: Cornell University Press.

Jwa SH. 2017. *The Rise and Fall of Korea's Economic Development: Lessons for Developing and Developed Economies*. Cham, Switzerland: Palgrave Macmillan.

198 | References

Kaiwar V. 2014. *The Postcolonial Orient: The Politics of Difference and the Project of Provincialising Europe*. Leiden: Brill.

Kalberg S. 1980. "Max Weber's Types of Rationality: Cornerstones for the Analysis of Rationalization Processes in History." *American Journal of Sociology* 85 (5): 1145–79.

Kalinowski T. 2013. "Regulating International Finance and the Diversity of Capitalism." *Socio-Economic Review* 11 (3): 471–96.

Kalinowski T. 2015. "Crisis Management and the Diversity of Capitalism: Fiscal Stimulus Packages and the East Asian Neo-Developmental State." *Economy and Society* 44 (2): 244–70.

Kan HW. 2021. "Anti-Corruption Agency Summons Seoul Education Chief in Power Abuse Probe." *Korea Herald*, July 27. http://koreaherald.com/view.php?ud=2021072 7000805

Kang D. 2002. *Crony Capitalism: Corruption and Development in South Korea and the Philippines*. Cambridge: Cambridge University Press.

Kang D, Leheny D, and Cha V. 2013. "Dialogue about Elections in Japan and Korea." *Journal of Asian Studies* 72 (2): 233–50.

Kang HK. 2011. "Park Geun-hye Starts 'Anything but Lee' Drive: GNP to Overhaul President's Major Policies." *Korea Times*, December 28. http://www.koreatimes.co.kr /www/news/nation/2011/12/116_101749.html

Kang JI. 2017. *Contemporary Korean Political Thought and Park Chung-hee*. Lanham, MD: Rowman & Littlefield.

Kang JK. 2013. "Torture's Scars Take Time and Therapy to Heal." *Joongang Daily*, November 11. http://koreajoongangdaily.joins.com/news/article/article.aspx?aid=2980239

Kang JM. 2008. "The Death of Politics." *Hankyoreh*, June 30. https://english.hani.co.kr/arti /english_edition/english_editorials/296158.html (accessed January 2018).

Kayatekin S. 2009. "Between Political Economy and Postcolonial Theory: First Encounters." *Cambridge Journal of Economics* 33: 1113–18.

KCTU. 2005. *KCTU Report on Recent Situation of Labour Laws and Industrial Relations, For the Meeting with OECD Mission*. http://kctu.org/index.php?mid=documents&listt itle=gallery&sort_index=readed_count&listStyle=gallery&page=2&document_srl=1 2600

Kelsall T, Schulz N, Ferguson W, vom Hau M, Hickey S, and Levy B. 2022. *Political Settlements and Development: Theory, Evidence, Implications*. Oxford: Oxford University Press.

Kim A. 2011. "Left Out: People's Solidarity for Social Progress and the Evolution of Minjung after Authoritarianism." In *South Korean Social Movements: From Democracy to Civil Society*, edited by Shin G and Chang P, 245–69. London: Routledge.

Kim CY. 2009. *87nyŏnch'ejeron: Minjuhwa ihu han'guksahoeŭi inshikkwa sae chŏnmang* [The 1987 system thesis: Consciousness and the new prospects of South Korean society after democratization]. Seoul: Changbi.

Kim DC. 2006. "Growth and Crisis of the Korean Citizens' Movement." *Korea Journal* 46 (2): 99–128.

Kim DC. 2010. "The Truth and Reconciliation Commission of Korea: Uncovering the Hidden Korean War." *Asia-Pacific Journal*, September 5. https://apjjf.org/site/show _list/id/258/start/70

Kim EM. 1997. *Big Business, Strong State: Collusion and Conflict in South Korean Development, 1960–1990*. Albany: SUNY Press.

Kim H. 2017. "'Spoon Theory' and the Fall of a Populist Princess in Seoul." *Journal of Asian Studies* 76 (4): 839–49.

Kim HA. 2013. "Industrial Warriors: South Korea's First Generation of Industrial Workers in Post-Developmental Korea." *Asian Studies Review* 37 (4): 577–95.

Kim JB. 2013. "Chaebol Policy for Suppression of Economic Power Concentration." In *Republic of Korea Knowledge Sharing Program*. Seoul: Ministry of Strategy and Finance.

Kim JC. 2012. "Korea's Anti-Neoliberal Critic Chang Ha-Joon Defends Chaebol." *Hankyoreh*, September 20. http://english.hani.co.kr/arti/english_edition/e_business/552 592.html

Kim JH. 2022. *Kimyusŏn sodŭkchudo sŏngjangt'ŭgwi wiwŏnjang int'ŏbyu* [Interview with Kim Yu-seon, chairman of the Special Committee on Income-Led Growth]. *Kyunghyang Shinmun*. April 3. https://www.khan.co.kr/politics/politics-general/article/20 2204031011001

Kim JI. 2012. *Chigŭm wae kyŏngjeminjuhwain'ga: Han'guk kyŏngjeŭi miraerŭl wihayŏ* [Why economic democracy now? For the future of the Korean economy]. Seoul: Donghwach'ulpansa.

Kim JJ. 2017. *Seoul Labour Policy: Restoring Labour to Its Proper Place in Society*. Seoul: Seoul Institute.

Kim JT. 2011. "The Discourse of Seonjinguk: South Korea's Modern Identities and Worldviews." PhD diss., University of Illinois at Urbana Champaign.

Kim JT. 2012. "The West and East Asian National Identities: A Comparison of Korean Seongjinguk, Japanese Nihonjinron, and Chinese New Nationalism." In *Globalization and Development in East Asia*, edited by Pieterse J and Kim JT, 80–97. New York: Routledge.

Kim KM. 2020. *The Korean Developmental State*. Berlin: Springer.

Kim KS. 2021. *Yangdae noch'ong, inyŏmdo nosŏndo ŏpsŭni kwŏnwiga ttŏrŏjinŭn kŏt* [The two major trade unions have no ideology or line, so their authority is falling]. *Hankyoreh*, October 15. https://www.hani.co.kr/arti/society/labor/1015290.html

Kim KW. 2004. "Chaebol Restructuring and Family Business in Korea." Unpublished working paper, Department of Economics, Korea National Open University (Seoul).

Kim N. 2018. "The Color of Dissent and a Vital Politics of Fragility in South Korea." *Journal of Asian Studies* 77 (4): 971–90.

Kim PH and Jung W. 2018. "Ownership and Planning Capacity in the Asian-Style Development Cooperation: South Korean Knowledge Sharing Program to Vietnam." *Korea Observer* 49 (2): 349–68.

Kim SJ. 2002. "Financial Sector Reform in Korea: A Dilemma between 'Bank-Based' and 'Market-Based' Systems." *Korea Journal* 42 (1): 42–73.

Kim SJ. 2006. "Pitting Foreign Capital against Domestic Capital Is Undesirable." *Korea Focus*, May 3. Via http://www.koreafocus.or.kr (accessed July 2018, no longer available, copy in author's possession).

Kim SJ. 2012a. *Chonghoeng mujin han'gung kyŏngje: Chaebŏl kwa mop'ia ŭi hamjŏng esŏ t'alch'ul hara* [The Korean economy inside out: Escaping the trap of the chaebol and MOF-ia]. Seoul: Ohmybooks.

Kim SJ. 2012b. *Kyŏngje minjuhwanŭn 'chaebŏlgaehyŏk' 'yanggŭk'wa haesoota* [Economic democratization is 'chaebol reform' and 'polarization resolving']. *Solidarity for Economic Reform*, September 18. http://www.ser.or.kr/bbs/board.php?bo_table=B31& wr_id=19547&page=14&ckattempt=1

200 | References

Kim SK. 1997. *Class Struggle or Family Struggle? The Lives of Women Factory Workers in South Korea.* Cambridge: Cambridge University Press.

Kim SH and Park SH. 2007. "A Reappraisal of the Park Chung-hee Regime." In *Marxist Perspectives on South Korea in the Global Economy,* edited by Hart-Landsberg M, Jeong SJ, and Westra R, 183–201. Burlington, VT: Ashgate.

Kim ST. 2018. *Changhajun: Han'gung kyŏngjenŭn chigŭm kukka pisangsat'aeda* [Ha-joon Chang: The Korean economy is now in a state of national emergency]. *Joongang Ilbo,* August 9. https://www.joongang.co.kr/article/23192759#home

Kim W. 2011. "Changes in the 1980s Nationalist *Minjung* Academic Communities and the Alternative Academic Communities." *Korea Journal* 51 (3): 140–68.

Kim Y and Baek B. 2021. "Samsung to Invest $205 Bil. in Bio, Foundry, Memory Businesses." *Korea Times,* August 24. https://www.koreatimes.co.kr/www/tech/2023/08/129_314428.html

Kim YC. 1990. "Politics of Emergency Powers: The Case of Korea." In *Coping with Crises: How Governments Deal with Emergencies,* edited by Leng SC, 129–71. Lanham, MD: University Press of America.

Kim YM. 2022. "The 2022 Election in South Korea: The Politics of Resentment and Revenge Confirms Older Trends and Cleavages and Reveals New Ones." *Georgetown Journal of Asian Affairs* 8 (1):14–22.

Kim YS. 2021. "Korea Fastest in Growth of Household Debt in OECD." *Korea Herald,* November 1. http://www.koreaherald.com/view.php?ud=20211101000269

Kim YT. 1999. "Neoliberalism and the Decline of the Developmental State." *Journal of Contemporary Asia* 29 (4): 441–61.

Kipfer S. 2012. "City, Country, Hegemony: Antonio Gramsci's Spatial Historicism." In *Gramsci: Space, Nature, Politics,* edited by Ekers M, Hart G, Kipfer S, and Loftus A, 83–103. Chichester, UK: Wiley-Blackwell.

Kleibert J. 2018. "Exclusive Development(s): Special Economic Zones and Enclave Urbanism in the Philippines." *Critical Sociology* 44 (3): 471–85.

Ko SH. 2011. "Is 'Progressive Liberalism' in Korea Progressive Enough? An Essay on Social Democracy as a Progressive Alternative." *Korea Observer* 42 (3): 345–75.

Kong TY. 2004. "Neo-Liberalization and Incorporation in Advanced Newly Industrialized Countries: A View from Korea." *Political Studies* 52:19–42.

Korea Herald. 15 July 2011. "Chaebol-Driven Economy." http://www.koreaherald.com/view.php?ud=20110715000554

Korea Labor Institute. 2022. "KLI Statistical Archive." https://www.kli.re.kr

Korea Times. 2003. "Opposition Threatens to Impeach President." June 13.

Krippner G, Granovetter M, Block F, Biggart N, Beamish T, Hsing Y, Hart G, Arrighi G, Mendell M, Hall J, Burawoy M, Vogel S, and O'Riain S. 2004. "Polanyi Symposium: A Conversation on Embeddedness." *Socio-Economic Review* 2:109–35.

Krueger A. 1987. "The Importance of Economic Policy in Development: Contrasts between Korea and Turkey." *NBER Working Paper* Series No. 2195. Cambridge, MA: National Bureau of Economic Research.

Kuruvilla S and Liu M. 2010. "Tripartism and Economic Reforms in Singapore and the Republic of Korea." In *Blunting Neoliberalism,* edited by Fraile L, 85–127. London: Palgrave Macmillan.

Kwak JS. 2012a. *Kyŏngje minjuhwa chŏndosat' Kimsangjo kyosu* [Professor Kim Sang-jo: Evangelist of economic democratization]. *Hankyoreh,* September 9. http://www.hani.co.kr/arti/economy/economy_general/550845.html

References | 201

Kwak JS. 2012b. "The Origins and Need for Economic Democracy." *Hankyoreh*, October 4. http://www.hani.co.kr/arti/english_edition/e_business/554271.html

Kwak JS. 2014. "Samsung Special Law Being Debated by the Company and Civic Groups." *Hankyoreh*, August 4. http://www.hani.co.kr/arti/english_edition/e_business/649719.html

Kwak JS. 2019. "Progressive Scholars Denounce Moon's Recent Meeting with Samsung Electronics Vice Chairman." *Hankyoreh*, May 3. http://english.hani.co.kr/arti/PRINT/892565.html

Kwon D. 2015. "Damage Claims and Provisional Seizure as a Means of Union Busting." *International Union Rights* 22 (1): 8–9.

Kwon HJ. 2006. "Democracy and the Politics of Social Welfare: A Comparative Analysis of Welfare Systems in East Asia." In *The East Asian Welfare Model: Welfare Orientalism and the State*, edited by Goodman R, Kwon HJ, and White G, 27–74. London: Routledge.

Lakatos I. 1970. "Falsification and the Methodology of Scientific Research Programmes." In *Criticism and the Growth of Knowledge*, edited by Lakatos I and Musgrave A, 91–196. Cambridge: Cambridge University Press.

Lee B. 2007. "Militant Unionism in Korea." In *Strikes around the World: 1968–2005*, edited by Velden S, 155–72. Amsterdam: Aksant.

Lee BC. 2006. "The Political Economy of Developmental Dictatorship." In *Developmental Dictatorship: The Shaping of Modernity in the Republic of Korea*, edited by Lee BC. Paramus, NJ: Homa and Sekey Books.

Lee BC. 2012a. *Chaebŏlgaehyŏgi nalgŭn hwadu? Kŭdŭrŭn k'waedonanmahaji mot'aetta* [Chaebol reform is an old topic? They failed to cut the Gordian knot]. *Pressian*, May 2. http://www.pressian.com/news/article.html?no=38700

Lee BC. 2012b. *Chaebŏlgwa t'ahyŏp'agi chŏne him itke puditch'yŏra* [Before compromising with the chaebol, stand up to them firmly]. *Pressian*, July 3. http://www.pressian.com/news/article.html?no=106606

Lee BC. 2019. *Munjaein chŏngbu kyŏngjejŏngch'aeng p'yŏngga t'oronhoe kihoek* [Debating Moon Jae-in's economic policy]. *Kyunghyang Shinmun*, April 20. http://news.khan.co.kr/kh_news/khan_art_view.html?art_id=201904200600005#csidx810929225b583c68946d19fa71a7af2

Lee BC and Jeong JH. 2014. *Samsŏngjŏnjaŭi ch'ukchŏkpangshing punsŏksegyehwa shidae han'gung illyu kiŏbŭi pitkwa kŭrimja* [Analysis of the accumulation mode of Samsung Electronics: The positive and negative sides of a super-chaebol firm in a globalizing world]. *Donghyang-gwa Chŏnmang* [Trends and Prospects] 92:129–73.

Lee BC and Yoon SY. 1988. *Chŏnhu Hangookkyoungjehakkyŭi Yŏngudonghyang* [Trends and tasks of postwar studies in economics in Korea]. Seoul: Yŏksa Bipyŏngsa.

Lee CK. 2019. *Take Back Our Future: An Eventful Sociology of the Hong Kong Umbrella Movement*. Ithaca: Cornell University Press.

Lee CS. 2016. *When Solidarity Works: Labor-Civic Networks and Welfare States in the Market Reform Era*. Cambridge: Cambridge University Press.

Lee CS and Yoo HG. 2023. "Unions in Society, Unions in the State: New Forms of Irregular Workers' Movements beyond the Factory in South Korea." *Economic and Industrial Democracy* 44 (2): 432–53.

Lee DK. 2018. *Cho Kuk: Minjunoch'ongmanŭi chŏngbu anya, hamkke panbo naeditcha* [Cho Kuk: It is not the KCTU's government: Let's take a half-step together]. *MBC*

202 | References

News, November 24. https://imnews.imbc.com/replay/2018/nwdesk/article/49565 83_30181.html

Lee GS. 2006. *Chon sŭt'yuŏt'ŭ mirŭi jinbojŏk chayujuŭi* [John Stuart Mill's progressive liberalism]. Seoul: Kiparang.

Lee GS. 2010. *Chinbojŏk chayujuŭiwa han'guk chabonjuŭi* [Progressive liberalism and Korean capitalism]. *Pressian*, June 26. https://www.pressian.com/pages/articles /60867

Lee GS, Choi JJ, Ko SH, You JI, and Choi TW. 2011. *Chayujuŭinŭn chinbojŏgil su innŭn'ga?* [Can liberalism be progressive?] Seoul: Politeia.

Lee HY. 1991. "South Korea in 1991: Unprecedented Opportunity, Increasing Challenge." *Asian Survey* 32 (1): 64–73.

Lee IH. 2008. "Lifting Our Politics to a Higher Level." *Dong-a Ilbo*, January 15.

Lee JH. 2004. "Taking Gender Seriously: Feminization of Nonstandard Work in Korea and Japan." *Asian Journal of Women's Studies* 10 (1): 25–48.

Lee JH. 2017. "More Protection, Still Gendered: The Effects of Non-Standard Employment Protection Acts on South Korean Women Workers." *Journal of Contemporary Asia* 47 (1): 46–65.

Lee JH. 2019. "Promises and Reality of Labor Reform in South Korea." *Cadernos do CEAS: Revista Crítica de Humanidades* 248: 766–87.

Lee JS. 2010. "Is Korea an Advanced Country?" *Korea Focus*, February 12. Original article available at https://www.chosun.com/site/data/html_dir/2010/02/18/201002180 1700.html

Lee JT and Jeong SI. 2014. *Samsunge 'Che-3-uihim'ul T'uamhaja* [Let's place a third power against Samsung]. *Sisa-in*, September 2. Accessed July 2022. https://www.sisa in.co.kr/news/articleView.html?idxno=21125

Lee JW. 2007. "Moving Forward in the Wrong Direction." *Hankyoreh*, July 2. http://engl ish.hani.co.kr/arti/english_edition/e_editorial/219678.html

Lee JW. 2013. "The In-House Contracting Paradox: Flexibility, Control, and Tension." *World Development* 45:161–74.

Lee N. 2007. *The Making of Minjung: Democracy and the Politics of Representation in South Korea*. Ithaca: Cornell University Press.

Lee N. 2011. "From Minjung to Simin: The Discursive Shift in Korean Social Movements." In *South Korean Social Movements*, edited by Shin G and Chang P, 41–58. London: Routledge.

Lee N. 2019. "Social Memories of the 1980s: Unpacking the Regime of Discontinuity." In *Revisiting Minjung: New Perspectives on the Cultural History of 1980s South Korea*, edited by Park S, 17–45. Ann Arbor: University of Michigan Press.

Lee N. 2022. *Memory Construction and the Politics of Time in Neoliberal South Korea*. Durham: Duke University Press.

Lee SE. 2012. "Chang Ha-jun: 'Chaebolhaej'aega Kyeongjaeminjuwha? Sunjinhan Saeng-gak'" ["Chang Ha-joon: 'Dismantling Chaebol Is Economic Democratization? It's Naive to Think So.'"] *Joongang Ilbo*, 23 December. https://www.joongang.co.kr/artic le/10248267#home

Lee SSY and Kim Y. 2020. "Female Outsiders in South Korea's Dual Labour Market: Challenges of Equal Pay for Work of Equal Value." *Journal of Industrial Relations* 62 (4): 651–78.

References | 203

Lee TH. 2012. "Liberal Candidate to Be Finalized on November 22." *Hankyoreh*, November 22. http://english.hani.co.kr/arti/english_edition/e_national/561827.html

Lee TK. 2018. *Kidŭkkwŏnŭi nollie p'ohoektanghan minjujuŭi* [Democracy captured by the logic of vested interests]. *Newsmin*, November 26. https://www.newsmin.co.kr/news/35315/?ckattempt=2

Lee Y. 2005. "Law, Politics, and Impeachment: The Impeachment of Roh Moo-Hyun from a Comparative Constitutional Perspective." *American Journal of Comparative Law* 53 (2): 403–32.

Lee Y. 2015. "Sky Protest: New Forms of Labour Resistance in Neo-Liberal Korea." *Journal of Contemporary Asia* 45 (3): 443–64.

Lee Y. 2021. "Neo-Liberal Methods of Labour Repression: Privatised Violence and Dispossessive Litigation in Korea." *Journal of Contemporary Asia* 51 (1): 20–37.

Lee Y. 2022. "Between the Streets and the Assembly." In *Between the Streets and the Assembly: Social Movements, Political Parties, and Democracy in Korea*, edited by Lee Y. Honolulu: University of Hawaii Press.

Leftwich A. 1995. "Bringing Politics Back In: Towards a Model of the Developmental State." *Journal of Development Studies* 31 (3): 400–427.

Levine A. 2016. *South Korean Civil Movement Organisations: Hope, Crisis, and Pragmatism in Democratic Transition*. Manchester: Manchester University Press.

Lew SC. 2013. *The Korean Economic Development Path: Confucian Tradition, Affective Network*. New York: Palgrave Macmillan.

Liguori G. 2015. *Gramsci's Pathways*. Leiden: Brill.

Lim KF. 2019. *On Shifting Foundations: State Rescaling, Policy Experimentation, and Economic Restructuring in Post-1949 China*. New York: John Wiley & Sons.

Lipset SM. 1959. "Some Social Requisites of Democracy: Economic Development and Political Legitimacy." *American Political Science Review* 53 (1) (March): 69–105.

Marx K. 1982. *Capital: Volume 1*. London: Penguin Books.

McCormack G. 2011. "The Park Chung Hee Era and the Genesis of Trans-Border Civil Society in East Asia." In *Reassessing the Park Chung Hee Era, 1961–1979: Development, Political Thought, Democracy, and Cultural Influence*, edited by Kim HA and Sorensen C. Seattle: University of Washington Press.

McCurry J. 2017. "South Korea Spy Agency Admits Trying to Rig 2012 Presidential Election." *The Guardian*, August 4. https://www.theguardian.com/world/2017/aug/04/south-koreas-spy-agency-admits-trying-rig-election-national-intelligence-service-2012

Medley J. 2000. "The East Asian Economic Crisis: Surging US Imperialism?" *Review of Radical Political Economics* 32 (3): 379–87.

Metzler M. 2013. *Capital as Will and Imagination*. Ithaca: Cornell University Press.

Meulbroek C and Akhter M. 2019. "The Prose of Passive Revolution: Mobile Experts, Economic Planning and the Developmental State in Singapore." *Environment and Planning A: Economy and Space* 51 (6): 1242–56.

Mikuni A and Murphy R. 2003. *Japan's Policy Trap: Dollars, Deflation, and the Crisis of Japanese Finance*. Washington, DC: Brookings Institution Press.

Miller J. 2021. "Neoconservatives and Neo-Confucians: East Asian Growth and the Celebration of Tradition." *Modern Intellectual History* 18 (3): 806–32.

Miller O. 2010. "The Idea of Stagnation in Korean Historiography: From Fukoda Tokuzo to the New Right." *Korean Histories* 2 (1): 3–12.

204 | References

Mitchell T. 1999. "Society, Economy, and the State Effect." In *State/Culture: State Formation after the Cultural Turn*, edited by Steinmetz G. Ithaca: Cornell University Press.

Mkandawire T. 2001. "Thinking about Developmental States in Africa." *Cambridge Journal of Economics* 25 (3): 289–314.

Mobrand E. 2019. *Top-Down Democracy in South Korea*. Seattle: University of Washington Press.

Moon JI. 2017a. "Remarks by President Moon Jae-in of the Republic of Korea at the 2017 Atlantic Council Global Citizen Awards Dinner." Atlantic Council. https://www.atlanticcouncil.org/commentary/transcript/remarks-by-president-moon-jae-in-of-the-republic-of-korea-at-the-2017-atlantic-council-global-citizen-awards/

Moon JI. 2017b. "Inaugural Address by President Moon Jae-in." Ministry of Foreign Affairs Available online at https://overseas.mofa.go.kr/ir-en/brd/m_11371/view.do?seq=759666&srchFr=&amp%3BsrchTo=&amp%3BsrchWord=&amp%3BsrchTp=&amp%3Bmulti_itm_seq=0&amp%3Bitm_seq_1=0&amp%3Bitm_seq_2=0&amp%3Bcompany_cd=&amp%3Bcompany_nm=&page=1

Moon S. 2005. *Militarized Modernity and Gendered Citizenship in South Korea*. Durham: Duke University Press.

Moon S. 2009. "The Cultural Politics of Remembering Park Chung Hee." *Asia-Pacific Journal* 7 (19). http://apjjf.org/-Seungsook-Moon/3140/article.html

Morton AD. 2007. *Unravelling Gramsci: Hegemony and Passive Revolution in the Global Political Economy*. London: Pluto Press.

Mosler H. 2023. "Out of Proportion: The 2019 Electoral Reform and the State of Representative Democracy in South Korea." In *Politics, International Relations and Diplomacy on the Korean Peninsula*, edited by Lim S, 1–30. London: Routledge.

Mouffe C. 2000. *The Democratic Paradox*. London: Verso.

Munck G and Snyder R. 2007. *Passion, Craft, and Method in Comparative Politics*. Baltimore: Johns Hopkins University Press.

Nam CH. 1995. "The Role of Trade and Exchange Rate Policy in Korea's Growth." In *Growth Theories in Light of the East Asian Experience*, edited by Ito T and Krueger AO, 153–79. Chicago: University of Chicago Press.

Nam H. 2021. *Women in the Sky: Gender and Labor in the Making of Modern Korea*. Ithaca: Cornell University Press.

National Human Rights Commission of Korea. 2015. "Jaenguihaeng-e taehan Sonhaebaesang Gamapsryu silt'ae p'ak mit Gaesonbangan Malyeon-eul wihan T'oronhui" [*Forum on Damage Claims and Provisional Seizures and for Improvements to Industrial Action Disputes*]. Accessed June 2018. https://www.humanrights.go.kr/base/board/read?boardManagementNo=17&boardNo=610385&menuLevel=3&menuNo=115

Noh H. 2016. "Temp Agencies Abuse the Law While Workers Suffer." *Hankyoreh*, March 20. http://english.hani.co.kr/arti/english_edition/e_national/735820.html

Oh CM. 2013. "Economic Democratization in Retreat." *Kyunghyang Shinmun*, July 29. http://english.khan.co.kr/khan_art_view.html?artid=201307291442287&code=710100

Oh JKC. 1976. "South Korea 1975: A Permanent Emergency." *Asian Survey* 16 (1): 72–81.

Paik NC. 2011. "How to Think about the Park Chung Hee Era." In *Reassessing the Park Chung Hee Era, 1961–1979: Development, Political Thought, Democracy, and Cultural Influence*, edited by Kim HA and Sorenson CW. Seattle: University of Washington Press.

Paik NC. 2013. "South Korean Democracy and Korea's Division System." *Inter-Asia Cultural Studies* 14 (1): 156–69.

Pan K. 2019. *Mun chŏngbu chaebŏlgaehyŏkŭn F Chaebŏl ppajin kŏmch'algaehyŏkŭn pantchoktchari* [Interview with Park Sang-in: Moon's chaebol reform is an F, and prosecution reform without the chaebol is half-price]. *Kyunghyang Shinmun*, October 6. https://www.khan.co.kr/politics/politics-general/article/201910060917011

Park A. 2018. "The Parallax Visions of Economic Democracy in South Korea: A Critique." In *Korea's Quest for Economic Democratization: Globalization, Polarization and Contention*, edited by Kim Y, 171–208. London: Palgrave Macmillan.

Park A. 2022. "A Recycling of the Past or the Pathway to the New? Framing the South Korean Candlelight Protest Movement." *Journal of Asian Studies* 81 (1): 101–5.

Park BG. 2005. "Spatially Selective Liberalization and Graduated Sovereignty: Politics of Neo-Liberalism and 'Special Economic Zones' in South Korea." *Political Geography* 24 (7): 850–73.

Park BG. 2012. "Social Movements and the Geographies of Economic Activities in South Korea." In *Wiley-Blackwell Companion to Economic Geography*, edited by Jamie Peck, Eric Sheppard, and Trevor Barnes, 486–500. London: Wiley-Blackwell.

Park BG and Choi YJ. 2014. "Relations between the State and the Local in the Construction of Masan Exporting Processing Zone." *Journal of the Korean Geographical Society* 49: 113–38.

Park BG, Hill RC, and Saito A, eds. 2011. *Locating Neoliberalism in East Asia: Neoliberalizing Spaces in Developmental States*. Hoboken, NJ: John Wiley & Sons.

Park CG. 1991. "Dead-End Democracy: Who Can Lead It in Korea?" *Korea Times*, August 25.

Park CJ. 2014. "The Transformation of Debt-Economy in South Korea: Focusing on the State–Industry–Finance Relationship." PhD diss., Sociology, Seoul National University.

Park GS and Kim KP. 2008. "Financial Crisis and the Minority Shareholders' Movement in Korea: The Unfolding and Social Consequences of the Movement." *Korean Journal of Sociology* 42 (8): 59–76.

Park HC and Cho HY, eds. 1989–92. *Hanguk Sahoe Kuseong Nonchaeng* [The Korean social formation debates]. Vols. 1–4. Seoul: Hanul Publishing.

Park, HJ. 2013. *Chaebŏl, han'gukŭl chibaehanŭn ch'ogukchŏng chabon* [The Korean chaebol as dominant transnational capital]. Seoul: Chaeksaesang.

Park HJ and Doucette J. 2016. "Financialization or Capitalization? Debating Capitalist Power in South Korea in the Context of Neoliberal Globalization." *Capital and Class* 40 (3): 533–54.

Park HO. 2015. *The Capitalist Unconscious: From Korean Unification to Transnational Korea*. New York: Columbia University Press.

Park HO. 2022. "The Politics of Time: The Sewŏl Ferry Disaster and the Disaster of Democracy." *Journal of Asian Studies* 81 (1): 131–44.

Park HS. 2017. "Democratic Transition and Economic Democracy in South Korea." *Journal of Contemporary Korean Studies* 4 (2): 61–91.

Park JH. 2019. "No. of Irregular Workers Hits Record 7.48 Million." *Korea Times*, October 29. https://www.koreatimes.co.kr/www/biz/2019/10/488_277892.html

Park KY and Lee JH. 2018. "Labor Community in Fierce Opposition to Expansion of Unit Periods in Flexible Working Hour System." *Hankyoreh*, November 21. http://english.hani.co.kr/arti/english_edition/e_national/871183.html

206 | References

Park M. 2008. *Democracy and Social Change: A History of South Korean Student Movements, 1980–2000*. Bern: Peter Lang.

Park SH and Ko JA. 2020. "Moon Blew His Big Chance, Says Scholar" [interview with Choi Jang-jip]. *Joongang Daily*, January 6. https://koreajoongangdaily.joins.com/ne ws/article/Article.aspx?aid=3072297

Park SH, Shin HB, and Kang HS. 2020. *Exporting Urban Korea? Reconsidering the Korean Urban Development Experience*. London: Routledge.

Park SI. 2019. *Kŏmch'al kaehyŏng myŏngbun talsŏnghan choguk, sat'oero chŏngguk haebŏm ch'ajaya* [Cho Kuk has achieved the cause of prosecution reform, but must find a solution to the political situation through resignation: Park Sang-in interview]. *Sisa Journal*, October 14. https://www.sisajournal.com/news/articleView.html?idxno=191420

Park, SI. 2021. "Economic Power: Chaebol Reforms Are Crucial for South Korea's Future." *East Asia Forum Quarterly* 13 (1): 21–25.

Park SJ. 2013. "Developmental State in Korea (60–70ties) Revisited: Institution-Building for the Making of 'Coordinated Market.'" *Ordnungspolitische Diskurse: Discourses in Social Market Economy*, no. 2013-02.

Park SJ. 2016. "The Critiques of Liberalism in Korea and the New Liberalism." *Trans-Humanities Journal* 9 (1): 5–28.

Park SY and Cho SE. 2021a. *Mun chŏngbu 4nyŏn, sahoet'pkyŏngje kaehyŏng wae shilp'aehaenna "kaehyŏkp'ullong kuch'ukshilp'ae, 't'ŭkchŏng chŏngp'a' insa"* [Why social and economic reforms failed in the four years of the Moon government: "Failure to build a reform bloc, 'partisan' appointments." Interview with Lee Byeon-cheon, Cho Don-mun, and Jeon Kang-su]. *Pressian*, April 9. https://www.pressian.com/pages/ar ticles/2021040817271997577

Park SY and Cho SE. 2021b. *K'o ap'e tagaon 20tae taesŏn, tashi ch'otpurŭn muŏsŭl murŏya halkka?* [The 20th presidential election is approaching, what should the candlelight ask for again? Interview with Lee Byeon-cheon, Cho Don-mun, and Jeon Kang-su]. *Pressian*, April 10. https://www.pressian.com/pages/articles/2021040817311859158

Park YC. 2006. *Economic Liberalization and Integration in East Asia: A Post-Crisis Paradigm*. Oxford: Oxford University Press.

Peck J. 2023. *Variegated Economies*. Oxford: Oxford University Press.

Peck J and Theodore N. 2007. "Variegated Capitalism." *Progress in Human Geography* 31 (6): 731–72.

Peck J and Theodore N. 2012. "Follow the Policy: A Distended Case Approach." *Environment and Planning A* 44 (1): 21–30.

Pels D. 2004. "Strange Standpoints, or How to Define the Situation for Situated Knowledge." In *The Feminist Standpoint Theory Reader: Intellectual and Political Controversies*, edited by Harding SG, 273–90. New York: Routledge.

Pirie I. 2018. "Korea and Taiwan: The Crisis of Investment-Led Growth and the End of the Developmental State." *Journal of Contemporary Asia* 48 (1): 133–58.

Rehmann J. 2013. *Max Weber: Modernisation as Passive Revolution. A Gramscian Analysis*. Leiden: Brill.

Republic of Korea. 2009. *Criminal Act*. http://www.moleg.go.kr/FileDownload.mo?flSe q=31320

Rho HK. 2004. "From Civil Society Organization to Shareholder Activist: The Case of the Korean PSPD." *Brunel Research in Enterprise, Innovation, Sustainability, and Ethics Working Paper*, no. 15. Uxbridge, UK: Brunel University.

Rhyu SY. 2018. "Moon Jae-in and the Politics of Reform in South Korea." *Global Asia* 13 (3): 26–32.

Roh HC. 2007. *Nohaech'anŭi che 7 konghwagung kŏn'gugundong sŏnp'o* [Roh Hae chan's proposal for a movement to build the 7th Republic]. Roh Hae Chan Archive. https://www.archivecenter.net/hcroh/archive/srch/ArchiveNewSrchView.do?i_id=51606

Roh KC. 2002. "Historical Characteristics of Korea's Social Democracy." *International Journal of Korean History* 3 (December): 295–319.

Roland A and Hwang HR. 2010. "Time Running Out on South Korea's Truth and Reconciliation Commission." *Stars and Stripes*, January 19. http://www.stripes.com/news/time-running-out-on-south-korea-s-truth-and-reconciliation-commission-1.98156

Rose G. 1981. *Hegel contra Sociology.* London: Athlone.

Ryu M. 2019. "Ratification of C87 and C98: A Means of Regression?" *International Union Rights* 26 (3): 8–10.

Ryu Y, ed. 2018. *Cultures of Yusin: South Korea in the 1970s.* Ann Arbor: University of Michigan Press.

Ryu Y. 2016. *Writers of the Winter Republic: Literature and Resistance in Park Chung Hee's Korea.* Honolulu: University of Hawai'i Press.

Salzman J. 2000. "Labor Rights, Globalization, and Institutions: The Role and Influence of the Organization for Economic Cooperation and Development." *Michigan Journal of International Law* 21: 770–848.

Selwyn B. 2014. *The Global Development Crisis.* London: Polity.

Selwyn B. 2016. "Elite Development Theory: A Labour-Centred Critique." *Third World Quarterly* 37 (5): 781–799.

Seo H. 2018. "Intelligence Politicization in the Republic of Korea: Implications for Reform." *International Journal of Intelligence and CounterIntelligence* 31 (3): 451–478.

Seol K. 2021. "President of South Korea's Militant Union Federation Arrested for Organizing a Rally." *Labor Notes*, September 7. https://labornotes.org/2021/09/president-south-koreas-militant-union-federation-arrested-organizing-rally

Seoul Metropolitan Government. 2015. *A City with Respect for Labor.* http://english.seoul.go.kr/city-respect-labor/

Seoul Metropolitan Government. 2017. *The Seoul Declaration on Decent Work City.* Declaration adopted at the International Forum on Transforming Cities for Decent Work, Seoul, South Korea, September.

Shin GW. 2020. "South Korea's Democratic Decay." *Journal of Democracy* 31 (3): 100–114.

Shin GW. 2022. "In Troubled Waters South Korea's Democracy in Crisis." Walter H. Shorenstein Asia-Pacific Research Center Freeman Spogli Institute. https://fsi.stanford.edu/news/troubled-waters-south-korea%E2%80%99s-democracy-crisis

Shin HB and Kim SY. 2016. "The Developmental State, Speculative Urbanisation and the Politics of Displacement in Gentrifying Seoul." *Urban Studies* 53 (3): 540–59.

Shin JW. 2022. *Kŭrŏn sedaenŭn ŏpta: Pulp'yŏngdŭng shidaeŭi sedaewa chŏngch'i iyagi* [There is no such generation: Politics and generation in an era of inequality]. Seoul: Gaemagowon.

Shin JS and Chang HJ. 2003. *Restructuring "Korea Inc.": Financial Crisis, Corporate Reform, and Institutional Transition.* London: RoutledgeCurzon.

Shin KY. 2010. "Globalisation and the Working Class in South Korea: Contestation, Fragmentation and Renewal." *Journal of Contemporary Asia* 40 (2): 211–229.

Shin KY. 2021. "The Rocky Road to New Democracy in South Korea." In *The Volatility*

208 | References

and Future of Democracies in Asia, edited by Hsiao H and Yang A, 31–48. London: Routledge.

Sial F and Doucette J. 2020. "Inclusive Partners? Internationalising South Korea's Chaebol through Corporate Social Responsibility-Linked Development Cooperation." *Third World Quarterly* 41 (10): 1723–39.

Sidaway JD. 2013. "Geography, Globalization, and the Problematic of Area Studies." *Annals of the Association of American Geographers* 103 (4): 984–1002.

Sioh M. 2010. "The Hollow Within: Anxiety and Performing Postcolonial Financial Policies." *Third World Quarterly* 31 (4): 581–97.

Skocpol T. 1979. *States and Social Revolutions: A Comparative Analysis of France, Russia, and China.* Cambridge: Cambridge University Press.

Skocpol T. 1985. "Bringing the State Back In: Strategies of Analysis in Current Research." In *Bringing the State Back In*, edited by Evans P, Rueschemeyer D, and Skocpol T, 3–43. Cambridge: Cambridge University Press.

Slater D and Wong J. 2013. "The Strength to Concede: Ruling Parties and Democratization in Developmental Asia." *Perspectives on Politics* 11 (3): 717–33.

Slater D and Wong J. 2022. *From Development to Democracy: The Transformations of Modern Asia.* Princeton: Princeton University Press.

Sohn HY. 2000. *The Road of Progressive Liberalism.* [In Korean.] Seoul: Saengkakui Namu.

Son WJ. 2012. "Moon Jae-in's Presidential Platform." *Hankyoreh*, September 17. http://www.hani.co.kr/arti/english_edition/e_national/552012.html

Song CK. 2020. "South Korean Chaebols Comprise 84% of GDP but Only 10% of Jobs." *Hankyoreh*, June 14. https://english.hani.co.kr/arti/english_edition/e_business/9492 36.html

Song HY. 2013. "Democracy against Labour: The Dialectic of Democratisation and De-democratisation in Korea." *Journal of Contemporary Asia* 43 (2): 338–62.

Song HY. 2019a. "From Getting the Development Question Wrong to Bringing Emancipation Back In: Re-reading Alice Amsden." *Development and Change* 50 (6): 1554–78.

Song HY. 2019b. *The State, Class and Developmentalism in South Korea: Development as Fetish.* New York: Routledge.

Song J. 2009. *South Koreans in the Debt Crisis: The Creation of a Neoliberal Welfare Society.* Durham: Duke University Press.

Song J and Hae L, eds. 2019. *On the Margins of Urban South Korea: Core Location as Method and Praxis.* Toronto: University of Toronto Press.

Sonn JW and Shin HB. 2019. "Contextualizing Accumulation by Dispossession: The State and High-Rise Apartment Clusters in Gangnam, Seoul." *Annals of the American Association of Geographers* 110 (3): 864–81.

Stiglitz J. 2002. *Globalization and Its Discontents Revisited: Anti-Globalization in the Era of Trump.* New York: W.W. Norton.

Stockhammer E. 2008. "Some Stylized Facts on the Finance-Dominated Accumulation Regime." *Competition & Change* 12 (2): 184–202.

Suh JJ and Kim M, eds. 2017. *Challenges of Modernization and Governance in South Korea: The Sinking of the Sewol and Its Causes.* Singapore: Palgrave Macmillan.

Suh JJ, Park SW, and Kim HY. 2012. "Democratic Consolidation and Its Limits in Korea: Dilemmas of Cooptation." *Asian Survey* 52 (5): 822–44.

Suh S. 2001. *Unbroken Spirits: Nineteen Years in a South Korean Gulag*. Lanham, MD: Rowman and Littlefield.

Thomas P. 2009. *The Gramscian Moment: Philosophy, Hegemony, and Marxism*. Leiden: Brill.

Thurbon E. 2016. *Developmental Mindset: The Revival of Financial Activism in South Korea*. Ithaca: Cornell University Press.

Tikhonov V. 2019. "The Rise and Fall of the New Right Movement and the Historical Wars in 2000s South Korea." *European Journal of Korean Studies* 18 (2): 5–36.

Tilton T. 1979. "A Swedish Road to Socialism: Ernst Wigforss and the Ideological Foundations of Swedish Social Democracy." *American Political Science Review* 73 (2): 505–20.

Van der Zwan N. 2014. "Making Sense of Financialization." *Socio-economic Review* 12 (1): 99–129.

Wade R. 1990. *Governing the Market: Economic Theory and the Role of Government in East Asian Industrialization*. Princeton: Princeton University Press.

Wade R. 2004. *Governing the Market: Economic Theory and the Role of Government in East Asian Industrialization*. Second ed. Princeton: Princeton University Press.

Wade R and Veneroso F. 1998. "The Asian Crisis: The High Debt Model versus the Wall Street-Treasury-IMF Complex." *New Left Review* 228: 3–22.

Wainwright J. 2010. "On Gramsci's 'Conceptions of the World.'" *Transactions of the Institute of British Geographers* 35 (4): 507–21.

Wang H. 2011. *The Politics of Imagining Asia*. Cambridge: Harvard University Press.

Weber M. 1946. "Politics as a Vocation." In *From Max Weber: Essays in Sociology*, translated by H. H. Gerth and C. Wright Mills. Oxford: Oxford University Press.

Weber M. 1958. *The Religion of India: The Sociology of Hinduism and Buddhism*. New York: Free Press.

Weber M. (1903) 1975. *Roscher and Knies: The Logical Problems of Historical Economics*. New York: Free Press.

Weber M. 1978. *Economy and Society*. Berkeley: University of California Press.

Weber M. (1922) 1988. *Gesammelte Aufsätze zur Wissenschaftslehre*. Tübingen: Mohr.

Weiss L. 1998. *The Myth of the Powerless State*. Ithaca: Cornell University Press.

West C. 1988. "Between Dewey and Gramsci: Unger's Emancipatory Experimentalism." *Northwestern University Law Review* 81 (4): 941–52.

Whitehead J. 2015. "Au Retour a Gramsci: Reflections on Civil Society, Political Society and the State in South Asia." *Journal of Contemporary Asia* 45 (4): 660–76.

Won JW. 2001. "The Ideal and Reality of the Korean Legal Profession." *Asian Pacific Law and Policy Journal* 2 (1): 45–68.

Wong J. 2005. "Re-Making the Developmental State in Taiwan: The Challenges of Biotechnology." *International Political Science Review* 26 (2): 169–91.

Wong J. 2011. *Betting on Biotech: Innovation and the Limits of Asia's Developmental State*. Ithaca: Cornell University Press.

Woo J. 1991. *Race to the Swift: State and Finance in Korean Industrialization*. New York: Columbia University Press.

Yang JJ. 2017. *The Political Economy of the Small Welfare State in South Korea*. Cambridge: Cambridge University Press.

Yang M. 2021. "The Spectre of the Past: Reconstructing Conservative Historical Memory in South Korea." *Politics & Society* 49 (3): 337–62.

210 | References

Yang S. 2021. "An Old Right in New Bottles: State without Nation in South Korean New Right Historiography." *Journal of Asian Studies* 80 (4): 889–909.

Yeung H. 2016. *Strategic Coupling: East Asian Industrial Transformation in the New Global Economy.* Ithaca: Cornell University Press.

Yi I and Mkandawire T, eds. 2014. *Learning from the South Korean Developmental Success: Effective Developmental Cooperation and Synergistic Institutions and Policies.* New York: Palgrave Macmillan.

Yi KM. 2022. "The Fragility of Liberal Democracy: A Schmittian Response to the Constitutional Crisis in South Korea (1948–79)." *Journal of Asian Studies* 81 (2): 305–21.

Yonhap News. 2013. "6 Organizers of Railway Union Searched for Violating National Security Law." April 29. http://www.yonhapnews.co.kr/bulletin/2013/04/29/0200000000AKR20130429129800004.HTML?from=search

Yoon SY. 2023. "Address by President Yoon Suk Yeol on Korea's 78th Liberation Day." Office of the President of the Republic of Korea. https://eng.president.go.kr/speeches/ChFr4MEm

You JS. 2016. *Sewŏlho-wa Ch'oesunshil, yegodoen ch'amsa* [The Sewol ferry tragedy and Choi Soon-sil were predictable]. *Pressian,* November 14. http://www.pressian.com/news/article.html?no=144221

You JS. 2019. "State Intervention Can Cut Inequality, but the Current Approach Is Wrong." *Global Asia* 14 (1). https://www.globalasia.org/v14no1/debate/state-intervention-ca

You JS and Park YM. 2017. "The Legacies of State Corporatism in Korea: Regulatory Capture in the Sewol Ferry Disaster." *Journal of East Asian Studies* 17:95–118.

Yuk J. 2019. "Cultural Censorship in Defective Democracy: The South Korean Blacklist Case." *International Journal of Cultural Policy* 25 (1): 33–47.

Yun A. 2007. *The ILO Recommendation on the Employment Relationship and Its Relevance in the Republic of Korea.* Global Union Research Network, Discussion Paper 4. Geneva: International Labour Office.

Zhang J and Peck J. 2016. "Variegated Capitalism, Chinese Style: Regional Models, Multi-Scalar Constructions." *Regional Studies* 50 (1): 52–78.

Znaniecki F. 1934. *The Method of Sociology.* New York: Reinhardt and Company.

Index

accumulation, 29, 31, 34–35; finance-led regime of, 74–76

administrative democracy, 151–52

agonism, 20, 128

alliance making, 5, 14, 42, 46, 141–42, 145, 150, 162, 168–71

alter-globalization, xi, 16

Alternatives Network (Taean Yeondae), 91, 97, 102

alt-right, 163, 172

Amsden, Alice, 26, 42, 58

anticommunism, 7n6, 9, 14, 106, 114, 143–59

Asian financial crisis, 2, 15, 53, 87–88, 97–101, 173; and developmental state theory, 23, 25, 35, 54; financialization, 19, 55–57, 73–77; and financial transformation, 61–66; and income distribution, 66–70; and labor restructuring, 55, 68–71, 113, 117

Asian values. *See* orientalism

authoritarianism, 3–9, 14, 23, 27, 30, 51, 72, 119, 141, 147, 152, 156, 178

authoritarian populism, 50

awkward affinity, 23, 25, 27, 37, 48, 177

banks, 61, 93, 101; banking system, 58; lending regulations, 59; restructuring, 63

blacklist, 1, 149, 152

bloc politics, 21, 139, 158, 172

Burawoy, Michael, 15–16. *See also* case study method

bureaucratic thinker (*penseur fonctionnaire*), 37

Candlelight Democracy, 3, 22, 78, 110, 141, 143, 164, 165, 174, 185–86

Candlelight Revolution, 1–3, 8–11, 19–22, 79, 129, 139, 159–62, 167, 174, 180–81

case study method, 15–16, 183–86. *See also* methodology

Castells, Manuel, 29, 31

Center for Good Corporate Governance, 102

chaebol, 2, 10, 12–13, 19–21, 23, 73, 113, 135, 150–51, 156–57, 160–62, 170, 183; concentration of economic power, 95–96, 108; cross-shareholding structure, 63–64, 87–88; and economic democracy debate, 77–111; and labor, 2, 12–13, 20–21, 55, 66, 80, 86, 100, 104–6, 108, 111, 135, 151; politics of debt, 55–66; 2012 elections, 80–91, 103, 183

Chang, Ha-joon, 85–89, 97–98, 100, 104–7

Chang, Sok-joon, 176

Chin, Jung-kwan, 160

Cho, Hee-yeon, 7, 91, 145, 163

Cho, Kuk, 13, 21, 100, 142, 159–62, 165, 172, 186; and tension within CSOs, 160 n6

Cho Soon (reformative Keynesianism), 94. *See also* Chung Un-chan

Choi, Jang-jip, 8–11, 85, 99, 144–45, 165, 175

Choi, Soon-sil, 1, 155–57

212 | Index

Choo Mi-ae, 167n1
Chun Doo-hwan, 153
Chung, Tae-in, 81, 87–89
Chung, Un-chan, 94–96
Citizens Committee for Economic Justice (CCEJ), 84, 92, 95, 108, 161
"city that respects labour," 130
civil society organizations (CSO), 16–17, 84, 86–, 90–91, 97, 102–3, 116, 129, 135–38, 143, 160, 171–73, 184–87; strategic appointments from 10–13, 78, 110, 131–32, 173
class relations, 34–35, 76, 168; inter- vs intra-, 20, 89, 95, 103; transnational, 41
Cold War, 2–3, 7n6, 11, 42, 51, 81, 139, 144, 150–51, 179. See also anticommunism; authoritarianism
Committee on Freedom of Association (of the International Labour Organization), 116, 120, 124
concentration of economic power. See chaebol
conjunctural analysis, 22, 50, 166
conservative bloc, 4, 10–11, 13–15, 21, 73, 94, 166, 172, 175, 181; and integral state, 139–64; moderate conservatives, 79, 90, 106–7, 146. See also New Right
conservative democratization, 8–11, 22, 110, 114, 143–46
Conservative Party, 3–4, 60, 81–84, 94, 147, 153–55, 160–64, 172. See also conservative bloc
Constitutional Court, 1, 149, 151, 153
consumption, as part of GDP 75, household 73
cooperatives, 109
corporate governance, 3–4, 20, 63, 79–80, 84–87, 102–3, 106–11, 146, 168, 179. See also chaebol
corporatism, 118, 126
corruption, 82, 145, 159, 163; and chaebol, 60, 87, 107; history of capitalism, 100
COVID-19, 64, 73, 132
creative economy, 146
cross-shareholding. See chaebol

damage claims, 119–26, 129, 133, 135, 138, 161, 163, 185

"deep-rooted evils" (*jŏkp'ye chŏngsan*), 2, 165
deferral, logic of, 71, 174
democratic deficit, 5–6, 18, 22, 24–26, 29, 43, 51–52, 100, 167, 169, 176. *See also* developmental state
democratic experimentalism, 134, 169
Democratic Labor Party, 82, 128, 131, 132, 134, 137–38
Democratic Party, 3–4, 8, 10–14, 53, 81–85, 94, 99, 102, 107, 113–15, 130, 133, 137–39, 143, 154, 164, 171, 174–75. *See also* prodemocratic bloc
democratization, 27, 51, 175; political economy of, 4, 23, 40–43; revisionist historiography of, 154–58. *See also* conservative democratization; economic democracy
deregulation, 61–62, 146; and Park's "chulp'use" platform, 83
developmental dictatorship, 6–7, 21–22, 35, 59, 111, 114, 143, 177
developmentalism, 4, 7, 12, 19, 21–22, 30, 35, 37, 42, 46, 50–51, 55–56, 78–79, 86, 103, 109, 111–14, 146–47, 164, 168, 172–74, 179–80
developmental state, 5–7, 17–18, 22, 23–52; neo-Weberian theories of, 6, 18, 24–33, 35, 46–48, 177. *See also* democratic deficit
disguised subcontracting and employment, 2, 67, 121–22. *See also* irregular work; precarious work; staffing agencies; user-enterprises
division system, 7, 105, 181. *See also* Paik Nak-chung

economic democracy, 3–15, 19–21, 23, 49, 52, 53, 56–57, 76–77, 78–110, 111–13, 137–41, 145–46, 153, 158–60, 164, 165–74, 177, 183; and chaebol, 4, 12, 20, 77, 78–110, 139, 145, 161, 170, 183; constitutional basis for, 82–83; and labor, 3, 9, 11, 19–21, 56, 77, 86, 89, 100, 105–6, 109, 111–13, 137–41, 159–61, 168–76; rival camps, 85–103
Economic Planning Board, 86, 95, 178

Index | 213

Economic, Social, and Labor Council (ESLC), 14, 128–37, 163, 185

'87 regime, 9–11, 105, 143, 169; '97 regime, 106

elections, 114–15, 129, 139, 149, 153; 1997 presidential election, 53, 117; 2007 presidential election, 84; 2012 presidential election, 19–20, 79–85, 103, 106, 147, 183; 2017 presidential election, 2–3; 2022 presidential election, 3, 8, 15, 162, 167

electoral interference, 1, 147–48

embedded autonomy, 24, 28–34

embeddedness, 28–30, 137

environmental issues, 9, 14, 22, 145, 173, 181. *See also* Four Rivers Project

epistemology, 18, 24, 43–50

Evans, Peter, 28–32, 34, 42n8, 43, 44n9, 54n1. *See also* developmental state

events, democratic, 2, 8, 19, 155, 174, 180

exploitation, 24, 72, 100; direct vs indirect, 66; of irregular workers and subcontractors, 132, 158

export-oriented economy, 2, 4, 7, 19, 23, 26, 55–60, 72–76, 98, 151

Fair Trade Commission, 78 107, 136

Fascism, 37; and Carl Schmit,t 27n1, 151. *See also* Yushin Constitution

Federation of Korean Industries, 83

Federation of Korean Trade Unions (FKTU), 113, 116–19, 126–27, 133, 138, 171

feminism, 49, 110, 173–74; feminist political economy, 35; feminist standpoint theory, 49–51. *See also* #MeToo

financialization, 19, 54, 56, 63–66, 73–76; subordinate, 75. *See also* financial restructuring

financial restructuring, 2, 54–66, 73, 77, 96–97, 106, 117; financial imperialism, 62

First Republic (1948–60), 150; Third and and Fourth Republic, 151; Sixth Republic, 176; Seventh Republic, proposal for, 176

Four Rivers Project, 82, 145

gapchil (abuses of power), 80

gender, 35; activism, 174; antidiscrimination legislation, 171; and irregular work, 68–70, 77, 130, 131, 133; Ministry of Gender Equality, 162–63; and social reproduction, 35. *See also* #MeToo

generation (386/586 generation), 17, 160, 162, 167, 174; generational politics, 160, 166–67

geographical political economy, 7–8, 22, 51, 177

geopolitics, 42, 167, 170, 178

German historical school of economics, 25

Glassman, Jim, 40–43, 58–59

global production networks, 41

gold spoon/dirt spoon, 2, 160, 185

Gong, Jiyoung, 160

Gramsci, Antonio, 6–8, 18, 24–25, 43–44, 48–52, 168–69, 181; dialectical approach, 38–39; historical blocs, 14, 38, 175; passive revolution, 42n7, 94n8; study of intellectuals, 36–38; war of position/war of maneuver, 175–76. *See also* integral state; politico-gnoseology

Grand Social Compromise, 117–19, 124, 126, 131, 134

Gross Domestic Product (GDP) growth, 5, 59–60, 73–75; "747 Plan," 82, 145

Habermas, Jürgen, 31

Hak'yŏn School, 94

Hall, Stuart, 50

"*Hell Chosŏn*," 2

heterodox economists, 184

"high-debt model," 4, 56–61, 77

history textbooks, 155

Hong, Gibin, 104

Hong, Jang-pyo, 135–36

Hope Bus, 72

household debt, 55–58, 65–66, 73, 75, 77–78, 173

Hyundai, 60 125, 156

ideal type method, 24–25, 42–51, 59, 101, 103, 169, 170, 172, 176–77. *See also* methodology

214 | Index

ideographic-nomothetic distinction, 30, 45, 50
ideology, 3, 7, 29, 157; competition between, 8–9; and knowledge, 49; and Korean left, 91; and method, 50; and values, 46
impeachment, 1–2, 140, 142, 152, 158, 165. *See also* Park Geun-hye; Roh Moo-hyun
indefinite term contract workers, 21, 68, 118, 131, 135
industrial policy, 26, 34–35, 41–42, 57–64, 96–98, 103
inequality, 8–9, 12, 51, 54–56, 82, 164, 166, 172–73, 176; and income, 65–72, 77–78, 145–46
infrastructure projects, 58, 82, 173. *See also* Four Rivers Project
institutional fetishism, 77, 103, 170
institutionalist economists, 94, 117, 184
integral state, 7, 13–14, 17–19, 24, 36–42, 49, 53, 77–79, 110, 112–13, 132, 139, 157, 166, 172–75, 177–80. *See also* Gramsci, Antonio
Intellectuals Declaration Network, 136, 168–69
interested interaction, 17, 49, 51, 177. *See also* standpoint
international development cooperation, 22, 155, 157, 178
International Labour Organization, 116, 120–21, 124; core conventions, 132–33, 138, 146, 161, 185
International Monetary Fund (IMF), 62, 64, 96–97, 117, 120; IMF crisis, 15, 53, 66, 126. *See also* Asian financial crisis
inyŏn (connection, providence), 131
irregular work, 13, 19–20, 55–56, 66–73, 77–78, 118–19, 131–34, 166, 170–75. *See also* non-standard employment

Jang, Ha-sung, 84, 86 n5, 88, 96, 102, 107–8, 135–36, 167n1
Jeong, Seong-jin, 35, 66, 74, 91
Jeong, Seung-il, 85, 97–98, 102
Johnson, Chalmers, 27–28, 32

June Democratic Uprising (1987), 82, 92, 115, 117, 155
Justice Party, 138, 160, 174, 176
Jwa, Sung-hee, 27, 151, 157

Keynesianism, 94; post-Keynesian economists, 13, 169, 184
Kim Chung-yum, 82, 157
Kim, Dae-jung, 9, 53, 62, 70, 72, 96, 99, 117, 124, 148, 152, 154
Kim, Geun-tae, 102
Kim, Jong-in, 80–83, 90, 94, 107, 146
Kim, Ki-choon, 152, 157
Kim, Kum-soo, 126, 134
Kim, Kyung-yul, 160
Kim, Sang-jo, 81, 85–89, 95–96, 99, 101–2, 107, 136, 167n1
Korea Development Institute, 95, 157
Korea Labour and Society Institute (KLSI), 126, 128, 130, 136, 185
Korean Confederation of Trade Unions (KCTU), 69–70, 116–17, 125–28, 131–34, 161, 163
Korea Tripartite Commission (KTC), 117, 124, 126, 129
KTX (high speed railroad) workers, 146, 149

labor rights, 114–16, 130–35, 146, 171
labor standards, 12, 112, 114, 116, 161
labor unions, 12–13, 20–21, 27, 72, 77, 104n12, 113–37, 146, 149, 171, 185; and employment status, 70, 72, 119, 122, 131
laissez-faire, 37, 101
Lee, Byeong-cheon, 6–7, 88–89, 91, 99, 136, 168
Lee, Joung-woo, 84
Lee, Myung-bak, 21, 82–83, 94, 145–46
Lee, Yoonkyung, 12, 171, 175
left-nationalism, 62, 91, 148, 149
legitimacy, 29–33, 110, 113, 148, 158, 165, 171; politics of legitimation, 12–13, 21, 31–32, 53, 112, 129, 137–39, 143, 151, 171
Lew, Hyuck-in, 48n13
Lew, Seok-choon, 48n13
liberalism, 37, 143–46, 171; developmental liberalism, 114; economic liberalism 99,

113; progressive liberalism, 99–100, 109, 113, 138. *See also* neoliberalism

Lipset, Seymour Martin, 30

market for corporate control, 55, 98, 103; and professionalization of management, 95–96

Marx, Karl, 34

Marxism, 24, 29, 34–35, 50, 59, 66, 74, 88, 91, 92–94, 184

Mass Participatory Economy, 9, 111. *See also* Kim Dae-jung

methodological nationalism, 39–40, 42

methodology, 15–18, 38, 40, 49–52, 177, 183–87. *See also* case study method; ideal type method

#MeToo, 13, 159, 162, 167n1

Ministry of Strategy and Finance, 61, 107, 168; "MOFia," 86

minjung (people's movement), 9, 14, 105

minority shareholder movement (MSM), 80, 84, 88–89, 92–98, 101–4, 108, 111. *See also* Center for Good Corporate Governance; Jang Ha-sung; Kim Sang-jo; People's Solidarity for Participatory Democracy

misogyny, 162, 166

Monopoly Regulation and Fair Trade Act, 59–60, 84–85, 107

Moon, Jae-in, 2–3, 8–12, 20–22, 78–81, 84, 100, 108, 110, 113–17, 129–39, 142, 147, 158–76, 185–86

moral hazard, 62, 90, 97

mortgages, 64

National Human Rights Commission (NHRC), 132, 144

National Intelligence Service (NIS), 1, 141, 147–49, 152–53, 155, 159

national liberation (NL), 91. *See also* left-nationalism

National Security Law, 81, 148–51, 153

neo-Kantianism, 30, 44–46

neoliberal accounts of Asian development, 25

neoliberalism, 4, 37–38, 50, 56, 62, 86, 168,

172, 177; alternatives to, 26, 51, 78, 103, 106, 109, 133, 164, 176; inclusive neoliberalism, 118

neo-Weberianism. *See* developmental state

New Right, 14, 142, 145, 153–58, 162–63

nodal ministries, 26, 86

nonbank financial institutions (NBFIs), 61–63

non-standard employment, 2–4, 19–20, 35, 66–67, 70–71, 118–21, 126–27, 130–31, 138. *See also* precarious work

North Korea, 3, 14, 81, 147–51, 154–56; sunshine policy toward, 148. *See also* division system

occidentalism, 46–47, 169

Organisation for Economic Co-operation and Development (OECD), 2, 65, 70, 116, 124

orientalism, 47–49, 179; and Confucianism, 48n13

Paik, Nak-chung, 6, 9. *See also* division system

Park Chung-hee, 6–7, 18, 27, 40, 59, 81–83, 94, 99–100, 150–51, 154–58; memorial foundation, 27, 156–58. *See also* Park Geun-hye; Yushin Constitution

Park, Geun-hye, 1–3, 21, 79–83, 105–6, 107, 126, 129, 140, 142, 145–65. *See also* Choi Soon-sil; Park Chung-hee

Park Won-soon, 129, 167

parsimony (and economic thought), 18, 43, 55, 73, 100, 193. *See also* democratic deficit

Participatory Government, 9, 111 161. *See also* Roh Moo-hyun

people's democracy, 91, 99

Peoples Solidarity for Participatory Democracy (PSPD), 84, 91–97, 102, 109, 129, 132, 135, 145, 160–61; participatory economy committee of, 92–93, 96

personality, 8, 157; politics of personality, 5, 16, 139, 143, 163–64, 173, 180 (*see also* Cho Kuk; Park Chung-hee); Weberian theory of, 45–48

Index

plaza democracy, 9, 165, 175. *See also* Choi, Jang-jip

policy coordination, 13, 118, 135, 171, 175; and Seoul Labor Policy, 130–31

political society, 4–8, 35–43, 141, 157; political party names 3n2. *See also* integral state

politico-gnoseology, 18, 24, 43–50, 183

politics by public security, 21, 106, 142, 146–53, 163, 167

populism, 50, 93, 165–66

postcolonial critique, 18, 25, 47–49; of political economy, 7–8, 43, 49. *See also* orientalism

postdevelopment, 52

postdevelopmental state, 4–8, 11–12, 15, 19, 22, 50, 52, 54–56, 72, 75–78, 80, 111, 114, 174; political economy of, 53–77; strategic dilemma of, 4–5

precarious work, 10, 55, 66–68, 72, 130–31. *See also* irregular work; nonstandard employment; regularization

pro-democratic bloc, 3, 10–12, 14–15, 19–21, 79–80, 109–14, 137–43, 166–67, 172, 174–77, 181, 184. *See also* bloc politics; Gramsci, Antonio; integral state

productive welfare, 86, 118

progressive liberalism. *See* liberalism

project finance, 64–65, 82

proportionate representation system, 135, 139, 149, 164

prosecution service, 3, 10, 139, 141–42, 156, 158–59, 167; Corruption Investigation Office for High-Ranking Officials, 159, 163; prosecutors-cum-politicians, 142, 150, 153

provisional utopia, 104. *See also* Hong, Gibin; Wigforss, Ernst

public intellectuals, 5, 8–9, 17, 87–88, 166. *See also* Intellectuals Declaration Network

public sphere, 11

rationality, 6,17, 26, 33, 37, 46, 54, 178; bureaucratic, 6, 48, 59, 178

real estate, 2, 10, 55, 64–65, 77, 108, 173

regularization (of employment contract),

3, 10, 21, 118, 122, 127, 131, 135, 171; and use of subsidiaries, 131, 135. *See also* indefinite term contract

Rehmann, Jan, 43–47

relational comparison, 52, 105, 169, 180

representative democracy, 8–11, 166

resentment, 18, 33; politics of, 162, 166

Rhyu, Shimin, 160

Roh, Hae-chan, 176

Roh, Moo-hyun, 9, 16, 62n3, 81, 84, 87, 97, 102, 111, 124, 128–29, 137, 147, 152–54, 160–61, 183

Roh, Tae-woo, 60, 150

sambo ilbae ("three steps one bow"), 72

Samsung, 41n6, 61, 63–64, 80, 87, 102, 105, 107, 156, 170

savings (household), 56, 58, 64–65

Seoul Metropolitan Government, 129, 130–31

Sewŏl ferry disaster, 1, 149, 155–56

shareholder value, 33, 55, 63, 77, 89, 90, 103, 108, 111. *See also* minority shareholder movement

Skocpol, Theda, 30–32, 44

social democracy, 20, 27, 50, 81n1, 104–5, 111–13, 136, 138, 168–71

social dialogue, 3, 20–21, 39, 112–19, 124, 126–34, 137, 170–71, 176, 185. *See also* Economic, Social, and Labor Council; social partnership

social formation debate, 12, 91, 99, 106

socialism, democratic, 104

social justice, 2, 20, 51, 77, 79–80, 89, 93, 95, 103, 108, 159, 163, 170, 173, 181

social partnership, 20, 112–13, 117, 124–28, 130–31, 141, 170, 179

social protection, 55, 70–72, 87, 111, 115, 126, 138, 163, 181; social insurance, 19, 70–71, 116, 119

social reproduction, 35, 100

social welfare, 9, 14, 55, 66, 77, 80–82, 85–87, 104, 112–13, 117–18, 145, 176, 181. *See also* welfare state

"society that respects labor" (*nodongja chonjung sahoe*), 3, 12, 20–21, 76, 111, 113–14, 117, 128–37, 143, 159, 167–70, 174

Sogang School (of economics), 82, 94. *See also* Kim Jong-in
solidaristic scholarly practice, 50–52, 178
Solidarity for Economic Reform, 102, 108
sŏnjinhwa (joining the advanced countries discourse), 82–83
speculation, financial, 2, 10, 19, 54–55, 64–66, 77–78, 86, 97, 102, 108, 173, 179. *See also* financialization; real estate
Ssangyong Motor, 125, 129
staffing agencies, 122, 126. *See also* irregular work; precarious work
standpoint, 5, 7, 17–18, 20, 22–26, 43–44, 46, 49, 51–53, 100, 118, 177, 183. *See also* feminist standpoint theory
state autonomy, 6, 18, 24, 26, 28–30, 32–35, 41, 44n9, 58, 176, 178
state-society distinction, 38–39
state vs. market framework, 73, 177
strategic/spatial selectivity (of the state), 42, 179
subprime crisis, 65, 75
suicide: protest, 72, 123, 185; Roh Moo-hyun, 160; workers, 129
surplus value, 66. *See also* Marxism

taxation, 65, 76, 86–87, 104, 173
teachers' unions, 117, 129, 146, 155, 163
Thatcherism, 50, 96
Trade Union and Labor Relations Adjustment Act (TULRAA), 121, 133, 161, 171
Truth and Reconciliation Commission (TRC), 144, 154

union democracy, internal, 117, 127, 134
United Progressive Party (UPP), 104n12, 148–49

urban development, 19, 22, 42, 59, 65, 173, 184
urban labor policy, 21, 129. *See also* "city that respects labor"
user-enterprises (employers), 121–22. *See also* precarious work; staffing agencies

values, 26, 31–33, 44n9, 48n14; neo-Kantian philosophy of, 44–45; value-free science, 46–47; value judgement, 46; Weber, Max, 45–48

Wade, Robert, 26–27, 62
Washington Consensus, 25
wealth inequality, 65, 84, 167, 173
Weber, Max, 18, 24–25, 42–48, 59; definition of the state, 31–32; irrational hiatus, 44–46. *See also* developmental state; ideal type method; personality
welfare state, 66, 70, 77, 79, 85–87, 89, 100 103–4, 111, 113, 168. *See also* social democracy, social welfare
welfare state camp (WSC), 86–89, 97–106. *See also* Chang, Ha-joon
Wigforss, Ernst, 104
Won, Sei-hoon, 148
Woo, Jung-en, 26, 41, 58
workfare, 70

Yellow Envelope Law, 133, 171
Yoo, Jong-il, 84, 95
Yoon, Seok-yeol, 133 n9, 147–48, 162–63, 172, 174
Yushin Constitution, 27, 83, 151–52, 157. *See also* Kim, Ki-Choon